"In *Unshrinking,* Kate Manne ... searched history of how anti-fa........voped and develops within us all, as well as a thorough dissection of our modern moral panic about fat—all interwoven with her powerful story of reclaiming her own body. If you have ever struggled to feel safe in your body as it is; if you have ever wondered who your body is for, Manne has articulated the answers: Our bodies belong to us. We are all better for her work."

—Virginia Sole-Smith, author of *Fat Talk*

"[Manne] writes in harrowing detail of her own experiences of discrimination and the cycle of shockingly disordered eating. . . . She is striving for 'body reflexivity,' which 'prescribes a radical evaluation of whom we exist in the world for, as bodies: ourselves, and no one else.' Claiming total ownership of one's own body ought not to feel radical, but perhaps it is."

—*The New Statesman*

"Kate Manne lays bare the sinister power of fatphobia—its pervasiveness, its roots in anti-Blackness, its shoddy logic—and argues beautifully and clearly for the moral necessity to resist it. Both trenchant and moving, *Unshrinking* is a long overdue reckoning and a manifesto for true intersectionality."

—Kimberlé Crenshaw, distinguished professor of law, UCLA School of Law, and editor of *Critical Race Theory*

"*Unshrinking* is a tour de force that only someone with Kate Manne's particular mix of rigor, clarity, and writerly skill could pull off—a must-read, no matter your body size, and an unignorable call to action."

—Anne Helen Petersen, author of *Can't Even*

"A potent and unsettling piece of social philosophy . . . Manne's case for the harmfulness of fatphobia is compelling. But the book's greatest strength is its author's personal narrative and the sense of justified grievance that runs through the prose like a line of fire. . . . *Unshrinking* demonstrates amply the importance of aspiring to care a little less about the unruly behaviour of our irrepressible flesh."

—*The Times Literary Supplement* (UK)

"An essential book of impossible-to-overstate importance; *Unshrinking* is a lucid, vital addition to the fat canon."

—Carmen Maria Machado, author of *In the Dream House*

"A breathtaking work of meticulous research, philosophical rigor, and personal anecdote . . . Manne brilliantly ushers forth scientific studies and powerful anecdotes to dispel us of the notions that a fat body is necessarily an unhealthy body. . . . [A] superb book full of insight and hope."

—*Chicago Review of Books*

"In her new book [*Unshrinking*], philosopher Kate Manne tears down the fortress of Western fatphobia, excavating its foundations in racism, misogyny, and classism, and clearing a space to build a better moral paradigm through which to relate to our bodies. *Unshrinking* is a project of deconstruction, archaeology, and care—of listening to the stories medical professionals have ignored or disdained, hearing the plaintive notes in speeches by fictional characters most people mock, and reading between the lines of physicians' reports and autopsies. . . . Manne's paradigm is radical."

—*Los Angeles Review of Books*

"Kate Manne's *Unshrinking* is an incisive polemic that brilliantly dissects fatphobia, the way it encroaches upon our lives, and how, ultimately, we can, if we are willing, do the challenging work of unlearning damaging ideas about fatness, health, and happiness.

Manne is a beautiful writer with a consummate research ethic. The depth of her knowledge and how she synthesizes it is clear from the first page to the last, and she deftly navigates personal narrative and cultural examination to demonstrate that the personal truly is political, particularly when you live in a fat body. What elevates *Unshrinking* is the keen awareness that there is no universal experience of fatness and that fatphobia, like everything else, is affected by the intersections of the identities we inhabit. *Unshrinking* is required reading for everyone who lives in an unruly human body."

—Roxane Gay, author of *Hunger*

"[A] brilliant takedown of fatphobia . . . Combining rigorous research, well-reasoned arguments, and lucid prose, Manne examines how fatphobia shows up in every facet of life. . . . [Her] book is wide-ranging, accessible, and engaging. . . . An essential addition to the growing body of literature on the experiences of fat people and fighting fatphobia."

—*Booklist* (starred review)

"As someone raised in the era of 'nothing tastes as good as skinny feels,' I am beyond grateful to Kate Manne for ushering in the era of *Unshrinking*. This book is a tasty, tasty takedown of diet culture and a firm but gentle guide to finally getting free from fatphobia—individually, collectively, and within society at large. Is it too much to say that Manne has written a big, fat masterpiece?"

—Jessica DeFino, writer, *The Review of Beauty*

"Trust Kate Manne to provide the clearest statement of one of the major problems of the twenty-first century. Through science, reason, and human experience, she shows us the moral failure of fatphobia, in direct contradiction to the widespread and toxic narrative of fatness as a moral failing."

—Emily Nagoski, author of *Come as You Are*

"The personal is political when it comes to fatphobia, and Kate Manne has written this intimate and razor-sharp examination to expose the gaslighting, double standards, and conditioning behind size discrimination. Manne's new framework of 'body reflexivity' offers valuable new ways and words to fight the existing power structures of fat oppression."

—*Ms.*

"To be fat in a thin-obsessed world is to be treated as a moral failure all the time. Through impeccable research, compelling writing, and refreshing honesty, *Unshrinking* undoes so much of that undeserved shame. Kate Manne brings her razor-sharp analysis to the world we all inhabit, reminding us all that fatness isn't a deviance and should never have been treated as one to begin with. A rich text for the ages, one we should all read, especially if we desire to create a world that treats fat people with more dignity and less disdain than this one."

—Evette Dionne, author of *Weightless*

"Manne's book about fatphobia is a must-read in every way. A powerful, dare I say healing, text—it changed the way I view my own body."

—*Book Riot*

"Blisteringly brilliant . . . So many of us have been fed unhealthy messages about the shape and size of our bodies, which Manne makes her mission to reframe. The feminist philosopher doesn't hold back her own story, sharing intimate details of the agonizing pressure to be small."

—Amazon Editors' Picks

"Incisive . . . A brave, thought-provoking book. With rigorous research and personal experience, Manne tackles and dismantles fatphobia in all its forms."

—*Kirkus Reviews*

"*Unshrinking* is a deft auto-ethnographic work that brilliantly weaves together indisputable research with parts of Kate Manne's own personal story. I am thrilled and thoroughly impressed with the scholarship and pivotal citational practice displayed in this book."

—Da'Shaun L. Harrison, author of *Belly of the Beast*

"*Unshrinking* is a provocative argument for 'radical body autonomy.'"

—*The Sunday Times* (UK)

"A systematic takedown of fatphobia, addressing all the myths it convinces us to accept about the health, attractiveness, intellect, and willpower of fat people. [*Unshrinking*] lays bare the way the world is set up to alienate fatness, then suggests the start of a solution."

—*SheKnows*

"Manne brilliantly reveals . . . that fatphobia, not fatness, is the problem. In *Unshrinking,* Manne presents a personal and methodical account of fatphobia—the systemic devaluation of larger bodies—its history, and its harms."

—*Ms.*

"[Manne's] personal, unshrinking call to action should be widely read."

—*Nature* (UK)

BY KATE MANNE

Unshrinking
Entitled
Down Girl

UN-
SHRINK-
ING

CROWN
NEW YORK

UN-SHRINK-ING

HOW TO FACE FATPHOBIA

KATE MANNE

CROWN
An imprint of the Crown Publishing Group
A division of Penguin Random House LLC
crownpublishing.com

LIBRARY OF CONGRESS CATALOGING-IN-PUBLICATION DATA
Names: Manne, Kate, author.
Title: Unshrinking / Kate Manne.
Description: First edition. | New York: Crown, 2024 | Includes bibliographical
references and index.
Identifiers: LCCN 2023034032 (print) | LCCN 2023034033 (ebook) | ISBN
9780593593851 (paperback) | ISBN 9780593593844 (ebook) Subjects: LCSH:
Physical-appearance-based bias. | Fat-acceptance movement. | Weight loss.
Classification: LCC HM1091 .M37 2024 (print) |
LCC HM1091 (ebook) | DDC 305.9/08—dc23/eng/20230811
LC record available at https://lccn.loc.gov/2023034032
LC ebook record available at https://lccn.loc.gov/2023034033

ISBN 978-0-593-59385-1
Ebook ISBN 978-0-593-59384-4

Originally published in hardcover in the United States by Crown,
an imprint of the Crown Publishing Group, a division of
Penguin Random House LLC, in 2024.

Editor: Amanda Cook
Editorial assistant: Katie Berry
Text designer: Elizabeth A. D. Eno
Production manager: Mark Maguire
Managing editors: Allison Fox, Sally Franklin
Proofreaders: Julie Ehlers, Alissa Fitzgerald
Indexer: Thérèse Shere
Publicist: Stacey Stein
Marketer: Melissa Esner

Manufactured in the United States of America

2 4 6 8 9 7 5 3 1

First Paperback Edition

To my parents, who let me be

Not everything that is faced can be changed; but nothing can be changed until it is faced.

—JAMES BALDWIN,
"As Much Truth as One Can Bear," 1962

You only have to let the soft animal of your body
love what it loves.

—MARY OLIVER, "Wild Geese," 1986

I do not owe you shrinking.

—RACHEL WILEY, "Fat Joke," 2017

CONTENTS

Content note: Please note that this book contains frank descriptions of fatphobia in its intersections with racism, misogyny, ableism, transphobia, etc., and discussions of dieting, disordered eating, and body norms that may be triggering for some readers.

UN-
SHRINK-
ING

INTRODUCTION: FIGHTING WEIGHT

I should have been thrilled. My first book, which I wrote as an academic text, expecting an audience of just dozens, had been sold in paperback to a major U.K. publisher. A study of misogyny, *Down Girl* canvassed strangulation, sexual harassment, sexual assault, and rape culture. I wanted to get the word out, to talk about these issues that matter to me more than almost anything. But when my editor suggested an all-expenses-paid publicity tour of London, with book-store readings and television appearances, I flinched from the prospect. I felt too fat to be a feminist in public. I felt too big to speak out about the "down girl" moves that teach girls and women to be small, meek, and quiet. And as acutely aware as I was of the irony, it wasn't enough to shift my thinking in the moment.

The Australian author Helen Garner once remarked that

she felt the need to get down to her "fighting weight" before embarking on a publicity tour. I cursed myself for not doing that and in fact being at my heaviest. I clocked in then, in early 2019, at a weight that made me "severely obese" according to the BMI chart my doctor pointed to, frowning.[1]

My book had first come out late in 2017, the very week that Tarana Burke's #MeToo movement was popularized by celebrities. And so, much to my surprise, I found myself talking to journalists about misogyny almost daily. But I would not allow camera crews to come to my home or office. I hid my body from the public eye by only ever appearing on camera via Skype so I could control the angle. I had a handful of carefully curated headshots from when I was thinner—though I have never been thin in my adult life—that I used for every interview. I would agree to give interviews only when they promised to use one of them, rather than sending their own photographer. (Sometimes this was a battle.) When I gave talks, I asked audience members not to take any photos. When people occasionally took them anyway and posted them on social media, I begged them to take them down. I explained, in a partial truth, that I was subject to a lot of misogynist trolling, and that new photos of me that appeared online would attract mockery and vitriol. And, indeed, I'd been called a bitch and worse too many times to mention—"dumb cunt writing dumb things" was one of the first tweets I saw after publishing my first *New York Times* piece—and subject to anti-Semitic slurs too. ("Your people will burn in ovens now," someone DMed me the night Trump was elected.) Rape threats are not uncommon in my little corner of the internet.

But there was one reaction I really dreaded: being called fat. Which I was. I was fat, but I couldn't hear it—not even in my own voice—without wanting to disappear myself. I knew that would be all it took to silence me.

You might expect that as a lifelong feminist, not to mention the author of now two books on misogyny, I would be one of the last people to be suckered into policing my own body and trying to force it into a size and shape more acceptable to the patriarchy. You'd be wrong about that, sadly. Since my early twenties, I have been on every fad diet. I have tried every weight-loss pill. And I have, to be candid, starved myself, even not so long ago.

I can also tell you what I weighed on any significant occasion from the age of sixteen onward. I can tell you precisely what I weighed on my wedding day, the day I defended my PhD dissertation, the day I became a professor, and the day I gave birth to my daughter. (Too much, too much, too much, and much too much, to my own mind then.) I even know what I weighed on the day I arrived in Boston—fresh off the plane from my hometown of Melbourne, Australia—to begin graduate school in philosophy, nearly twenty years ago. I had packed my scales with all of my worldly possessions in one of two overflowing suitcases. They were among the first things I unpacked, second only to my toothbrush.

In coming of age—and size—in a fatphobic society, I learned to avoid certain key opportunities, risks, and pleasures. I have been swimming just once since the age of sixteen. (I wore leggings and an oversize T-shirt.) I haven't been dancing since I was twenty. And nobody, save my husband and doctors, has seen the dimpled, stretch-marked backs of my knees over the same time period. (My wardrobe is approximately 80 percent leggings.)

So fatphobia has made me miss out on a lot in life. It has made me undertake a careful social calculus whereby the risk of being judged, scorned, and discredited for my fat body has often not been worth the potential benefits of putting myself out there. And so I have shrunk from public scrutiny.

I begged off the London book tour, vaguely citing health reasons. I told myself, again, it was true: my mental health was terrible, and surely I couldn't be physically healthy either at my size—no matter how strangely good were my blood pressure, blood work, and other relevant markers. I bought a best-selling book with the optimistic title *How Not to Die* and listened to it on Audible while walking slowly around the supermarket buying chia seeds and green tea and complicated probiotics. I had checked out with hundreds of dollars' worth of overpriced, un-filling, mostly nonfood items long before I got to the conclusion. The author Michael Greger's dear friend Art, an avid runner and health nut and the founder of a "natural foods" empire, had died at just forty-six, in the shower of his own health retreat, while Greger was writing the book. It turned out to be a random, though preventable, tragedy: carbon monoxide poisoning from a poorly vented water heater.

I wept for Art, and Dr. Greger, and myself. I restarted the audiobook. For some months, I ate endless, impossibly bland lentils and unseasoned greens and earnest goji berries. I lost nary a pound; I didn't feel any different. And so I continued to hide. As I began to write my second book that spring, I was already dreading the publicity. I added the phrase "aspiring recluse" to my Twitter bio as a warning not to expect too much of me.

Lockdown, when COVID hit in March 2020, came as

something of a relief. To be clear, I was as upset by the pandemic itself as anyone, especially as someone who lives with a young child and an immunocompromised and immunosuppressed partner. But I did enjoy the reprieve from public scrutiny as a side effect of the situation. I could now keep my weight a secret without even making an effort. I could finally hide at home, safely, and let my mind wander, explore ideas, without worrying about the body that would eventually have to defend them. (I had the decency, of course, to delete the pseudo-joke about my reclusive ways from Twitter when this became a widespread reality.) The same holds for many people, especially fat ones, who've confessed to me similar truths: their relief that the pandemic spared them the sense of exposure that comes with teaching college students in person, or eating lunch alongside judgmental co-workers, or having to participate in the office "health challenges" that seem almost designed to shame and bully larger employees.

And, as my mind wandered, I began to wonder: What if I didn't have to hide? What if I didn't have to feel this way? What if the fat activist, Health at Every Size (HAES), and intuitive eating content that I'd consumed for decades at a safe distance—thinking good for thee, but not for me—could actually change my life? What if I accepted my own fatness and began to think through fatphobia?

As I did this, I became convinced that my own internalized fatphobia was but a hazy reflection of the fatphobia rampant in society. And I came to understand that what I hated was less my body than the way it made me vulnerable: to being put down and ridiculed and belittled. But I, of all people, recognize that the answer to bullying and abuse is not to alter the victims but instead to address the culprits and, ultimately, change the system.

I began to hear, and use, the word "fat" not as an insult but as a neutral description of some bodies—as I do throughout what follows. I began to realize that fixating on people's weight, an infinitely gradable quality, was a perfect way to construct the pernicious social hierarchies that I'll argue underlie fatphobia. I began to view fatphobia as a serious, and underestimated, form of structural oppression. I began to understand that by perpetually trying to shrink myself, I had been complicit in this system. And I began to gather the strength and the tools to do what had long seemed impossible: to stop dieting, to stop obsessing, and to live peaceably with my body. I vowed to be, in a word, unshrinking.

It took a long time for me to get there. Once, in a fit of desperation, I left a voice message with a local weight-loss-surgery mill. (I never returned their phone call; they seemed a bit too eager.) There was even one final, mad, last-ditch diet in the interim that put me in real danger. Even now I have bad days. My relationship with my body remains a work in progress. But diet culture—which privileges thinness and insists that dieting is the means to it—no longer has its claws in me. And this book is partly a product of that mundane but hard-won victory.

For, as I've realized, our bodies are not the problem. Rather, the world is, so mired as it is in fatphobia. And we can fight it.

I know it can be a struggle. Trust me, I have been there. If you are there at this moment, fighting against your own body rather than a society that unjustly punishes fatness, this book is for you too. But it is primarily a political and structural, as opposed to a psychological and individualistic, intervention. It is written in the tradition of calls for fat justice, fat pride, or—my favorite term—fat liberation.[2] I believe that when it comes to fatphobia, the solution is not to improve our self-image or love our bodies better. It is nothing less than to *remake the world* to properly fit fat bodies, and to effect the socially transformative recognition that there is truly nothing wrong with us.[3] We must trenchantly resist the fatphobia that has oppressed, controlled, and constrained us, for the sake of ourselves and—most importantly—still larger people. We must face the violence of anti-fatness, wherein fat bodies are put down, cut down, and cut up, all for no good reason.

It's important to tackle fatphobia not just because it does so much damage but also because it is on the rise, according to some measures. Harvard researchers reported in 2019 that of all of the six forms of implicit bias they investigated— race, skin tone, sexual orientation, age, disability, and body weight—anti-fatness is the only one that had gotten worse since 2007, when they began to research them. And the majority of people canvassed still harbored *explicit* anti-fat biases in 2016, at the end of the study.[4]

This gives the lie to the popular idea that contact with members of a marginalized group will reduce the biases they face from the rest of the population. In fact, most Americans are now arguably somewhat fat, with nearly three-quarters of us classified as "overweight" or "obese," according to the BMI charts—which, as we'll see later, are highly problematic.[5] And yet we have faced no less fatphobia because of our ubiquity.[6]

We can usefully conceptualize fatphobia as a straitjacket: it threatens most people not to get any fatter, and causes dis-

comfort and even pain to anyone over a certain size. It restricts our freedom, our movement, and our capacity to take
up space in a world that is already telling girls and women, in
particular, to diminish ourselves dutifully. Moreover, we are
often prevailed upon to submit to this oppressive garment
ourselves, on the grounds it's for our own good—contrary to
the best current evidence, which suggests that repeatedly losing and regaining weight is a bigger problem than simply
being heavy, as we'll see in the pages that follow.

The straitjacket of fatphobia is bad for most, perhaps all,
of us. But it cuts into the very flesh of the largest bodies, who
must therefore be centered and prioritized in a viable politics
of anti-fatphobia. In the language widely adopted both in fat
activist circles and in the narrower but highly overlapping
domain of fat studies, these people are termed "superfat" or
"infinifat"—the latter being a word coined by Ash Nischuk,
the creator of *The Fat Lip* podcast.[7] Others of us may be
termed "small fats," "mid fats," and "large fats."[8] Of course,
as with most concepts in natural language, these are all somewhat vague and admit of borderline cases. But we are the
people who, to varying degrees, struggle to find clothing
large enough for our bodies—exceeding so-called straight
sizes at major clothing retailers—and are sometimes unable
to fit our breadth and girth into the space designated for us
in society. If you don't face these challenges, then you are
probably *not* fat in my parlance, even if you have "felt fat" on
certain occasions or struggle with body image. For, in this
work, fat is not a feeling—nor, again, an insult, nor a problem.[9] It is simply the way some bodies are. And that is not
regrettable or in need of euphemisms like "fluffy," "husky,"
"curvy," and so on. Still less welcome in my book is the
pathologizing language of being "overweight" or "obese,"

which I use in scare quotes or similar only when unavoidable, as when reporting the results of various scientific studies.[10] As for the term "persons with overweight/obesity," currently favored by some medical researchers: don't even get me started on these clunky, patronizing formulations, which make the general mistake of thinking that "person-first" language is superior, whatever the stigma of the categorization that follows.

So: I am fat. Maybe you are; maybe you aren't, according to these definitions. Whatever the case, we can and must face the fact together that it's not fatness but fatphobia that is collectively plaguing us.

Fatphobia can be defined as a feature of social systems that unjustly rank fatter bodies as inferior to thinner bodies, in terms of not only our health but also our moral, sexual, and intellectual status. Fatphobia is thus partly a misguided ideology, or a set of false beliefs and inflated theories, that our culture holds about fat people: that we are necessarily unhealthy, even doomed to die of our fatness; that we are to blame for our own fatness, in lacking moral fiber or willpower or discipline; that we are unattractive, even disgusting; and that we are ignorant, even stupid.[11]

Fat bodies thus lie on a continuum not only of weight but of *value,* according to this hierarchy. And the fatter one is, the more one is affected by fatphobia, all else being equal.

However, all else is *not* equal, because of other inequalities and injustices within the social world. Like all oppressive systems, fatphobia intersects with a gamut of others, including racism, sexism, misogyny, classism, ableism, ageism, homophobia, and transphobia.[12] And, as the fat activist Kate Harding has pointed out, it privileges "good fatties"—those who perform supposedly healthy behaviors, such as dieting, or who duly regard their own fatness as a failing—over their more unruly, less apologetic counterparts.[13] The less obedient you are, the less you get to speak out, according to the logic of fatphobia.

But speak out we must, and I want to start by identifying three common myths about the nature of fatphobia that this book will help to dismantle.

First, the idea that fatphobia is purely the product of individuals' biased attitudes, toward themselves and others, is deeply mistaken. Fatphobia is an inherently structural phenomenon, which sees people in fatter bodies navigating a different world, containing numerous distinct material, social, and institutional barriers to our flourishing. Even if everyone woke up magically free from fatphobic attitudes tomorrow, the world would need to change, sometimes in radical ways, to accommodate fat bodies and actively support us. However, it would also be a mistake to dismiss the interpersonal contempt and hostility faced by fat people as hence beside the point. Not only are these forms of prejudice hurtful and isolating, but the people who harbor them may be gatekeepers for vital institutional benefits and resources in healthcare, employment, and education, just for starters. We can thus ill afford to have such individuals be fatphobic, especially for the sake of those most vulnerable to oppression.

Second, despite its name, fatphobia may feel neither hateful nor fearful to the people who practice it; it may not even feel hostile. (To people on the receiving end, it is often another story.) True, there is disgust toward fat bodies in the origin story of fatphobia, as we'll see. And it's not unusual to fear fatness, in part because of what the philosopher Alison Reiheld calls the "porousness" of the category, with many people destined to enter it and exit it as their weight fluctuates over their lifetimes.[14] But particular instances of fatphobia may lack any distinctive "feel"—or, as philosophers put it, phenomenology. Instead, they may feel like dispensing sound medical advice, picking the best person for the job, or objectively assessing the abilities of your pupils.[15] In reality, fatphobia leads to many common mistakes and omissions and biased judgments in these arenas. And some of these have serious repercussions, especially in the aggregate.

Third, and finally, there is a common tacit assumption, even among progressives, that fatphobia is vastly less important than other kinds of oppression. (It felt telling that while writing this book, I had to add the word "fatphobia" to my own phone and computer dictionaries.) But, as we'll see, there is no deep understanding of some of the more well-recognized forms of bigotry—including racism, misogyny, classism, ableism, and transphobia—without a keen appreciation of their intersection with fatphobia. Fatphobia is a powerful weapon that serves to oppress the most vulnerable of the vulnerable. Moreover, it harms people in some of the most fundamental ways, with regard to their education, their labor, their health, and their reproductive freedom. If we care about justice, we simply cannot afford to take fatphobia lightly.

✦ ✦ ✦

Let me address the elephant in the room: I am not very fat at the time of writing. Though I still identify as a "small fat," I lost more than sixty pounds shortly before throwing away my scales and feeling the initial sparks of this project forming.

(The last time I looked, the BMI charts told me that I could still stand to lose another twenty to fifty-five pounds—the latter of which would put me at a weight I haven't been since before puberty.) I do not view this weight loss, however, as a success story. In fact, it was a failure to realize the implications of my own politics and to live by them authentically.

More than that, my body bears the battle scars. It is a body I have fought with, literally and figuratively. I am usually cold. I am always tired. Like many people who have gone on extreme diets, my metabolism has slowed to a crawl now. And, before I gave up dieting once and for all, I was chronically hungry.

Accounts of fatphobia written by authors who have experienced its effects even more acutely than I have—because of either the size of their bodies or the intersecting forms of oppression to which they are subject—are immensely valuable, and I draw on these accounts throughout. My aim is both to summon these voices—of Roxane Gay, Linda Gerhardt, Aubrey Gordon, Da'Shaun L. Harrison, Marquisele Mercedes, Tressie McMillan Cottom, Ash Nischuk, and Lindy West, among many others—and to add my own to the growing choir, informed by my perspective as a feminist philosopher. I also mine my personal experiences. Like many others, I'm a living testament to the way our bodies may change dramatically over a lifetime; weight may oscillate, decreasing temporarily after disordered eating or an illness, but returning almost inexorably if we are lucky (and, often, privileged) enough to recover.

By the time you read these words, I fully expect to be fatter, and do not regard that as a problem. Indeed, it would be more me: my body runs to fat. And I am ready not to fight it, nor to hide from the world in consequence.

CHAPTER 1

THE STRAITJACKET OF FATPHOBIA

When Jen Curran, thirty-eight, went to see a kidney doctor, she was prescribed weight loss. "Can you start dieting and exercising? Try to lose some weight," she was counseled. Jen played along, despite serious misgivings. "Okay, yeah. I can do that." Jen had a five-month-old baby at home. The doctor continued, "Take the baby out for walks, eat less salt, nothing from a box, eat plants."[1]

Jen noted that she didn't need the instructions: she was already "painfully well-versed" in weight loss. She had lost some 115 pounds earlier in her life, not for the sake of her health, but for the sake of her appearance. She had since decided, some years earlier, to let go of her self-described obsession with her weight and to embrace her body as it was. She felt strong and resilient, despite the high levels of protein in her urine that her ob-gyn had flagged with concern during her pregnancy, along with high blood pressure. She had been put on bed rest during her second trimester and induced at thirty-seven weeks, before delivering her baby daughter, Rose.

But, contrary to her ob-gyn's hopes, the protein in Jen's urine had not resolved itself after the pregnancy was over. She was advised to see a kidney specialist at the earliest opportunity.

"And if I lose weight, the protein will go away?" Jen asked the doctor at her appointment. "Yes. Lose weight, the protein will go away. Come back four months from now."

Jen's weight was not the problem, though: she had bone marrow cancer. If she hadn't been suspicious of this doctor's advice and sought out a second opinion a month later, the cancer would have continued to ravage her body, and her protein levels would have remained as high as ever. "There's nothing diet or exercise can do to touch this much protein," the second kidney specialist told her.

Fortunately, Jen's cancer—multiple myeloma—was caught in time to allow it to be treated with six months of chemotherapy and steroids. Jen's prognosis is, at the time of this writing, a good one.

Other people are not so lucky. When Laura Fraser's sister, Jan, fifty-nine, came to visit her, Laura told her she looked great. Jan had lost sixty pounds. She hadn't been trying to: for months she had been in so much pain that she hadn't had much of an appetite. She was experiencing postmenopausal vaginal bleeding and near-constant pelvic pain. Her eyes welled with tears as she described her attempt to get help from an ob-gyn. He had performed a routine examination and then effectively shrugged. Jan felt dismissed as a "fat, complaining older woman." She tried to address her own pain by experimenting with dietary restrictions—cutting out dairy and gluten—and taking over-the-counter pain medications. A physician's assistant she saw months later thought she was jonesing for an opiate fix. But at least he ordered blood work.[2]

Jan received a call early the next morning, telling her to go straight to the ER. She was admitted to intensive care in critical condition, with extremely high levels of calcium in her blood. An MRI revealed a huge mass in her abdomen: the largest endometrial tumor her surgeon had ever seen. Her pelvis was filled with cancer; her bladder had also been invaded; there were even spots on her lungs.

Jan lived just six months longer. She continued to waste away throughout her rounds of chemotherapy. And people continued to compliment her on her weight loss.

✦ ✦ ✦

The straitjacket of fatphobia is a source of pressure and discomfort for most, if not all, of us. But it makes life even harder when our bodies do not fit within certain rigid confines, which some bodies—including mine—will always strain against and spill over. And much like a straitjacket, fatphobia serves as a powerful social marker: it signals that some bodies should be ignored, disregarded, and mistreated. It marks fat bodies as undeserving of care—and of education, employment, and other basic forms of freedom and opportunity.

The straitjacket starts tightening early. It's well known that fat children face widespread ridicule in school; a child's weight appears to be the most common basis for schoolyard bullying.[3] I remember being seated in a circle of kids, eating our lunches in a grassy playground, when a prepubescent boy pointed at each of us in turn: "skinny," "medium," or "fat," he casually pronounced us. When I was the only girl classified as fat, the sound of social static buzzed in my ears. There was no doubt in my mind that I had been accorded the lowest ranking. And it affected not just how I perceived myself but how my peers did too. "Mangoes make you fat!" one said, turning up their nose in disgust at the contents of my lunch box. "And mangoes make your breath stink!" another added for good measure.

Such treatment, like any form of early weight stigmatization, places larger children at increased risk for depression, anxiety, low self-esteem, and body dissatisfaction. There is even increased risk, in extreme cases, of suicidal behaviors.[4]

Fat children are also subject to discrimination and bias from their teachers—yes, their *teachers*. Educators frequently express negative weight-based stereotypes about their larger pupils, assuming they will perform worse in reasoning tasks, struggle more with physical education, and have poorer social skills.[5] I flash back to a teacher clapping an avuncular hand on my shoulder and declaring me a "brick house" when I was fourteen years old. I immediately felt my stomach lurch, seeing myself through his eyes as stocky, stolid, stupid. And indeed, teachers tend to perceive children classified as normal weight as having above-average abilities and children classified as obese as having academic challenges.[6] It's true that there is some (mixed and inconsistent) evidence that students classified as overweight or obese do tend to perform worse in school. But this is plausibly because, as one study showed, these students tend to disengage from school, and even avoid going altogether, when they are subject to weight-based teasing.[7] Another study showed that when such weight-based teasing was duly controlled for, the performance gap disappeared.[8] Hence, inasmuch as educators hold larger children responsible for not performing as well as their peers, this is effectively victim blaming—and the result of noxious, wrong-headed stereotypes about fat people's lack of acumen.[9]

Moreover, even if students perform just the same, they are perceived differently as they gain weight. One large longitudinal study found that, from fifth to eighth grade, an increase in a student's BMI led teachers to deem them less academically capable, despite unchanging objective measures in the form of their standardized test scores.[10] Specifically, girls were perceived as less able readers and boys as less able mathematically—which, interestingly, tracks the areas in which each group is expected to do the best according to gender stereotypes.

Some studies suggest that these forms of fatphobic educational bias may be particularly pronounced for girls. Adult women classified as overweight or obese frequently report having experienced weight stigmatization from an educator, with a third recalling at least one such incident and 20 percent recalling more than one.[11]

One of the most galling studies I came across while researching this book showed that parents in the 1990s were less willing to offer financial support to their fat daughters to attend college, compared with their thinner ones.[12] I am grateful that my own parents never saw me, whatever my weight, as any less bright or industrious or worthy of a good education. Indeed, they celebrated my intelligence along with my appetite. But many girls and women are not so fortunate. Many of us never have the chance to develop our voices, owing to the sense that someone with a body like ours wouldn't have anything valuable to contribute. It strikes me as a heavy, if seldom-noticed, silence.

Fatphobia is also a potent source of discrimination in employment. A wealth of research indicates that applicants with a higher BMI are less likely to be hired, compared with our thinner counterparts with the same profile and qualifications.[13] Fat people are perceived as less competent in general.[14] One study showed that the stigma against fat people is so powerful that even being caught *next* to a fat body is enough to deter prospective employers: when a fictional so-called normal-weight male applicant was pictured in a photograph sitting next to an "obese" woman, he was rated as significantly less desirable as an employee than when he was pictured sitting next to a thin one. In other words, "the hiring bias has spread to a person proximal to an obese individual."[15]

Some studies suggest that fat women are particularly subject to such biases.[16] In a 2016 study by Stuart Flint and his collaborators, hypothetical candidates of various genders and weights (revealed by a photo) were rated on their suitability for a range of employment opportunities.[17] These candidates were all depicted, via their CVs, as highly qualified for the positions to which they were applying (as an administrative assistant, a retail salesperson, a manual laborer, and a university lecturer). Both male and female participants ranked the so-called normal-weight man as the best person, and the so-called obese woman as the least suitable candidate, for each and every job opening.[18] Subsequent analyses confirmed that personnel suitability was judged differently depending on the candidate's perceived weight, as well as their gender. This suggests that fatphobic discrimination in employment is common, and that fat women are even more likely to be discriminated against than their fat male counterparts.

When I interviewed for academic jobs during my final year of grad school at MIT, I worried about the usual things: the pithiness of my dissertation summary, the sharpness of my research talk, the aptness of my answers to questions about my teaching plans. But I also worried, more than anything, about how my fat body would look in the process of giving them. I struggled to find professional-looking suits that fit my big hips and struck out epically on the knee-high boots that were practically mandatory during the New England winter that provided the snowy backdrop to most of my interviews.[19] The one pair I ordered that even approached fitting me was so difficult to haul over my fat calves that I grazed my knuckles deeply trying to get them on one morning. On my final day of interviews, I had to shake hands wearing Band-Aids. The tight kneesocks I wore to help the boots fit cut off my circulation so badly that they left deep red rings around each of my calves. I felt ridiculous—and damaged.

Interviewing at a small liberal arts college in Southern California, during what is known as a "fly out" to visit the campus, was no better. I was acutely self-conscious about sweating through the "walk and talk" with faculty members in the bright hot January sunshine. I worried about what to order at lunch, and then again at dinner, to seem like a "good fatty" with a healthy lifestyle and modest appetite. (I ended up eating almost nothing and was too afraid to order room service later, lest my potential employer get wind of it—not impossible since the university covered all job candidates' hotel expenses.) When I unwisely made a remark about enjoying horseback riding, trying to seem vaguely active, a faculty member jeered at a local equestrian outfit. "It's just for fat American tourists to sit on fat lazy horses on their fat American asses" was the gist of it. He blushed beet red as another—similarly lean, white, male—professor shot him a look. "My own fat ass is Australian," I thought without saying, struggling to regain my foothold in the conversation. But the damage was done. And I didn't get the job offer.

Of course, there might have been many reasons for that, including entirely valid ones. And, in the end, I was fortunate enough to receive several good offers, thereby exceeding my own modest expectations. Still, I wish I hadn't had to worry so much that my fat body would make my mental acuity as a philosopher seem that much less impressive and suitable for employment. And I still wish that knee-high boots came in bigger calf sizes. (Yes, I know "wide calf" boots exist. I have pored over so many. Unfortunately, they are often nasty, brutish, and shorter than one would wish for.)

More importantly, many fat people are less lucky than I am, not to mention less privileged, and lose out entirely on employment opportunities due to fatphobic biases. And lest you think this must surely be illegal, fat people are protected from discrimination on the basis of their size in only two states at the time of writing—thanks, Michigan and Washington.[20] The results of large national surveys in the United States as well as Canada and several European countries show that people classified as obese are more often unemployed.[21] An increase in BMI is also associated with a lower percentage of total working years throughout one's life span, even adjusting for relevant socioeconomic and health-related factors.

And it is more difficult for heavier people to regain employment once they have lost it. These effects are especially pronounced, again, among fat women.[22]

In addition to this lower workforce participation, fatter people tend to end up in lower-status occupations: so-called obese people are underrepresented in technical and managerial positions, and "obese" women are dramatically overrepresented in administrative and service roles.[23] Even within the same profession, fat people tend to earn considerably less than their thinner counterparts. Fat women are, yet again, disproportionately affected. According to one recent state-of-the-art analysis, published in 2018, so-called obesity is associated with an 8 to 10 percent wage penalty for women, on average, compared with only about 2 percent for men.[24] (Other studies showed no such penalty for men whatsoever, or even a modest pay increase for all but the very fattest male employees.[25])

Disturbingly, the wage gap for fat women seems to have only grown over time. The researchers Christian Brown and P. Wesley Routon analyzed two sets of longitudinal data that suggested that fat people born in the 1960s saw a smaller wage gap than those born twenty years later. The highest earners among the "obese" younger women were liable to be penalized particularly heavily—as much as 27 percent—for our fatness.[26] This is more than three times the penalty faced by the highest-earning fat men, and more than five times the penalty faced by the lowest-earning fat women, within this age demographic.[27] Other research has put a dollar figure on such fatphobia, suggesting that very fat women in the United States earn $19,000 less annually than their "average"-weight counterparts; and gaining twenty-five pounds as a woman was associated with upwards of a $13,000 annual salary loss.[28]

"This may suggest that, at least for women, the growing prevalence of obesity has not had a normalizing effect in the workplace," Brown and Routon noted.[29] If anything, this is an understatement: fat people generally seem more despised than ever.

The straitjacket of fatphobia is something fat people experience in public spaces when we simply try to move through the world and go about our business. Sometimes we literally don't fit—as became salient to me as a teaching assistant at Harvard, when I would have to get to class forty-five minutes early to secure a seat at one of the roomier fixed-desk benches. I dreaded the day when the narrower ones beckoned. When that day finally arrived—a meeting with my dissertation adviser ran late—I felt choked up with anxiety as I folded myself into the smallest shape I could and squeezed myself precariously into the one remaining space in the lecture theater. I held back tears of relief that my body was, just, containable. I still have nightmares about not fitting.

Recently I found myself giving a guest class at another campus on the topic of fatphobia. Some of the students were sympathetic; others scoffed, openly skeptical that fatphobia was really such a big deal. At the end of the session, where one student had held forth about his own fitness regimen and the benefits of lean protein, I couldn't help but point out that every single seat was a narrow fixed-desk bench. Who was not even potentially privy to this debate, this conversation? Fat people are frequently squeezed out of their proverbial place at the table, from the classroom to the boardroom to restaurants and theaters and stadiums. Recently, Universal

Studios Hollywood's Mario Kart virtual reality attraction came under fire for seats that fit only people with waists under forty inches—slightly less than the average American man's waist circumference.[30]

Travel is also inaccessible to many fat people. Seats on buses and trains and planes are simply not built for us. Air travel is particularly traumatic, with fat passengers regularly frog-marched back down the aisle if they are held to take up too much space for other people's comfort. Others pay a premium for an extra seat or first-class tickets. Requests for seatbelt extenders are often met with dirty looks, from both flight attendants and other passengers. And some passengers are positively vicious about being seated next to a fat person. When the plus-size model Natalie Hage boarded a flight from Texas to L.A. for a photo shoot, she noticed her seatmate sighing heavily and texting a friend. He joked that the plane would not be able to take off due to her weight. "Hopefully she didn't have any Mexican food," the friend replied. "I think she ate a Mexican," quipped Hage's seatmate via text message. He complained he was leaving a neck mark against the window because she left him so squashed against it.

When Hage confronted this man about his behavior, in a video that went viral, he initially apologized. But later, off camera, he doubled down—holding he was concerned that Hage wouldn't be able to do her duties as a passenger, since they were seated in an exit row. (She had paid for the privilege of a little extra legroom.) As Hage put it, "This is a fat person's daily reality and not just on a plane. This is on a bus, standing in line at the grocery store, at a concert, on the internet. You can be completely in your own space, not bothering anyone, and people will still fuck with you and try to hurt you." She added, "All you can do is know you haven't done anything wrong just by existing and move on."[31] Although you'll be encumbered in the process, still, by the fatphobia of transportation.

Perhaps nowhere is fatphobia more evident than in the healthcare system. Fat patients face a litany of barriers to equitable, effective care right from the moment we enter a doctor's office. The encounter itself typically begins with a weigh-in, regardless of whether any aspect of our care requires knowing what our weight is. And while all patients are weighed routinely, this is a particularly fraught experience for fat people, who step onto the scale bearing a lifetime of weight stigma. We can also expect expressions of disapproval, and sometimes outright shaming, during the appointment on the basis of the number. Aspects of this process have even been automated. I remember one doctor's visit where my weigh-in prompted a flashing red alert to appear on the screen of my patient records, adverting to my weight gain. I looked up my patient notes in the clinic's online system afterward. Under "appearance," there were just three words: "She is obese." I have rarely felt so ashamed of myself, or so reduced to my body, as an adult.

But even bigger patients face even bigger problems. Often, doctor's scales do not accommodate the largest patients, who may need to know their weight in order to gauge the appropriate dose for a medication or, as the case may be, to see if a weight-loss plan urged on them by their doctor is working. Such patients report having been advised to seek out the scales of junkyards and zoos. This could scarcely be more humiliating.[32] Many facilities lack chairs, blood pressure cuffs, gowns, examination tables, and needles suitable for very fat bodies too. And some patients are told they will not fit into an MRI machine, even when they would in fact fit comfortably.[33] Others are genuinely too large for standard machines, and so have to travel long distances to access one suitable for their bodies, or miss out entirely on this vital diagnostic service.[34]

When it comes to seeking emergency contraception, the first line of defense—Plan B—is known to be less effective for patients over 155 pounds. Even Ella, the medication touted as a solution, is only suggested for people up to 195 pounds.[35] If you weigh more than that, you may well be out of luck when it comes to avoiding a pregnancy—and, depending on where you live in the United States, good luck ending it, thanks to the draconian antiabortion laws that are being implemented across the country in the wake of the *Dobbs* decision.[36] Good luck too in obtaining adequate obstetric and gynecological care if you elect to keep the pregnancy. Some providers refuse to treat pregnant patients above a certain weight, allegedly due to our "high risk" status.[37] And, as fat people who can get pregnant, our needs are often denied, or we are rendered invisible. Or, sometimes, providers shrug. "I just have the feeling you'll get preeclampsia," one obstetrician blithely predicted when I was pregnant, despite my normal blood pressure and lack of other risk factors. It wasn't the hunch that bothered me, but rather the way she expressed it—at the very end of the appointment, casually, as if this potentially serious complication didn't warrant discussion or concern or extra monitoring. It was just something that someone like me should be expecting while pregnant. (Fortunately, it never happened.)

Provider attitudes are a prevalent site of injustice in medicine much more broadly. A comprehensive survey of the literature showed that fat patients are subject to numerous pernicious stereotypes. We are seen as lazy, undisciplined, weak-willed, and less likely to adhere to treatment or self-care recommendations.[38] In one study of primary care doctors and their patients, researchers also found that these doctors were less likely to build emotional rapport with fatter patients, and showed lower levels of empathy toward us—as was evident in their using significantly fewer expressions of care, concern, and reassurance during the appointment.[39] Another study revealed that a substantial proportion of nurses feel "repulsed" by our bodies and do not want to touch us.[40]

Providers report having less respect for fat patients and spend significantly less time with us.[41] In one study, primary care providers were asked to evaluate the medical records of a patient with migraine headaches who was classified as either obese, overweight, or "normal" weight, with otherwise identical records. (The researchers chose this condition because of the belief among consulting physicians that it is not linked to body weight.) The providers indicated that they planned to spend nearly one-third less time with the heaviest (that is, "obese") patients.[42] They also viewed heavier patients more negatively on twelve out of thirteen indices. These included "seeing this patient would feel like a waste of my time," "amount of patience I would have," "extent to which this patient would annoy me," and even "personal desire I have to help this patient."[43] Some of the physicians included notes in the margins of the files of the "obese" patients clearly indicative of stigma. For example: "This woman has a very unhappy life"; a second patient was "most likely a drug addict";

a third was held to be "suffering underlying depression." In more than a dozen instances, the provider suggested anti-depressant medications for heavier patients without any further information—a tad ironic, given that many tend to lead to weight gain.[44]

Fatphobic biases can lead to misdiagnosis, or no diagnosis at all—as the chapter's opening stories of Jen and Jan highlighted.[45] Nor are we limited merely to anecdata here: women classified as obese are significantly less likely to be screened for certain cancers.[46] In a study of more than three hundred autopsy reports, deceased people classified as overweight were also 1.65 times more likely to have serious undiagnosed medical conditions, including lung carcinoma and endocarditis (a heart infection).[47] This suggests, as the health writer and body positive advocate Jess Sims put it, that "other patients might be given life-saving tests and care such as CT scans and MRIs," while fat patients with the same symptoms are often "told to go home and lose weight."[48] Or we may not seek care in the first place, at least until we're in urgent need of medical attention. Some 45 percent of women across the size spectrum said in a 2016 survey that they had delayed going to the doctor until they lost weight.[49] In another study, the fear of being not only weighed but fat-shamed was disproportionately likely to make fatter women avoid going to the doctor.[50] In yet another, the fatter a woman was, the more likely she was to avoid healthcare altogether.[51] For all of these reasons, fatphobia can literally be a killer.

There is a final insult: as fat people, we may be precluded from donating our bodies to science after our passing. Cut-offs as low as 180 pounds are common, for no good scientific reason.[52] Seemingly, people in the medical establishment are reluctant to deal with our wayward bodies even postmortem.

✦ ✦ ✦

The above patterns of bias in healthcare, while grim, are likely to be familiar to at least some readers. What is less well known, and deserves emphasis, is how harmful fatphobia is to the most marginalized among us. This is due in part to compounding forms of oppression and stigmatization, and also because some marginalized people require specialized forms of care routinely denied to fatter bodies. There have been many reports of trans patients being denied gender-affirming care on the basis of their BMI, for example. One trans man, Nathan, twenty-five, undertook a grueling crash diet in order to try to get his BMI down from 38 to 35 to qualify for top surgery in Brighton, in the U.K. He managed to get it down to 35.8 by cutting out carbs completely and exercising nearly three hours daily. But he found his weight loss stalled at that point, because he was gaining muscle. He was asked to lose a further two kilograms (nearly four and a half pounds) in ten days so he could have his surgery.[53] It's hard to imagine that this rapid loss to meet an arbitrary cutoff made him any healthier, either before or after his surgery—especially since it led, he believes, to his developing an eating disorder.

Nathan later learned that, had he been a patient at another nearby clinic, he would have been approved for surgery all along; its BMI cutoff was 40. "If I had gone to Plymouth, I wouldn't have been asked to lose weight at all," he reflected.

Although BMI limits for surgery have been defended on the grounds that they supposedly yield better surgical outcomes and easier recoveries, the evidence on this score is limited and conflicting. Some studies have indeed found an association between a higher BMI and negative outcomes during and after surgery (intra-operative bleeding, atrial arrhythmia, deep vein thrombosis, and pulmonary embolism, for example). But other studies contradict these findings and detect "no association between peri-operative outcomes and elevated BMI alone," as the researchers noted.[54] The fact remains too that many fat patients would likely be approved for a particular class of major surgeries: bariatric ones. And whatever potential risks of gender-affirming surgeries there may be for heavier patients must also surely be balanced against others; for trans patients, being denied such care often decreases quality of life significantly and increases mental health risks—including suicidality.[55] Moreover, it is sometimes the surgeon's own aesthetic sense, as well as cis-centric beauty standards, that appears to be at stake in these decisions: one told a patient seeking bottom surgery that he wouldn't "look big and . . . right" unless he lost weight. In at least one aspect of body policing, size is considered an asset.

Disabled fat trans patients, for whom exercise may be difficult, may struggle even more to find the care they need. Lee Hulme, thirty-eight, a nonbinary transmasculine patient in the U.K., had long suffered from a knee injury and back pain, and then developed sciatica and arthritis. Despite these exercise-limiting conditions, they have been told they must lose weight before being approved for bottom surgery. "There's just utter despair sometimes that I'm never going to get the things that I need," they lamented.

Being denied gender-affirming care due to their weight is common for trans patients in the United States as well. In the first comprehensive study of this issue to date, published in 2020, researchers followed nearly fifteen hundred trans patients seeking various gender-affirming surgeries at a large

New York hospital, Mount Sinai.[56] More than a quarter of these patients were classified as obese; 14 percent had a BMI over 33 and thus were deemed ineligible for surgery at this facility.[57] Notably, *none* of these patients had lost the weight required in order to qualify for their surgeries by the follow-up visit. Other patients were even deemed ineligible because of subsequent weight gain.[58] This, even though, as the researchers pointed out, they are likely to be a highly motivated population. All in all, these draconian policies on weight are yet another form of gatekeeping that trans people face in trying to get the humane, gender-affirming healthcare to which they are entitled.[59]

Many fat patients—cis and trans alike—are prevented from accessing reproductive technologies too, which queer as well as trans people frequently need in order to grow their families. IVF clinics routinely impose BMI cutoffs, many of them similarly arbitrary and not well evidenced as necessary.[60] Adoption too is often denied to fat people, on the seeming assumption that we would not make good parents.[61] Recently, a fat woman was even prevented from adopting a dog from a shelter, since they doubted her ability to give her pet adequate exercise—notwithstanding her avowal that she was able and willing to do so.[62]

If we do have children, and our children turn out to be fat like us—quite likely, given the power of genetics to determine body weight—we will face widespread disapproval. The assumption will be that we eat and feed our children unhealthy food, and that the bullying they may face is thus a product of our own poor choices. Even thin parents of fat children will be blamed and shamed for their children's bodies, according to recent research.[63]

We thus see that fatphobia is a prevalent and pernicious

form of oppression, which is so much more than a matter of individual meanness or name-calling. It is a material, structural, and institutional phenomenon. Moreover, as the philosopher Madeline Ward, writing as G. M. Eller, has shown, fatphobia is *systemic*, because its effects in one aspect of our lives can easily pervade others. She writes:

> Fat prejudice begins early in life and continues throughout it. Earlier harms beget and compound later ones. Reduced self-esteem in adolescent years might induce greater weight gain or depression, affecting success. Being a fat teen might cause one to attend a less prestigious college than one would have otherwise, leading to an even more reduced income later in life. Moreover, the harms suffered by fat people extend to every aspect of their lives. Not only is there pervasive and obvious discrimination . . . there are "all the little things nipping at one's heels": difficulty fitting into airline seats or rides at an amusement park, unaccommodating restrooms, or having to shop at a specialty store to find clothes that fit. All of these harms are connected and omnipresent in the fat person's life.[64]

Fatphobia thus has the power to ruin lives and even end them. "The consequences of being denied jobs, disadvantaged in education, marginalized by healthcare professionals, or victimized by peers because of one's weight can have a profound impact on quality of life," as one research team put it.[65] Or, as the Black, trans nonbinary, fat activist Da'Shaun L. Harrison writes, fatness—like other forms of supposed Ugliness—"is the determiner for who does and does not work, who does and does not receive love, who does and does not die, who does and does not eat, who is and is not housed."[66]

What explains the straitjacket of fatphobia documented in this chapter? You might naturally assume that it is the unfortunate but understandable by-product of an obvious truth: that fat people are less healthy than thin ones. But, as we're about to see, matters are not so simple in reality: the relationship between fatness and health turns out to be intricate. Moreover, the conviction that fat people are unhealthy is, more often than not, a form of concern *trolling*—a way to dominate and humiliate, rather than stemming from a place of genuine concern with our well-being.

CHAPTER 2

SHRINKING COSTS

My final year of college was, in many ways, rough. I broke up with my long-term, live-in boyfriend and began living by myself for the first time, working two jobs between classes to pay the rent. (Though, to be clear, I always had the privilege of a safety net in the form of a supportive, middle-class family, even if I was determined to be financially independent as early on as possible.) I worked blisteringly hard at my studies during my fourth year, in the hopes of pursuing my dream of going to philosophy graduate school in America. I was about the busiest I have ever been, between writing my senior thesis and sending off the applications and studying for the GRE test.

And so I ate whatever was filling and quick and cheap: pasta, bread, cereal. I gained a lot of weight rapidly, leaving my upper arms flecked with stretch marks. I was so embarrassed by them that I didn't wear a short-sleeve, let alone sleeveless, shirt for several years afterward, until they eventually faded from a vivid, angry purple to a milky, jagged lattice. I sweated in three-quarter-length-sleeve tops for summer after summer after summer.

By the end of that year, I was feeling truly lousy—tired, achy, anxious—and my feet began to tingle. After an hour with Dr. Google, I became convinced that what I was experiencing must be diabetic nerve pain. I walked to a local pharmacy and purchased a pinprick test for diabetes. I spiked my index finger, leaked out a fat drop of blood, and, with my heart in my mouth, tested my own blood sugar. It was, and remains, perfectly normal. (The culprit for my tingling feet? A pair of ill-fitting shoes that I had been walking in for long distances.) But I have rarely felt so sick with guilt, fear, and panic as during that little episode. I had the same feeling, some fifteen years later, while waiting for the results of my three-hour test for gestational diabetes when I was pregnant with my daughter. I refreshed the medical portal site so many times that day that they must have wondered if there was a hacker or a glitch in the system. Both times, the test felt like not just a medical assessment but an impending commentary on my character. And when all was well, I wept with more than relief: I felt I had been granted a reprieve from a fate both dire and predestined.

Aspects of this fear are not entirely irrational. Type 2 diabetes does run in my family. I would not be surprised if this diagnosis awaits me in the future. On the other hand, and as I am now aware, the depth and contours of my anxiety reflect a potent stigma about an illness that affects almost one in ten Americans. It goes beyond dreading being sick, ill, or disabled (as problematically ableist as that can sometimes be): it is also a fear of being held to *have brought this on myself*, by virtue of my fatness. And even though diabetes is of course a serious medical condition, which requires careful treatment and management, that fear is frequently weaponized against those of us living in larger bodies.

In this chapter, I want to examine some of the specific and general health-related panics that fatphobia gives rise to. We must find a way to have a conversation that recognizes the complicated relationship between fatness and health, highlighting that fat bodies can be healthy, without insisting that fat people *must* be healthy in order to be valid. Both our well-being and our access to appropriate, compassionate healthcare hang precariously in the balance.

In 2005, a landmark study by Katherine M. Flegal, a senior scientist at the CDC, showed that the mortality risks associated with fatness were much lower than had often been assumed. In Flegal's study, "mild obesity" (having a BMI between 30 and 35) wasn't associated with a statistically significantly greater risk of death than being in the so-called normal-weight category (with a BMI of 18.5 to 25).[1] Moreover, being "overweight" (with a BMI of 25 to 30) was actually associated with a significantly *lower* mortality risk. Being more than "mildly obese" (with a BMI of 35 or more) *was* associated with increased mortality, but so was being underweight (with a BMI of less than 18.5).[2] (I use the BMI as a reference point here only when unavoidable. For the record, "severe obesity" is defined as having a BMI of 40 or more, as I myself once did; it is sometimes called "morbid obesity," a particularly stigmatizing label.)

This research was meticulous and consistent with previous research; it has also been further confirmed by subsequent studies.[3] Flegal is a highly respected scientist whose study won the CDC's highest research award and has since guided its recommendations. Yet despite this, her research was torn apart by other researchers pushing an anti-fatness agenda.

Granted, Flegal is far from the only scientist looking into the question, and some of the findings have been contradictory—including those in another CDC study conducted the previous year, led by Ali H. Mokdad. His team claimed that a huge number of "excess" deaths—that is, more than the number of deaths we'd expect based on average life expectancy—were due to fatness (some 385,000 annually, compared with Flegal's modest estimate of fewer than 26,000 for the "overweight" and "obese" categories combined, concentrated among people with a BMI of more than 35).[4] But as the sociologist Abigail C. Saguy explains, Mokdad's study, unlike Flegal's, was flawed in numerous ways: it drew on data not representative of the U.S. population; it failed to adjust for gender, smoking, and age; it assumed rather than demonstrated that the deaths in the overweight and obese categories were due to "poor diet and inactivity"; and it failed to draw on data from the entire "normal"-weight category, instead canvassing only people at the upper end of this range (who would likely have a lower mortality risk than thinner "normal"-weight people, extrapolating from Flegal's findings).[5] It also drew on self-reported data about weight, which is notoriously unreliable.[6] Moreover, Mokdad's initial estimate suffered from basic calculation errors: it had to be revised downward by 20,000 after publication. The CDC officially endorsed Flegal's findings over Mokdad's.[7]

Unsurprisingly, though, given widespread perceptions

about the health risks of fatness, the press covered the two conflicting studies very differently: tending, as Saguy's news media analysis reveals, to present Flegal's findings as suspect. Specifically, Saguy found that 75 percent of news reports on Mokdad's study suggested that the findings confirmed previous research, whereas less than 10 percent of the news reports on Flegal's did, despite her research being consistent with a large body of epidemiological evidence. Conversely, less than 3 percent of news reports on Mokdad's study framed it as surprising, whereas more than one-third of news reports on Flegal's did. Finally, more than 30 percent of the news reports on Flegal's study quoted outside researchers who questioned her findings; none of the news reports on Mokdad's did.[8] As Paul Campos, the author of *The Obesity Myth*, has shown, a similar tendency to exaggerate the slightly elevated health risks posed by COVID-19 for fat people has afflicted reporting during the pandemic. You wouldn't guess from looking at the headlines that, at the time of writing, being a man appeared to be riskier on this score than being even "severely obese"—or, again, that being "overweight" was associated with slightly better outcomes than being a so-called normal weight.[9]

The discrepancy between the reporting of the two conflicting CDC studies was driven partly by the dedicated efforts of one Walter Willett, a professor at the Harvard School of Public Health, who has written several diet books. When Flegal's results came out, Willett went on the attack, issuing a press release pooh-poohing her findings—calling them "really naive, deeply flawed and seriously misleading"[10]—and organizing a one-day conference devoted to discrediting them that was webcast live to reporters. These are highly unusual measures in the scientific community. But so moved was he by the supposed dangers of fatness, Willett became vehement: "Kathy Flegal just doesn't get it." ("I go by Katherine," Flegal corrected him.[11]) "This study is really a pile of rubbish and no one should waste their time reading it," Willett fulminated about Flegal's follow-up meta-analysis that lent further support to her findings.[12] Students at the Harvard School of Public Health reported that some of their professors had even poked fun at Flegal's own weight.[13]

We hence see that the deadliness of fatness has often been exaggerated, by both journalists and some researchers.[14] The most careful, credible, well-replicated studies on this topic show that the relationship between fatness and mortality can be represented by a U-shaped curve, with being either very fat *or* very thin correlated with—and not necessarily causing—premature death.[15] Being "mildly obese" is not associated with elevated mortality compared with being a so-called normal weight, and being "overweight" is actually associated with significantly lower mortality. Yet despite that, fatness continues to be widely considered lethal.

So weight is much less of a death sentence than we've been led to believe.[16] It's also far less controllable than we are accustomed to thinking. Though many people can lose weight in the short term through dieting, keeping it off is strikingly rare, according to the best available data.

In one important meta-analysis, UCLA researchers set out to establish that dieting helps people to lose weight in the long term. "We found that the evidence shows the opposite," said Janet Tomiyama, a member of the research team: in other words, it doesn't. They analyzed thirty one long-term diet studies—virtually every available study that tracked people for two to five years—in the most comprehensive and rigorous analysis of this kind to date.[17] The lead researcher, Traci Mann, summarized their findings thus: "You can initially lose 5 to 10 percent of your weight on any number of diets, but then the weight comes back. We found that the majority of people regained all the weight, plus more." Only a small minority of participants showed sustained weight loss. The majority showed complete weight regain. Many people—between one- and two-thirds—regained more weight than they lost within a four- to five-year period.[18] Far from helping people to lose weight, dieting may hence be counterproductive on this score. "Several studies indicate that dieting is actually a consistent predictor of future weight gain," said Tomiyama.[19]

There's another reason why diets are so problematic from the perspective of our health. Not only is weight loss incredibly difficult to maintain, but the process of losing and almost inevitably regaining weight repeatedly—known as "weight cycling"—turns out to be very hard on the human body. It is linked to a variety of health problems: cardiovascular disease and strokes,[20] metabolic conditions,[21] worsened immune function,[22] and yes, even diabetes.[23] For the majority of the people who were studied, Mann thus holds that they would have been better off not dieting to begin with; there would be no major difference to their weight, and their overall health would be better. "Dieting is not effective in treating obesity," Mann concluded. "The benefits of dieting are too small and the potential harm is too large."[24] And even if a person who has always been lighter is healthier on average than a very heavy person, it doesn't follow that the heavier person *herself* would likely be healthier if she lost weight, due to these, as we might call them, "shrinking costs."[25]

Mann and her team published their meta-analysis in 2007, and subsequent research has further supported their findings. In another comprehensive meta-analysis, published in 2020, researchers analyzed 121 trials of various diets (low fat, low carb, and so on), encompassing nearly twenty-two thousand participants. They found that, at twelve months, most of these diets made no significant difference to measures of cardiovascular health: blood pressure, LDL cholesterol, and C-reactive protein. Just two differences emerged—one positive, and one negative. The good news: there was a significant reduction in LDL cholesterol—the bad kind—at the twelve-month follow-up for people who followed the Mediterranean diet (which emphasizes fish, nuts, leafy greens, and olive oil). The bad news: there was a significant *adverse* reduction in HDL cholesterol—the good kind—for some kinds of diets (low fat and moderate macronutrient). Summarizing the effects of all of these diets, the researchers noted that "at 12 months the effects on weight reduction and improvements in cardiovascular risk factors largely disappear." And the average weight loss of the participants was well under five pounds.[26]

Research has also shown that exercise, once assumed to be the key to weight control, has surprisingly little effect on people's weight-loss efforts (though it consistently tends to make them healthier, and may have more of a role to play in weight maintenance).[27] This seems to be in part because people overestimate the number of calories they burn, and in part because exercise can increase hunger. "You cannot out-exercise a bad diet" is now a veritable slogan (whatever "a bad diet" amounts to, exactly).

In 2018, Mann was interviewed about the aftermath of her landmark 2007 study. It had been updated in 2013 to incorporate further studies, including more recent ones. Her team's conclusions were unaltered.[28] "The results were clear," says Mann. "The dieters had little benefit to show for their efforts, and the non-dieters did not seem harmed by their lack of effort. In sum, it appears that weight regain is the typical long-term response to dieting, rather than the exception."[29]

Mann has subsequently been studying why weight regain occurs. The answer is not willpower: though willpower is not wholly unrelated to BMI, it is at most a minor factor, accounting for between 1 and 4 percent of the variance in body weight across the population. (In contrast, willpower is a fairly strong predictor of other outcomes, like SAT performance.[30]) Instead, there appear to be a variety of factors at play here: dieting may cause increased appetite due to a subsequent fixation on food; the body may have a natural "set point" weight that is largely due to genetics (but that may be raised by dieting, ironically).[31] Moreover, a slowing of people's metabolism seems to be a predictable and long-term outcome of a period of severe caloric restriction.[32] A study of former contestants from the weight-loss reality show *The Biggest Loser* showed a startling reduction in the number of calories they burned per day for years after their drastic weight loss—nearly 30 percent, on average. Not only had most regained some weight, but some were heavier than when they started. And the few who had kept off most of the weight had to work harder and harder to maintain their current body size.[33] This casts grave doubt on the popular idea of "calories in–calories out" upon which *The Biggest Loser*, among many other diet and fitness practices, is premised.

The upshot is this: dieting won't make most fat people thin, at least in the long term. And, just as important, the resulting weight cycling also seems to worsen health outcomes considerably.

Still, you might wonder: What *about* type 2 diabetes? Even if the relationship between being fat and being unhealthy is less straightforward than many suppose, isn't diabetes an obvious exception?

The relationship remains complex, and it's worth emphasizing how much we still don't know about what causes this chronic illness and how best to treat it. Diabetes occurs when the body either doesn't produce enough insulin or produces insulin but is insensitive to it—a condition called "insulin resistance"—leading to impaired uptake of glucose (a sugar) by cells, which then accumulates in the bloodstream. (Both of these interrelated problems occur in type 2 diabetes. In type 1 diabetes, the insulin-producing beta cells in the pancreas are destroyed by the immune system, leaving the body with little or no insulin.[34]) Of potential causal relevance, for example, one study turned up a seemingly bizarre correlation: People who used mouthwash at least twice daily were 55 percent more likely to develop diabetes or prediabetes over the next three years.[35] (In prediabetes, blood glucose levels are elevated, but not to the level that would warrant a diagnosis of diabetes.[36]) This correlation persisted even after accounting for a number of possible confounds, including diet, oral hygiene, sleep disorders, medication use, fasting glucose levels, income, and education. The researchers suggested that mouthwash may destroy "good" bacteria in the mouth that help with the formation of nitric oxide, a chemical in the body that helps to regulate insulin. But, at the time of writing, we are still a long way from knowing what is going on here. The same is true of research showing that the prevalence of type 2 diabetes was significantly lower in those who habitually drink coffee.[37]

It's undoubtedly true that most (by no means all) people who develop type 2 diabetes are classified as overweight or obese according to the BMI charts.[38] So a higher body weight and type 2 diabetes are certainly highly correlated. But some researchers have suggested, in a hypothesis currently gaining traction, that it's not that weight gain causes type 2 diabetes; rather, the high amounts of insulin in the blood that are a hallmark of developing type 2 diabetes precede and may cause weight gain.[39] Meanwhile, many other fat people are metabolically normal.[40]

Still, regardless of cause, doesn't weight loss improve health outcomes for patients with type 2 diabetes? This is, after all, a common prescription for those newly diagnosed or found to have prediabetes. To be sure, weight loss often improves blood glucose control and lessens other symptoms in the short term. But in the long term, the evidence is, again, much more equivocal. The well-known Look AHEAD (Action for Health in Diabetes) study sheds important light here. The researchers followed more than five thousand people, aged forty-five to seventy-six, who were classified as overweight or obese and had type 2 diabetes. Half received standard care in the form of diabetes support and education (DSE); the remaining half underwent an "intensive lifestyle intervention" (ILI), wherein they received comprehensive behavioral weight-loss counseling. They also received other services—structured meal plans and free meal replacements—and were advised to follow a low-calorie, low-fat diet. They were instructed to keep a food diary. Finally, they were prescribed at least 175 minutes of moderate-intensity exercise each week (and then more, if they managed to meet this goal). "Look AHEAD provides the largest and longest randomized evaluation to date of an intensive lifestyle intervention for weight reduction," the researchers noted. "The trial offers invaluable information about the feasibility of inducing and maintaining clinically significant weight loss, defined as more than a 5% reduction in initial body weight."[41]

The results? People in the ILI group did manage, unlike with many other studies, to lose an average of 8.5 percent of their starting weight at the one-year mark, compared with less than 1 percent for the DSE group. Many ILI participants maintained more than half of this weight loss, leaving them with an average loss of nearly 5 percent of their starting weight after eight years (compared with just over 2 percent for the control group). A person who initially weighed two hundred pounds would have ultimately lost around ten pounds, then, on average, as the result of this intensive lifestyle intervention. And significantly more ILI than DSE participants had lost more than 5 or even 10 percent of their starting weight after eight years.[42] However, notwithstanding their greater weight loss, the ILI group of participants showed no significant improvement on cardiovascular mortality or morbidity (illness) compared with DSE participants. Since this was the trial's primary target outcome, the researchers called a halt to it after ten years for ethical reasons, following what is called—rather poignantly—a "futility analysis."[43]

These results are incredibly disappointing. People did about as much as one can do by way of diet and exercise for around a decade, and many thereby *did* defy the odds by losing a modest amount of weight and maintaining some of this loss via these stringent and highly supervised measures. They also garnered certain benefits compared with the DSE group during the early years of the study: some had reduced urinary incontinence, sleep apnea, and depression; and these participants self-reported a significantly improved quality of life.[44] (Though whether these benefits were due to the weight loss itself, or improved diet, or exercise, or some combination of these factors, remains an open question—as does the question of whether these initial benefits were ongoing.) Still, there were *no statistically significant improvements* in the outcomes that pose the biggest risk to people with type 2 diabetes, in the form of illness and death due to cardiovascular issues, compared with people treated using the standard (much less intense and interventionist) protocols.[45]

A study published in 2016 further supported these findings. Rasmus Køster-Rasmussen and his co-authors examined the effect of weight loss on long-term morbidity and mortality in so-called overweight and obese patients with type 2 diabetes. The team was testing the hypothesis that intentional weight loss, under the supervision of a doctor, would lead to a longer life and reduce the risk of cardiovascular disease for patients with this profile. They monitored more than four hundred Danish patients' BMIs and intentions to lose weight every three months over a six-year period. They then tracked these patients' outcomes during the ensuing thirteen years, making for a nearly twenty-year study. To the researchers' surprise, they found that weight loss (regardless of intention) was not predictive of better outcomes, and even proved to be an independent *risk factor* for increased all-cause mortality.[46] The team found "a V-like association between weight change and all-cause mortality, suggesting the best prognosis for those who maintained their weight." (And suggesting, by the same token, that a large weight loss and a large weight gain were both problematic.) And they concluded, "In this population-based cohort of overweight patients with type 2 diabetes, successful therapeutic intentional weight loss, supervised by a doctor over six years, was not associated with reduced all-cause mortality or cardiovascular morbidity/mortality during the succeeding 13 years."[47]

Of course, in any study like the ones above, there are and will be outliers. This is true much more broadly: there *are* people who lose large amounts of weight through diet and exercise, and some do keep off at least a large proportion of it, according to self-reports available via the National Weight Control Registry.[48] And we also can't rule out the possibility that some people do get significant medical benefits from such weight loss. My point is just that these outliers are exactly that: outliers. They don't provide a good basis for individual health advice or public policy interventions.

Given these discouraging outcomes, you might well wonder what *does* make a difference for people—with or without diabetes—trying to minimize their risk of cardiovascular disease and other major drivers of mortality. Many studies do suggest that exercise helps, even quite independently of weight loss. One meta-analysis of fourteen studies of people with type 2 diabetes found that both aerobic and strength training reduced levels of hemoglobin A1C in the blood— a standard measure of blood glucose control—"by an amount that should decrease the risk of diabetic complications," despite the lack of significant weight loss in there people.[49] Another meta-analysis of more than ten studies of the general population (that is, *not* specific to people with type 2 diabetes) showed that, compared with "normal weight" fit individuals, unfit individuals had twice the risk of mortality regardless of BMI. However, "overweight and obese-fit individuals had similar mortality risks as normal weight-fit individuals," the researchers summarized. They added, "Researchers, clinicians, and public health officials should focus on physical activity and fitness-based interventions rather than weight-loss driven approaches to reduce mortality risk."[50]

Similarly, in a study of more than five thousand people in Rotterdam, aged fifty-five or older, participants were classified according to both BMI and levels of physical activity (low or high) and followed for around ten years on average. Although those classified as overweight and obese with low physical activity had a higher risk of cardiovascular disease (CVD) than people classified as normal weight with low physical activity, the same did *not* hold for highly active people. "Overweight" and "obese" participants with high physical activity had no more CVD risk than their "normal"-weight (and similarly highly active) counterparts.[51] A study of more than twenty-two thousand Americans, aged thirty to sixty-four, also found that being physically active was associated with a larger reduction in cardiovascular disease risk than having a so-called normal BMI.[52]

When it comes to our health, then, there is considerable evidence that it is fitness, not fatness, that matters most, and that fitness mitigates many if not all of the health risks associated with living in a larger body. And yet many continue to mistake fatness for the biggest problem.

✦ ✦ ✦

A common refrain in fat activist circles is that correlation is not causation: the fact that very heavy people are less healthy, on average, than their thinner counterparts—in being more likely to have type 2 diabetes, for example—doesn't imply that a higher weight in itself *causes* ill health. Male-pattern baldness and heart disease are highly correlated, for example, but that doesn't mean that this type of baldness *causes* heart disease (or vice versa); they both appear to be caused by a third intervening, or "confounding," variable: high testosterone.[53] Likewise, both fatness and certain kinds of ill health may be correlated not because the former causes the latter but because, for example, a lack of exercise causes the relevant health problems *and* a higher body weight—among many other possibilities.

These points are important and generally well taken. Still, there are lots of correlations established by science that *do* lend themselves to a plausible causal story: smoking clearly causes lung cancer, and opiates clearly cause addiction in some people. Why not think that fatness causes ill health, given the correlation between them?[54]

We've already seen several reasons, in the form of alternative explanations for this particular correlation. First, there's reason to believe that those of us with a higher body weight will diet more, due to potent social pressures, and thus suffer more of the negative health effects that are due to weight cycling. Second, some researchers believe that it's not that weight gain causes diabetes; rather, early diabetic processes such as insulin resistance may tend to cause weight gain.[55] Although more research is required to fully evaluate this hypothesis, it jibes with the finding that simply removing fat from a person's body, via liposuction, doesn't tend to improve health markers such as fasting glucose, insulin levels, and insulin sensitivity.[56] Conversely, if somewhat confusingly, bariatric surgeries can *improve* certain health markers, such as blood glucose control in people with type 2 diabetes, well before their weight has decreased substantially. Some researchers have speculated that this may be due to a change in the release of gut hormones.[57] Other research suggests that the difference is due not to the surgeries themselves but to the ensuing extreme caloric restriction—which of course isn't a livable long-term option for people who choose not to have these procedures that, as we'll see later, are fraught with risks and drawbacks.[58]

Perhaps the most vital complication, when it comes to the relationship between health and weight, is stigma. People in larger bodies routinely face social stigma, as we saw in the opening chapter. And there is now considerable evidence of the adverse health effects of being subject to these biases. One study divided people classified as obese into two groups: those who demonstrated strong forms of internalized fatphobia—for example, the idea that they were lazy or unattractive because of their weight—and those who did not. The "high internalized weight stigma" participants were some three times more likely to have metabolic syndrome—a cluster of risk factors including high blood pressure, high blood glucose, abnormal cholesterol levels, and a high waist circumference—compared with "low internalized weight stigma" participants of the same age, race, gender, and so on. Members of the "high internalized weight bias" group were also six times more likely to have high triglycerides than their "low internalized weight bias" counterparts.[59] "There is a common misconception that stigma might help motivate individuals with obesity to lose weight and improve their health," noted the lead researcher, Rebecca Pearl. "We are finding it has quite the opposite effect."[60] And, as the writer and health reporter Virginia Sole-Smith summarizes in connection with this emerging body of research, researchers have found that the stress of stigma increases inflammation and cortisol levels, both of which are associated with negative health outcomes.[61]

Moreover, as we've seen, weight stigma causes fat people to avoid seeking medical care, and results in our getting inadequate care when we do seek it out. Fat patients are less likely, in particular, to receive screenings for cervical, breast, and colorectal cancer.[62] These findings are important to bear in mind when responding to the oft-cited fact that a higher body weight is correlated with developing certain cancers, including these three specific ones.[63] While we certainly shouldn't discount the possibility that a higher body weight does play a role in cancer development, it's difficult to separate out the health effects of fatness itself from the health effects of not being screened or treated for early cancer markers.[64] Yet another complication is that, although a higher weight is correlated with *developing* such illnesses, the survival rate is frequently better for so-called overweight and obese people with these diagnoses than it is for their thinner counterparts. This is known as the "obesity paradox," which some researchers view as a misnomer for the likelihood that fat can be protective in some cases against the risk of "wasting away" due to severe illness.[65]

The health effects of weight stigma don't end there, either. Some studies show that experiencing it led people to avoid exercise[66]—which, as we've seen, does have clear health benefits according to the majority of studies.[67] This avoidance makes sense: as Sole-Smith points out, if you expect to be harassed or belittled at the gym, at the pool, or even just walking around in public, you're less likely to engage in the exercise you might have done otherwise. And so, as she puts it, "in obesity research, fatphobia is always the X factor": a hidden variable that underlies many of the relationships between weight and health that we often make easy—and biased—assumptions about.[68] In one study of more than twenty-one thousand people classified as overweight or obese, those who reported weight discrimination had a significantly higher risk of arteriosclerosis, high cholesterol, heart attack, minor heart conditions, stomach ulcers, and diabetes, even after adjusting for BMI, physical activity, and sociodemographic factors. "Such added health risk . . . posed by perceived weight discrimination warrants public health and policy interventions against weight discrimination to reduce the socioeconomic burden of obesity," the researchers concluded.[69] Another team of researchers found that, of nearly fourteen thousand older adults, those who reported experiencing weight stigma had a 60 percent increased risk of dying overall, again independent of their BMI.[70] It appears to be weight stigma, more than weight, that is deadly.

To summarize, when it comes to the relationship between weight and health, we have now seen that the following causal mechanisms are all plausible, where an arrow → indicates a likely causal relationship of some kind:

Higher weight → Weight cycling (due to the pressure on fatter people to diet) → Poorer health

Poorer health (for example, early diabetic processes) → Higher weight[71]

Higher weight → Weight stigma → Stress → Poorer health

Higher weight → Weight stigma → Medical fatphobia → Poorer health

Higher weight → Weight stigma → Less access to exercise → Poorer health (and, sometimes, further weight gain)

And all of that is even before we take into account other social determinants of health—including features of the built environment that are due to systemic classism and racism—which we'll consider later in these pages.

The question of whether fatness itself is *also* a causal risk factor for ill health—and, if so, to what extent, compared with numerous other causal factors—continues to be hotly debated by epidemiologists and other medical researchers. Some argue in the affirmative, based on methods like Mendelian randomization[72] and animal studies;[73] others make the negative case, based on principles like the Bradford Hill criteria and clinical studies that point to hyperinsulinemia and inflammation as important confounding variables.[74] Regardless of how this shakes out, here are some things we *do* know, which should be at the center of this conversation: the health risks of fatness have frequently been overstated; a person's weight is typically highly resistant to deliberate change, at least in the long term; there is currently no known reliable, safe, and ethical way to make fat people thin, at either an individual or a population level; fitness is at least as important as fatness in determining overall health; and weight stigma is hugely harmful to fat people's health, whatever the health risks of fatness simpliciter. So, in the end, even if fat people are subject to greater health risks purely on account of our fatness, how much does this matter, practically, and to the public discourse swirling around our bodies?[75] We still deserve support, compassion, and adequate healthcare. We still deserve to be treated like human beings, and not human failures—or walking, talking burdens on an anthropomorphized healthcare system. We still deserve to be seen through the lens of something more nuanced and humane than the bare statistics thin people often spit out to bully and belittle us. All of this I can say confidently as a moral philosopher. Indeed, it ought to be a no-brainer for anyone.

I confess I was reluctant to write this chapter. It felt, somehow, obscurely, that it was missing the point. But how could this be, when the unhealthiness of fat people is typically the *first* point that comes up in the discussion?

I suspect, precisely for this reason, that it is not really health that is on some people's minds when they ostensibly raise the issue. They are saying something else when they label us unhealthy. Namely, they are saying, or at least implying, that we are weak-willed, gross, lazy, lax, and stupid. They are saying that we are destined to be not just unhealthy but *unhappy*. And that we are responsible for our own ignominy.

In this way, the label "unhealthy" works as a dog whistle in the discourse around fat bodies—much as the terms "inner city" and "urban poor" encode racialized meanings, as the philosopher Jennifer Saul has argued.[76] To some of us, the meaning is the literal one, so we scramble to prove that fat people are not inevitably unhealthy and that, in any case, losing weight through dieting and exercise is ineffective and even positively counterproductive for most fat people. Many fat people are healthy, and many thin people are not, making reading someone's health off their appearance impossible—as well as, often, discriminatory. And so on. But to many in the audience—those laboring under the weight of fatphobic assumptions—these efforts are largely wasted. For them, "unhealthy" is a term that conjures up a litany of negative associations and stereotypes that much of the rest of this book serves to expose and dismantle: namely, that fat people are morally blameworthy, aesthetically inferior, and intellectually lacking.

So when the word "unhealthy" is used in discussing fatness, many people will inevitably respond to the dog whistle by barking loudly and aggressively in the direction of fat people. In fact, this meaning is so salient and readily available that "unhealthy" can be used in some contexts just to *mean* "fat" in the pejorative sense of the term. Imagine that your judgmental aunt has informed you that she just bumped into your childhood friend Cam. "They didn't look very *healthy*," she says with a contemptuous edge to her voice. In many circles, you'd probably be justified in thinking that your aunt is insinuating that Cam has gained weight.[77] Observe too that so-called healthy food is typically just whatever is assumed to be conducive to weight loss.

Hence, in many of the contexts in which fatness is under discussion, comments like "it's just not healthy" and "I worry about your health" don't just mean that fat bodies are subject to a greater chance of illness, disease, or early death. What is being said, or at least insinuated, is that fat people are undeserving of care and incapable of looking after ourselves. As the writer Claudia Cortese put it, in discussing the pandemic,

Health is weaponized against fat people: The gospel
of fatphobia says you're unhealthy and it's your fault,
so you don't deserve care and compassion. There's an
ingrained cultural myth that links wellness to goodness, so what's perceived as poor health—fatness,
chronic illness, or disability—is a result of poor
choices and thus poor character.[78]

And when health is weaponized in this way, it is particularly harmful to the fat people who are *not* healthy, or who
cannot perform certain health behaviors. Take Linda Gerhardt, who suffers from lipedema—a still poorly understood
condition estimated to affect more than 10 percent of
women, in which painful, lumpy fat deposits accumulate
under the skin, especially in the lower body.[79] In Gerhardt's
case, it has limited her mobility and made the currently popular idea of "joyful movement" a nonstarter. Let's be clear: a
lot of good has been done by the Health at Every Size paradigm, which emphasizes the possibility of being healthy
without weight loss, eating nutritious foods without restriction, as well as engaging in forms of exercise that are pleasur-
able and not punitive. But this framework tends to leave out
people like Gerhardt who suffer from health problems that
are not only chronic but also linked to their fatness, specifically. As she put it, in a moving conversation with Virginia
Sole-Smith,

> For me personally, there's a lot of shame in not being
> the Good Fatty and being the chronically ill fatty,
> who can't go on a long hike because my legs are heavy
> and swollen and hurt. There's this focus on "well,

you can be healthy at any size, just do the health behaviors." And, you know, some people can't.[80]

There should be no shame in not being healthy. And a
person's good health should never be a prerequisite for their
being treated with empathy and kindness and respect—least
of all by the medical professionals tasked with helping those
in ill health live the best lives they can, given the material,
physical, emotional, social, and financial constraints which
they may be facing.

But health is not just a weapon; it is also a smoke screen.
Our fear of fatness, and the disgust that fatness seems to
elicit, turn out to long predate credible medical concerns
about the so-called obesity epidemic. And it's not that we
abhor fatness because we discovered it is unhealthy. By and
large, we *decided* it is unhealthy because we came, over time,
to abhor it—for nefarious reasons we're about to delve into.

CHAPTER 3

VENUS IN RETROGRADE

O ne of the world's oldest surviving artworks, the Venus of Willendorf, is a fat female figurine rendered in limestone. Dating from the Paleolithic period, and created some twenty-five thousand years ago, she has heavy, pendulous breasts, a round belly, and thick thighs.[1] She is beautiful and faceless and devoid of sharp angles.

Though particularly famous, the Venus of Willendorf is far from a lone figure. There are hundreds of similar statuettes dating from this era, which have been found in a wide variety of locations across Europe and Asia.[2] (So much for the Paleo diet.) They are too ancient for us to be sure of their meaning; they might be fertility symbols, religious icons, dolls, tokens, pendants, representations of actual women, or perhaps an ideal—even yesteryear's pornography.[3] Whatever the case, they are only part of a sizable body of evidence suggesting that for much of human history, fatness wasn't typically viewed as a problem.

In ancient Egypt, the male fertility god Hapy (or Hapi) was often depicted as fat, with a large sagging belly and breasts. Some depictions of the pharaoh Akhenaten (who came to power around 1350 BCE and was likely the father of Tutankhamun) were similar, suggesting an association between fatness and not only fertility but also prosperity.[4] Later Egyptian figurines from the Hellenistic period, dated to the first century BCE, support the idea of an ongoing positive association between fatness and abundance in this region.[5]

In the Hebrew Bible, gluttony was condemned in no uncertain terms, but little comment was made on the fat body as such.[6] Similarly, the ancient Greek philosophers Plato and Aristotle had much to say about the vice of gluttony and the human tendency to eat to excess, as we'll see later. But fat bodies were acknowledged without much commentary.[7] As the historian Susan E. Hill puts it,

> Food scholars note that the equation of gluttony with fatness was rarely made in the ancient world, and not simply because ancient people did not have an understanding of calories, body metabolism, and the nutritional content of various foods. Rather, people in the ancient world usually distinguish being fat from being a glutton because anyone can behave gluttonously, and fat people are not inevitably gluttonous.[8]

This despite a general understanding that certain foods, consumed in large amounts, would lead to a fatter body. (God's promised land, after all, famously flowed with "milk and honey," on which people would "eat their fill and grow fat" before turning to worship other gods, as Deuteronomy 31 ominously predicted.[9]) Yet, far from being universally abhorred, "a fat body in the ancient world often positively represent[ed] wealth, abundance, and luxury."[10]

Following the Hellenistic Jewish philosopher Philo of Alexandria, early Christian writers developed the idea of gluttony as one of the seven deadly sins. But the fat body remained of little concern throughout the Middle Ages.[11] Meanwhile, in China, in the tenth century, the fat, cheerful Buddhist monk Budai came to be celebrated. He continues to be so today, depicted throughout China, Japan, Korea, and Vietnam carrying a bag filled with sweets for children. He is widely known, somewhat misleadingly, as "the laughing Buddha" and "the fat Buddha."[12]

Fatphobia is widespread across the world today, including in East Asia. But some places remain positive about the fat body, even to the point of policing via overfeeding. The ongoing practice of *leblouh* sees young women encouraged to become very fat prior to marriage, by having them eat around fifteen thousand calories per day, in certain parts of Mauritania, among other places.[13] This involves the cruelty of force-feeding, on some accounts.[14] Among Saharawi people, "overweight" bodies are simply preferred in (and by) both men and women.[15]

And so we see that fat people have always existed. Moreover, in many times and places, we have been and continue to be venerated, or regarded neutrally as a normal human variation. So when, where, and why did fatness fall out of favor?

✦ ✦ ✦

The admiration of relatively fat female bodies reached an artistic high point in sixteenth- and seventeenth-century Europe in the work of painters like Albrecht Dürer, Raphael, and, of course, Peter Paul Rubens.[16] As the sociologist Sabrina Strings explains in *Fearing the Black Body: The Racial Origins of Fat Phobia*, European beauty standards then dictated that white women in particular be fleshy and round, though still "proportionate."[17] Baroque painters notoriously celebrated ample female buttocks, breasts, hips, and fatty dimples—even cellulite—as well as what Rubens called a "snow white" skin tone.[18]

Ironically, given his proclivity for moderately fat women, Rubens himself kept to an abstemious diet, both so he could better devote himself to his paintings and to prevent weight gain.[19] The French figurehead of philosophy, René Descartes, similarly advised moderation in a letter written in the 1640s: one should have "a good diet, taking only food and drink that refreshes the blood and purges without any effort."[20] And during the seventeenth century, an ideology praising thinness began to develop in some circles. But it was *men* rather than women who were then supposed to be lean and lithe, due to an emerging association between this physique and mental quickness, intelligence, and rationality.[21] Such views, while influential in some quarters, were still far from the norm though: many people questioned the ideal of thinness and the wisdom of a meager diet, and thought it tantamount to a refusal to live healthily and heartily.[22] Shortly afterward, in the early eighteenth century, the nutritional teachings of the English physician George Cheyne stoked interest in a special diet to treat the gout, indigestion, and weight gain that were on the rise thanks to the advent of the coffeehouse.[23] Cheyne's "cure" involved drinking copious amounts of milk. The dairy industry should take note—perhaps it is due for a revival.

In the middle of the eighteenth century, when the trans-atlantic slave trade was growing rapidly in France and Britain, an association between Blackness and fatness began to be drawn. Strings points to the work of the Frenchman Georges-Louis Leclerc—who claimed the title "Comte de Buffon"—as pivotal. In his *Histoire naturelle, générale et particulière,* published in 1749, Buffon theorized human difference and made an early contribution to the nascent junk science of race. Following skin color, the size and shape of the body was, for Buffon, the most important marker of racial physiognomic difference. He rejected the extant stereotype of Africans as "meager . . . and very small" and argued that while this might be true of "Moors," Black Africans proper (*les nègres*) were "tall, plump . . . simple and stupid."[24] He attributed these traits to the lushness of the land they inhabited, and linked their supposed corpulence with laziness and slow-wittedness—a corollary to the idea of rationality as the exclusive property of the thin white men who were now regarded as both the norm and the standard of human excellence. Other thinkers of the time floated the idea that the supposed fatness of Africans was the result of hot climates, which encouraged the body to hold on to "excess" fat deposits.[25]

The work of Denis Diderot, the famous French rationalist, was even more contemptuous and laced with disgust toward fat Black bodies. In his *Encyclopédie,* first published in 1751, a certain group of Africans were described as follows:

> The least esteemed of all the nègres are the Bambaras; their uncleanliness, as well as the large scars that they give themselves across their cheeks from the nose to the ears, make them hideous. They are lazy, drunken, gluttonous, and apt to steal.[26]

Diderot's account, even more than Buffon's, was widely influential. Notably, neither man had ever been to the relevant parts of Africa.

Nor had the French naturalist Julien-Joseph Virey, who helped originate the derogation and othering of so-called Hottentot people—in particular, the women—nearly a century later. In his *Natural History of the Negro Race,* published in 1837, Virey asserted that "Negroes" generally were "of a mild disposition, robust, but slow, and very lazy." "Hottentot"—properly termed Khoisan—women were singled out in his treatment for their "big bottoms and bellies that push out."[27] Virey theorized these women as often sedentary or pregnant, leading to an accumulation of fatty liquid in their stomachs, breasts, hips, and buttocks. "The derrieres of Hottentot women . . . resemble those of four-legged creatures, at times growing so large that they could be supported with a small cart, like a domesticated animal," according to Strings's précis of Virey's horrifyingly dehumanizing impressions.[28]

The new revulsion toward fatness was no accident. It was an ideological tool wielded by a surging capitalist interest: slavery. It was the coding of fatness as a distinctively Black trait that led to the social construction of the fat body as something "other," as something grotesque, or even as deformed, Strings argues. It is not that fat bodies were first stigmatized and then Black bodies became associated with fatness; rather, Black bodies were first associated with fatness, and then fatness came to be stigmatized soon afterward. As Strings puts it, "Racial scientific literature since at least the eighteenth century has claimed that fatness was 'savage' and 'black.' . . . The phobia about fat 'always already' had a racial element."[29] And such fatphobia then served to justify and rationalize the burgeoning slave trade, and enabled white American Protestants to differentiate themselves from the people whom they had enslaved so brutally. By the end of the nineteenth century, thinness had become a marker of social status and "civility," especially among white American women.[30]

Nowhere are these social processes more evident than in the egregiously cruel and exploitative exhibition of the Khoisan woman, Saartjie "Sara" Baartman. Initially put on display in Cape Town, around 1806, for the pleasure of wounded and dying soldiers in a naval hospital, Baartman was forced to travel to England and then France to exhibit her "monstrous" body. She was consigned, in other words, to be the star attraction in one of the world's first freak shows. (Interestingly, she was immediately preceded in this ignominious fate by Daniel Lambert, a very fat white man, who reportedly weighed more than seven hundred pounds and became a popular spectacle.[31]) Marketed for an avid crowd as "the Hottentot Venus," Baartman was a real hit in London from 1810 to 1811. Strings writes,

> [Baartman] was simultaneously grotesque and exotic: a sexual specimen with a peculiar racial identity. For these reasons exhibitgoers came both to gawk at her proportions, especially her posterior, and to experience the sensory pleasure of touching her, which they could do for an additional fee. Although bustles exaggerating the derriere were fashionable in England at the time, there was something about the amplitude of flesh that, it was claimed, was amassed in her bottom and over her whole body, which made her a spectacle. Her figure was deemed "very different from the feminine standards of London" and its ladies' "long,

slender lines."[32] . . . Her "excess" fat was used as one sign of her primitivity.[33]

Some gawkers, however, were disappointed. They walked away complaining that she just looked like an ordinary woman.[34]

Cut to a century later. Following the advent of thinness as an aesthetic ideal, the U.S. medical establishment finally got in on the act. Health insurance was still a fairly recent innovation, and analysts tried to determine the risk of disease and mortality for people with various characteristics. They discovered that large deviations from the average weight-to-height ratio in either direction represented a mortality risk, statistically speaking, loosely anticipating Flegal's findings. Unfortunately, since the vast majority of salaried employees at the time were white men, their bodies were massively overrepresented in devising these early actuarial tables. And doctors soon began using these tables to treat individual patients, despite their never being intended for that purpose. They were used in part to justify turning away the "overweight" patients who doctors feared would be refused coverage by health insurers on the basis of their fatness.[35]

Even decades later, scientific studies and economic considerations weren't always the drivers of fatphobia: disgust remained a powerful factor. Ancel Keys, the famed Harvard physiologist, allowed in *Time* magazine in 1961 that "obesity" did not necessarily cause coronary heart disease. It was, however, "ugly"—not to mention "disgusting" and "ethically repugnant," as he wrote in other publications. Fat peo-

ple are "clumsy," and our bodies are "hard on furniture."
(Poor sofas.) As Strings writes, "These statements make it
hard to believe that [Keys's] work in this area was fueled exclusively by medical findings on the complex relationship between weight and health, as opposed to his personal opinion
that fat was unseemly and should be exorcised."[36]

It was Keys who developed the body mass index (BMI),
which came to replace actuarial tables such as the Metropoli-
tan Life Insurance ones, in the 1980s. Keys based his work
on that of the nineteenth-century Belgian astronomer and
mathematician Adolphe Quetelet. Quetelet was interested in
the nature of *l'homme moyen*—the average man—whom he
also took to be the ideal one, in a classic conflation of what *is*
the case with what *ought* to be.[37] Quetelet's "average" and
hence "ideal" models were exclusively white and European.
It's perhaps thus unsurprising that Quetelet's work eventually became pivotal in justifying the idea of an unfitness to
parent and the rising eugenics movement, which encom-
passed the systematic sterilization of people of color and disabled people, among others.[38]

If Keys realized this sordid backstory, he gave no sign of it
in his landmark 1972 paper, in which he and his collaborators
refer to Quetelet as "the great pioneer in anthropometry and
statistics."[39] Based on their measurements of samples of five
groups of men across the world—predominantly, though not
exclusively, white men—they adapted Quetelet's index into
the body mass index, a number given by a person's weight in
kilograms divided by the square of their height in meters.[40]
Keys and his team concluded, modestly, that the "body mass
index proves to be, if not fully satisfactory, at least as good as
any other relative weight index as an indicator of relative obesity."[41] But it had the advantage of simplicity over other mea-

sures.[42] The rest is, as we say, history—a history that includes millions of Americans becoming "overweight" on a single day in 1998, when the standard for that classification was lowered from a BMI of around 28 to 25. Why? In part to raise the red alert about fatness in America, and in part just because that number was deemed easier for doctors and patients to remember.

So the BMI is rooted in white-centrism, even racism; it was never designed to be a measure of individual health; and, notwithstanding the weight we put on it, it is an arbitrary and crude measure. Notoriously, it misclassifies many muscular people, including athletes, as overweight or obese despite their low percentage of body fat. More importantly, it is a terrible metric to apply to one of the most oppressed groups in our society: Black women—who have, it turns out, the highest average BMI of any comparable U.S. subgroup. This is partly because they (like Black men) have greater muscle mass and bone mineral density than their white counterparts. They also tend to suffer fewer health consequences at a supposedly elevated BMI than do others.[43] Ironically, the stigmatization that results from being classified as having too high a BMI *can* be expected to have deleterious health effects, as we saw earlier.

The moral panic over the "obesity epidemic" in the United States reached its zenith in 2013, when the American Medical Association declared obesity a disease—ignoring the advice of a council it had convened on the matter, who held that the measure it was based on, the BMI, was hopelessly flawed and simplistic.[44] And Black women once again became

the faces—or, rather, bodies—of ignominy during this cultural moment. Sabrina Strings notes the image accompanying the 2013 CNN headline "Obesity Kills More Americans
Than We Thought": a fat Black woman, with a tape measure
around her waist, held by the slender, benevolent hands of a
white female physician. The story adverted to the just-
published study claiming that obesity was killing more Black
women than any other such population in the country. But
many other studies, before and since, have contradicted this
one's findings and have received much less publicity.[45]

And no matter how fit and healthy a Black woman might
be, the sheer fact that she takes up space in a fatphobic, misogynistic, and racist world reliably attracts disgust, disapproval, and derogation. Serena Williams, one of the greatest
athletes of all time, was routinely mocked and criticized for
her muscular physique, and for being slightly "thicker" than
the archetype of the female tennis player, during her illustri-
ous career. One white player, Caroline Wozniacki, imitated
Williams in a stunningly racist display during an exhibition
match, by stuffing her bra and skirt with tennis balls, making
for an eerie visual echo of the Hottentot Venus image.[46] Such
derogation could not possibly have been based on concerns
about Williams's health, given her status as one of the fittest
and most athletic people in existence.[47]

Genuinely fat Black women, like Lizzo, attract yet more
consternation, notwithstanding their athletic prowess and
physical accomplishments. "It isn't going to be awesome if
she gets diabetes," complained Jillian Michaels, of *The Biggest Loser* fame, early in 2020, thereby deploying one of the
tiredest health faux concerns leveled against fat people online
whenever we are suspected of "glorifying obesity."[48] ("Look
forward to your amputations!" they yell at us, caringly.)

Again, it's difficult to see such negging as rooted in concerns about Lizzo's health, given that she manages to sing, play the flute, and dance for hours on end live in concert—feats that most thinner people can only dream of emulating.

Moreover, there is a palpable apathy about Black women's health in many other areas—maternal mortality, for example, with Black people being three to four times more likely to die during pregnancy, during childbirth, and following delivery than are their white counterparts.[49] If we really cared about Black women's health, wouldn't there be a wider outcry about this disgraceful situation?

The BMI is not the only white-centric, indeed racist, and arbitrary standard responsible for fatphobia. We must also consider beauty standards, which have similarly undergone numerous shifts during the past century. In Anglo-American culture, we have moved from revering the relatively buxom, hourglass figures of "Gibson girls" in the 1910s, to the thin, "boyish" flappers of the 1920s, to a slightly more rounded look in the 1950s, to a petite, waifish body in the 1960s, to "heroin chic" in the 1980s and 1990s, with "thin" becoming more "in" than ever then. Still, in many ways, these are small variations in the scheme of things. There was no point after the turn of the twentieth century in which fat female bodies were widely celebrated in the mainstream Anglo-American context. And these subtle shifts might have been caused by, rather than a cause of, the celebrities most beloved in the relevant eras: Marilyn Monroe in the 1950s, Twiggy in the 1960s, and Kate Moss in the 1990s. Despite persistent myths to the contrary, though, Monroe was a very slim woman.[50] Notably, Kim Kardashian recently boasted of the extreme diet she went on—losing sixteen pounds in three weeks—to fit into Monroe's gown for the 2022 Met gala.[51]

The example of Kardashian highlights the fact that it's not really a matter of fatness being fashionable in any recent era. Rather, different forms of fat *distribution* on enduringly thin frames are favored. This makes it easier to objectify and control us, as well as to take our money. Witness the current popularity of the Brazilian butt lift, which takes fat from someone's stomach, hips, or thighs and injects it into their buttocks. Witness too the way an increasing number of people now undergo buccal fat removal—surgically excising their cheek pads—to make them look sleeker, while others have long had fat injected into their cheeks to create the illusion of youth via facial fullness.

Such trends in fat distribution also give rise to pernicious forms of cultural appropriation, and even outright racism. In 2014, Kardashian posed for a magazine cover popping a bottle of champagne, which shot a thick stream above her head into the coupe glass balanced on her famously ample posterior. The image was captioned "break the internet." As Blue Telusma noted at the time, the photo recalled none other than Saartjie Baartman, the so-called Hottentot Venus. Though likely unintentional on Kardashian's part, the imagery was thus "steeped in centuries of racism, oppression, and misogyny" endemic in America.[52]

Kardashian—who is, notoriously, slightly racially ambiguous—performed a kind of Blackness here. Meanwhile, other unequivocally white women surround themselves with Black women as a point of contrast: and a source of status. In 2013, Miley Cyrus's MTV Video Music Awards performance featured Black female dancers in the background. As the sociologist Tressie McMillan Cottom pointed out, "Cyrus did not just have black women gyrating behind her. She had particularly rotund black women. She gleefully slap[ped] the ass of one dancer like she intend[ed] to eat it on a cracker." Cyrus's suggestive performance aimed to challenge the audience's image of her as sexually naive, by relying on the racist trope of fat Black female bodies as sexually deviant, McMillan Cottom argues. For "fat, non-normative black female bodies are kith and kin with historical caricatures of black women." Cyrus was thus "playing a type of black female body as a [wink-wink] joke to challenge her audience's perceptions of herself, while leaving their perceptions of black women's bodies firmly intact. [It was] a dance between performing sexual freedom and maintaining a hierarchy of female bodies from which white women benefit materially."[53] White women have indeed benefited from this hierarchy, and the subsequent means of differentiating themselves from Black women, since the advent of fatphobia in Anglo-American culture. This was and is, in many ways, fatphobia's original and ongoing purpose.

True, many other cultures, not necessarily steeped in historical anti-Blackness, are extremely fatphobic nowadays too. But this is no objection to Strings's argument that fatphobia is a product of anti-Black racism: as it turns out, fatphobia is largely a Western export, rather than having spontaneously arisen via different, parallel histories. Fatphobic attitudes and the preference for thin bodies tend to follow hot on the heels of the introduction of Western media—such as magazines and TV shows—into a culture. A spike in eating disorders, especially among young women, is reliably seen soon afterward.[54]

✦ ✦ ✦

Even though it might have been the Black female body that was originally singled out, and which continues to bear the brunt of fatphobia in America, fat Black male and masculine bodies have long been casualties of this system too. As Da'Shaun L. Harrison has shown, the anti-Blackness at the heart of anti-fatness can even prove fatal.[55] When the white police officer Darren Wilson felt threatened by the Black teenager Michael Brown, in Ferguson, Missouri, in August 2014, Wilson shot him down—and cited Brown's size afterward to justify his actions. "When I grabbed him the only way I can describe it is I felt like a 5-year-old holding onto Hulk Hogan," Wilson stated. He also labeled Brown a "demon" and said "it looked like he was almost bulking up to run through the shots, . . . like I wasn't even there, I wasn't even anything in his way."[56]

The difference in size between these two men was in fact not dramatic—with Wilson six feet four and 210 pounds to Brown's six feet five and 290-pound body.[57] Not to mention the fact that Wilson, unlike Brown, was armed with a deadly weapon. But Wilson, like the vast majority of such officers, was not convicted nor even indicted for this murder.

Neither was Officer Daniel Pantaleo, for his actions just weeks earlier in Staten Island. He had held Eric Garner in an illegal choke hold, facedown on the pavement, strangling him. "I can't breathe," Garner had famously protested, eleven times, on video. Pantaleo's defense rested on the idea that Garner was so fat that he was doomed to die anyway, and could have expired from something as benign as a "bear hug." Pantaleo's lawyer called Garner "morbidly obese" and a "ticking time bomb."[58]

And thus we see the fate of such fat Black bodies: to be too intimidating, or too vulnerable; a threat to others or themselves; and condemned to death either way. As Harrison writes,

It is true; Eric Garner was a six-foot-two, 395-pound man with asthma, diabetes, and a heart condition. However, before his interaction with Pantaleo and the other police officers that swarmed around him, what he was *not* was dead. This means that, no matter how much of an untamable Beast he was made out to be by the lawyers over the case, the grand jury, the medical examiner and other doctors, and the media, what led him to his dying breath was a police officer's arm around his neck.[59]

Apparently, some white people care so much about the health of fat Black people that they'll murder them and then shrug. Or, more plausibly, this was never about health to begin with. It is about the ongoing effort to stigmatize and derogate fat bodies, in service of anti-Blackness.

Fatphobia is not only rooted in racism; it continues to uphold it. For one thing, it gives privileged—and thin—white elites a way to believe in their superiority to other groups while maintaining plausible deniability of their racism and classism. This is especially true in leftist circles, where such prejudices are now widely frowned upon, and would be an occasion for guilt, shame, and self-censure if admitted, even inwardly. Hence, as Paul Campos has argued, fatphobia can serve as a powerful proxy—and outlet—for these forms of bigotry:

> Precisely because Americans are so repressed about
> class issues, the disgust the (relatively) poor engender

in the (relatively) rich must be projected onto some other distinguishing characteristic. In 1853, the upper-class Englishman could be quite unself-conscious about the fact that the mere sight of the urban proletariat disgusted him. [More recently], any upper-class white American liberal would be horrified to imagine that the sight of, say, a lower-class Mexican-American woman going into a Wal-Mart might some-how elicit feelings of disgust in his otherwise properly sensitized soul. But the sight of a fat woman—make that an "obese"—better yet, a "morbidly [sic] obese" woman going into Wal-Mart . . . ah, that is some-thing else again.[60]

The fact that this woman is poor and nonwhite will be dismissed, as Campos says, as "an irrelevant coincidence." It isn't. Fatness serves as a potent class and race signifier. And so, when we wring our hands or jeer at fatness, we are often tacitly and unwittingly expressing classism and racism. As Campos writes, "The disgust the thin upper classes feel for the fat lower classes has nothing to do with mortality statis-tics, and everything to do with feelings of moral superiority engendered in thin people by the sight of fat people."[61]

So eager are we to jeer that this has even given rise to new elements of the discourse. The website "People of Walmart" was, I'm ashamed to say, once popular in my—predominantly white, leftist or liberal, indeed progressive—circles.[62] This website didn't explicitly tell people to sneer in disgust at poor and Black and brown and disabled people's bodies. It didn't have to. It visually elicited disgust by posting photos of such predominantly fat and always supposedly ill-dressed people, their clothing frequently exposing unruly rolls of flesh, butt cracks, or "side boob." The invitation to look down on these people as hideous specimens of humanity, casting aspersions on their health and imagined characters, was thereby extended to the website viewer. What pretended to be a comment on consumerism in America was really a way of venting racism and classism, cloaked in the more acceptable garb of fatphobia.

Such objections to consumerism under late-stage capitalism would in fact be better leveled at the people—predominantly white elites—pursuing thinness at great cost. We are prevailed upon to buy exorbitantly expensive Peloton exercise bikes and subscriptions to overpriced salad delivery services. (And I do mean "we" here: I did both of these things at the beginning of the pandemic, expressly for the sake of weight loss, to my now great embarrassment.) These commodities are deemed investments in both our bodies and our supposed health, and become status symbols in their own right. And we may feel dutiful and virtuous for such exalted forms of consumerism.

The diet, fitness, and so-called wellness industries hence profit handsomely from the fatphobic hierarchies that make certain body types highly desirable, yet unachievable, for most people in our calorie-abundant social environment. As the feminist scholar Amy Erdman Farrell puts it, in her book *Fat Shame,*

> Before the end of the 19th century, only the privileged—in terms of both wealth and health—could become fat. Just as industrialization and urbanization transformed every other aspect of life in the United States, it also transformed bodies. As the 20th century progressed, more people experienced

sufficient wealth, lifestyles became more sedentary, the development of new farming methods and better transportation systems meant that food was more plentiful and relatively cheap, and healthcare improved. All of this meant that more people could gain weight and keep it on. At this point fatness became a marker dividing the rich and the poor, but now, unlike in earlier centuries, hefty weight connoted not high status but a person whose body was out of control, whose reason and intellect were dominated and overwhelmed by the weight of obesity. As the meanings of "fat" and "thin" shifted, moving up the socioeconomic ladder usually meant aspiring to a thinner body, even if that aspiration was unsuccessful.[63]

Being thin has thus become much harder over the course of the past century—and, at the same time, vastly more valued. This is surely no accident. It is indeed an example of what we might call the "harder-better" fallacy: that which is the most difficult to achieve is judged the most praiseworthy, regardless of its actual desirability or value.[64] Anything less effortful is regarded as contemptible, particularly by people who devote themselves assiduously to such efforts—in laboriously prepared "healthy" meals, grueling daily workouts, and so on—and thus grow heavily invested in maintaining their importance.

We are so prone, as human beings, to constructing ad hoc hierarchies that allow us to feel superior. Fatphobia, in its intersection with racism, owes its very existence to this tendency.

CHAPTER 4

DEMORALIZING FATNESS

Dieting, for me, long felt like virtue. Hunger seemed like evidence of goodness. The more I denied myself, the better I would feel not only about my body but about my moral character. The association was vague and unexamined—but no less powerful for being so.

In the old days, as a teenager, I mostly ate less, and sometimes almost nothing. Then, straight after college, nine months before moving from Australia to the United States for graduate school, I decided to embark on a "proper" diet: a low-carb one. I ate endless eggs and leafy greens and celery and almonds. I forced myself to eat meat, even though I neither particularly liked nor could afford it on my modest student budget. Although I believe it is probably wrong to eat meat, I convinced myself that being fat was worse. It's just one moral compromise I've made in my life for the sake of being thinner.

Although the low-carb, meat-heavy diet was fairly successful ("successful"), when combined with more than an hour of daily exercise, the weight inevitably came back. It was hence to be only the first diet of many. I can hardly think of a food now that I haven't given up, or at least severely restricted, at one time or another: bread; pasta; rice; white flour; all flours; all grains and starches; potatoes; sweet potatoes; all roots and tubers; legumes; beans; corn; deli meats; all meats; plant-based meat alternatives; white sugar; all sugar; all caloric sweeteners, such as honey and maple syrup; noncaloric sweeteners, from stevia to Splenda; anything that tasted sweet excluding a few berries. Finally, even berries went by the wayside.

I've tried low-fat and low-GI (glycemic index) diets—often euphemistically called "eating plans"—as well as low-carb ones. I tried the Shangri-La diet, which, bizarrely, involves ingesting flavorless oil on an empty stomach three times daily. (It was as disgusting as it sounds and, for me, as ineffective.) I've done keto, Paleo, South Beach, Atkins, the Whole30 (many times over), OMAD (one meal a day), and intermittent fasting (which turned into fasting, period). I've gone gluten-free and been plant based and briefly went vegan. I got progressively good at sticking to diets. I got increasingly bad at actually losing weight on them.

When I wrote a *New York Times* op-ed on the moral harms of dieting and being chronically hungry, in January 2022, many people wrote to me.[1] About half of my correspondents thanked me for what I'd said, and some pledged their own break with diet culture. The remainder told me about their latest diet and recommended—or, indeed, insisted—that I try it.[2]

Reader, in nearly every case, I already had done.

Like many chronic dieters, I've become fixated on foods I *could* eat while on a diet without feeling guilty: fresh apricots with coconut butter (which very vaguely resembles white chocolate); sweet potatoes with avocado (still not a bad combination); red peppers with cream cheese; and cheese, glorious cheese. (My "fat tooth" is voracious.)

Why do we feel virtuous, or at least better about ourselves, when we diet? And why do food and fatness come with such powerful guilt-inducing capabilities?

Part of the answer, of course, is that food was frequently in scarce supply for much of human history. A person's indulgence in more than their fair share would then have been a serious issue. But nowadays, hunger and food insecurity are huge problems that are products of rampant capitalism and neoliberalism and inequitable food distribution. It is not a simple matter of some people eating too much and not leaving enough for others.[3]

As human beings, I think we also don't quite trust pleasure. Most major religions have tapped into this reality, inspiring more devotion, not less, by adopting stringent food rules—what types of food we eat, how much we eat, when we eat, or all of the above. And much as with restrictions on sex, there is something deeply human in the desire to follow these rules to the letter. It is as if by resisting ourselves and our appetites, we reassure ourselves we are above nonhuman animals in an existential hierarchy. Occasionally, and exhilaratingly, we break the rules and prove to ourselves we are animals, despite ourselves.

Conversely, the idea of "eating crow" or "humble pie" is not entirely metaphorical.[4] I remember as a young child—perhaps four or five years old—committing some very minor sin and feeling horribly guilty. I decided to make amends by forcing myself to eat a small quantity of the putty that had been left lying around by some builders working on a deck for our kitchen. My parents (gentle, loving, liberal, nonpunitive people) were horrified—and puzzled—when I told them this. But, like many people, I had a deep instinct connecting what I consumed to my moral status, which impressed on me the idea of eating something bad as a kind of penance. (Luckily, I suffered no ill effects afterward.)

As we grow older, many of us continue to punish ourselves: eating only "virtuous" foods, or not eating at all, or eating to the point of discomfort—sometimes, before purging. Down this road, orthorexia, anorexia, and bulimia beckon. We feel impure, anxious, and try to make ourselves feel morally better through what we consume, or what we refuse to. And the supposed sin may be our fatness, our bodies, our very appetites.

No wonder we feel bad: the idea that fatness is a moral issue is everywhere. We get it via the news, in the alarmist reporting about the "obesity epidemic." We get it via social media, in the moral panics about fat children.[5] We get it from our own friends and families, who may variously adopt a tone of well-meaning hand-wringing, or disingenuous concern, or downright condemnation. In all of these ways and more, fat bodies are depicted as a moral problem, and fat people as a moral failure. And we are depicted in the process as lacking in key virtues: as lazy, unclean, weak-willed, greedy, slovenly, and selfish.

Experimental evidence confirms the moralism of fatphobia—and its unfairness. Fat people are deemed guiltier for the same actions as our thinner counterparts: One study showed that people in a hypothetical disciplinary case described as "obese" rather than "average-weight" were disciplined more harshly.[6] Another, more recent study showed a similar effect restricted to so-called obese women: defendants in a fictional court case were significantly more likely to be judged guilty if they were fat and female.[7]

Fat people's testimony highlights the weight of living under such moralism. Take Linda Gerhardt, a woman suffering from lipedema, whom we met earlier in these pages. As she points out,

> People have an expectation that . . . [your body] is the proof of your virtue. So, if you have a fat body, that is evidence that you have done something unvirtuous to get to that point. . . . It's so ingrained in our medical system that if you do the right things, and you follow the path, and you eat the right foods, and you exercise the right amount, if you do the correct things, you should be the ideal of the thin person. That is the expectation that most of us have is that we see a thin person and we think that they have done something correct. We see a fat person and we think they have done something incorrect and wrong and that they need to take some sort of corrective action, they need to change their behavior.[8]

Nowadays, within the framework of secular moral philos ophy, you typically need to show that someone has hurt *others* in order to demonstrate their lack of ethical virtue or—more or less synonymously—immorality. But the critics of fat people are not slow to wheel out just such an argument. According to the prevailing wisdom, we who are fat are a huge burden on the healthcare system, and because we are responsible for our fatness—by eating too much or exercising too little—we are morally culpable. It is time to examine this common and, to many, tempting line of thinking.

In addition to being inhumane—or at least often expressed in inhumane ways (think of the trope of "headless fatties"[9])—the argument fails on its own terms. Not being fat is simply not a moral obligation.

Philosophers routinely cite an "ought implies can" principle: the idea that you have a moral obligation to do something only if you *can* do it; or, equivalently, you are *not* obligated to do something that you *cannot* do. Under a plausible adaptation of this principle, someone's near inability to do something also makes it moot and unfair to demand that she do so. Hence the fact that most fat people cannot realistically make ourselves thin in the long term through diet and exercise has far-reaching moral implications: we cannot then be blamed for not doing the near-impossible.

There may be limited exceptions to an "ought implies can" rule, where trying to meet some near-impossible standard gets us closer to the mark, in achieving some valuable or desirable outcome. It might be a good idea as a keen student to aim for a perfect score on a test, say, even if that is a vanishingly rare outcome. But, as we've seen, this dynamic doesn't apply to weight loss: often, dieting is positively counterproductive, in making us fatter than ever over time, in part because it severely reduces metabolic function. Exercise is perhaps even less effective in inducing weight loss (although, again, it undoubtedly makes most people healthier). And although there are other weight-loss "treatments" that may be somewhat more reliable—pharmaceutical and surgical—these options frequently come with prohibitive costs, risks, and side effects. We surely cannot require people to go under the knife or take medications—potentially diminishing their quality of life greatly—in the name of morality.

And so we come to the first major problem with the idea of a supposed obligation not to be fat: we don't know *how* to make fat people thin in a reliable, safe, and non-drastic manner. Nor do we know how to prevent people from getting fat in the first place. For one thing, fatness has a strong genetic basis, with estimates suggesting a heritability upwards of 0.7—meaning that at least 70 percent of the variance in body mass we find in the human population is likely due to genetics.[10] To put this in perspective, human height's heritability is around 0.79: just a little higher.[11] Studies of identical twins show that these individuals' weight was consistently similar to their biological parents'. There was no relationship whatsoever between their BMI and that of their adoptive parents—that is, the people who raised them.[12] A picture is also emerging of many separate genes that function to make a person heavier, and some that, if a person has them, will almost inevitably result in their having a BMI that puts them in the "obese" category.[13]

Moreover, there is evidence that adults are likely to be

heavier when they experienced childhood trauma—including physical abuse, bullying, and sexual assault.[14] The writer Roxane Gay has written piercingly of the brutal gang rape she endured as a twelve-year-old girl at the hands of a group of adolescent boys: "There is the before and the after. Before I gained weight. After I gained weight. Before I was raped. After I was raped."[15] In the immediate aftermath of the assault, she describes herself as "disgusting because I had allowed disgusting things to be done to me. . . . I was no longer a good girl and I was going to hell."[16] In her shame and her fear, Gay turned to food—both as a source of comfort and to make her body a "fortress," impenetrable against the kind of attack she had lived through.[17] She writes,

> My memories of the after are scattered, fragmentary, but I do clearly remember eating and eating and eating so I could forget, so my body could become so big it would never be broken again. I remember the quiet comfort of eating when I was lonely or sad or even happy.[18]

More:

> I was lonely and scared and food offered an immediate satisfaction. Food offered comfort when I needed to be comforted and did not know how to ask for what I needed from those who loved me. Food tasted good and made me feel better. Food was the one thing within my reach.[19]

Sometimes, we fill our mouths not to have to speak; we swallow our pain and our words go along with it.

As powerful and important as Gay's account is, we of course shouldn't make the mistake of assuming that everyone fat has been traumatized—any more than we should infer someone's health status by reading it off their appearance. People become fat for a litany of other reasons—many common physical illnesses and health conditions, certain disabilities and mental health issues, taking common and vital medications (including birth control and antidepressants), pregnancy, stress, metabolic and hormonal changes (including polycystic ovary syndrome)—or for no particular reason.[20] Some people, like me, are just prone to fatness.

Or take Janet S., a 350-pound woman who was among thirty patients who agreed to be studied for three months in 1975 in exchange for free bariatric surgery. The researchers calculated the precise number of calories her body supposedly needed to maintain her weight and fed her exactly that number. She gained nearly twelve pounds in two weeks—a rate of nearly one pound daily. Janet wasn't surprised; they were feeding her a "tremendous amount of food" compared with her normal diet.[21]

And some people may become fat partly due to the foods and other resources available to them, either now or during childhood. Consider, for example, children raised in poverty and facing hunger, food insecurity, or highly limited food options. It is beyond understandable that they might want to fill up when they can, or that their subsequent food preferences would be shaped by what they had access to early on. We can only crave what we know when it comes to food.[22] And the foods that most comfort us later in life are often laced with nostalgia.

Of course, everyone should have access to fresh foods (among others), as well as the resources to exercise in ways that suit their body, as a matter of social justice. But this doesn't change the fact that in society as we know it, many people's weight is partly a function of their social, and "built," environment. This is especially true in countries like the United States, where so-called food deserts are prevalent, and many places make walking and other forms of exercise much more difficult than they should be. It's one thing to be idealistic about what this landscape *ought* to look like. It's quite another to be idealistic—and hence moralistic—about individual choices in view of this reality.

It's also important to recognize, as the fat activist and scholar Marquisele Mercedes has argued, that the specific term "food deserts" can obscure the fact that these are not naturally occurring features of the environment, but something inflicted by some groups of people on others. This is something dominant whites *do* to poor, brown, and Black folks, inasmuch as we live in a world of exploitative and oppressive social relations.

Such ostensible concern with "food deserts" may serve as a mask, or a fig leaf, for yet more fatphobia too. As Mercedes writes,

> The other major reason why the public health field loves talking about "food deserts" . . . is its general disdain for fat people. . . . "Food deserts" have long been connected to rates of "obesity," a long time fixation of public health. For those who are invested in "obesity prevention," the issue of "food deserts" is another way to link fatness to badness and moralized food. "Food deserts," with their typical overrepresentation of "ultra-processed" foods and underrepresentation of fresh "healthy" foods, are bad because

they have too much *bad food* and not enough *good food*. In turn, people in "food deserts" are fat and, as most in public health would say, fat is bad. Therefore "food deserts" are bad because they make people fat.[23]

But, as Mercedes goes on to argue, it's "entirely possible to talk about the equitable distribution of food and the predatory food industry without demonizing fatness or moralizing what we eat as *good* or *bad*." And there are far better reasons to advocate for food justice. Namely, everyone deserves access to the major kinds of foods they want to eat, and for most people in most communities, this will include a range of fresh *and* shelf-stable foods. We should understand these foods not as a source of bodily control or moral status, but as an important human resource—and a right for all communities.[24]

Similarly, when it comes to the undoubted truth that poor, Black, and brown communities in the United States face massive health injustices, we should care about this not because it arguably makes some people in these communities fatter than they otherwise might be *but because they are facing massive health injustices*.[25] Weight is at best a proxy for the health concerns that we can, and should, care about directly. Yet the moralism surrounding food as well as fatness often obscures this possibility—and leads to deeply misguided, patronizing interventions, such as restricting the kinds of foods that can be purchased using SNAP benefits.[26]

I am reminded of attending an event on locavorism during grad school in which the hosts not only extolled the virtues of local food but also downplayed worries about its expense and accessibility. One chef opined in a high-handed manner that poor people should eat beans cooked from scratch rather than McDonald's. My friend took the mic and explained that her family supported another family, who were living in poverty. She had recently wired them $10 to check that a new transfer method was working. The family had thanked her and said they'd been able to have hot dogs for dinner that night. Sometimes, as my friend pointed out, people in difficult circumstances want familiar, comforting foods, replete with salt, sugar, starch, and fat. Soaking and cooking dry beans from scratch is not always an adequate substitute, no matter their cheapness and nutritional value. And they require resources to prepare, in terms of time, knowledge, labor, cooking equipment, and clean running water, that many people in the United States and beyond unjustly lack access to.

And sometimes, when you just want a hot dog, nothing else will do. (I speak from experience.)

All in all, it is about as implausible to hold people responsible for *getting* fat as for staying fat, given the difficulties of weight loss. Fatness, in the vast majority of instances, is unchosen.

But even if getting and staying fat *were* up to us—that is, were purely discretionary—what is the moral problem supposed to be, exactly? Why do we regard other people's fatness as any of our business?

It will be spluttered: if fat people place a burden on the healthcare system, and thus on society, then surely it *is* our business if some people effectively choose to have fatter bodies. But this idea, as prevalent as it is, rests on a shaky premise. For one thing, as we saw earlier, the correlation between fatness and some forms of ill health does not establish causation. One study did conclude, however, that fat people die a few years younger on average (at around age eighty rather than eighty-four) than our so-called normal-weight counterparts. The twist? We may end up costing the healthcare system *less* because of this overall since, even if we do cost more during our lifetimes, we obviously do not require healthcare postmortem.[27] Admittedly, this study was done in the Netherlands, and it's not clear whether it generalizes to the U.S. context, where healthcare costs are notoriously ever rising. But these costs are a pressing problem to be solved, not a fact of life to be assumed uncritically in making an anti-fat argument.

We now see a second problem with the supposed obligation not to be fat: even to the extent to which fatness *is*, for some people, to some extent, under their control, it's empirically unclear that this represents a burden on the healthcare system.

Moreover, even to the extent that fatness is (again, for some people, and to some extent) under their control, and that this *does* represent a cost to the healthcare system, analogies suggest that this is not a genuine moral issue. People make all sorts of trade-offs to enrich their lives in some way, to pursue their desires and whims and pleasures, at the expense of potentially serious health problems and even increased mortality. Take the person who regularly goes BASE jumping, despite the risk of serious injuries and death; take the person who attempts to climb Mount Everest, despite the risk of altitude sickness and falls and frostbite; take the person who races cars, despite the risk of crashes and conflagrations;[28] take, to use the philosopher A. W. Eaton's pertinent example, the person who tans their skin, despite the risk of cancer.[29] Provided they take reasonable precautions, such as using the right equipment, and do not endanger others, we do not tend to condemn or shame these people. We regard them as entitled to live their lives, and to have humane and fitting healthcare if they do run into problems. We even generally regard them as entitled to run the risk of dying significantly younger. And we are *right* to regard them as having these entitlements.

So imagine a person who "lives to eat"—adventurously, pleasurably, comfortingly, or even just copiously—and does end up as a result with a significantly fatter body than they would have otherwise. And, suppose, controversially, that this person does run certain health risks as a result of this. The above analogies cast doubt on the idea that they are under a moral obligation to choose a different lifestyle. There's at least strong pressure on their critics to explain, if they don't object to the aforementioned risk takers and thrill seekers, what the difference is, exactly. Often, I suspect, these critics will not have a good argument, but rather an *image* of the above people as thin and thus, supposedly, "healthy"— which in this context means robust, lean, muscular, and non-disabled.

This highlights a third major problem with the idea of a moral obligation not to be fat: we regularly accept as much or more risk when it is carried by presumptively thinner bodies.

Some people will want to go further here, and say that there are no moral obligations to look after our health or ourselves in any way.[30] I myself would not want to go that far: when a preventative or curative health measure is easy and non-burdensome, and can reliably prevent very bad out-comes, I am inclined to say that we *do* have a duty, perhaps even a moral duty, to take it. Wearing a seatbelt or motorcy-cle helmet would be prime examples, thus highlighting the fact that the argument I'm making doesn't get us into dubi-

ous libertarian territory.[31] And of course we should all agree
that we have a moral duty to take small health measures that
protect the community at large, and not just ourselves, from
serious repercussions. Getting vaccinated against COVID-19,
and wearing a mask indoors during the height of the pandemic, are obvious examples.[32]

But the idea of a moral obligation not to be fat is very different from these duties. It is impracticable, as we have seen.
The health benefits are controversial, as I have also argued.
Being fat does not plausibly harm anyone else (contrary to a
few public health zealots who have argued that the "obesity
epidemic" is "socially contagious"[33]). And even setting these
points aside, choosing to be somewhat fatter in order to eat
more pleasurably or adventurously or comfortingly strikes
me as a valid choice—a potential trade-off of the kind people
make all the time and that they are entitled to make as their
lives unfold in all their individuality and richness and com-
plexity.[34] As Eaton puts it, in making a related argument:
"Modern life, especially modern urban life, is built around
this kind of trade-off which, in most cases, does not suffer
from any de-aestheticization, stigmatization, discrimination,
or other negative social consequences"—unlike fatness.[35]

Often the moralism I've been calling out here is criticized
under the aegis of "healthism": the idea that health has been
elevated to a supreme moral value in contemporary Anglo-
American culture, rather than recognized as one value among
many, and one that plausibly does not issue in an individual
moral mandate to be healthy.[36] (It certainly doesn't mean we
should be as healthy as humanly possible, given other com-
peting values such as the pleasure and community that par-
taking in supposedly "unhealthy" foods may foster.) But it's
worth reflecting how rarely such considerations figure in dis-

cussions other than fatness, drug use, and smoking—that is, bodily states and behaviors that are already heavily moralized. Healthism seems to be less a general moral mistake, then, than an ideological weapon wielded selectively against those who are already stigmatized and othered.

What *about* smoking, though? Don't we shame smokers, to great effect, and for their own good? It's true that the rates of smoking have decreased hugely since the public health campaign against it, due to this intervention, among other factors. But, for one thing, it's not clear to me that we *should* shame smokers, as opposed to continuing to educate them on the risks, given the very real social stressors and bodily vulnerabilities that lead people to develop this powerful addiction.[37] (Compare other addictions, like alcoholism, that we increasingly view through the lens of a disease model and do not take to be an appropriate basis for shaming in particular or moralizing generally.) For another thing, difficult as it is to quit smoking, it is a discrete behavior that can in some sense be given up. Whereas one cannot simply stop eating and live for long afterward. (I say this as someone who struggled mightily to quit smoking after a heavy-duty addiction I developed in my late teens; still, unlike becoming thin, quitting smoking was ultimately doable for me, given my acknowledged privileges, such as having enough money to buy nicotine patches to ease the worst of my cravings.) The health risks of smoking are also far greater and better established than the health risks of fatness. Finally, smoking confers real risks on other people, due to second- and thirdhand smoke, as well as modeling this ostensibly "cool" behavior to impressionable younger people. So fatness and smoking are in many ways disanalogous.

To sum up my argument in this section: fatness is by and

large out of our control, making the supposed moral obligation not to be fat likely moot from the beginning. But even
if we *were* in control of our body mass, fatness may not put a
burden on the healthcare system after all. And even if it does,
we tolerate people making all sorts of choices that markedly
increase their risk of diseases, injuries, and death. Why should
the choice to be somewhat fatter, in order to better enjoy the
profound pleasures of cooking, eating, and sharing food with
others, be regarded as fundamentally different? The answer is
not a rational one, I believe; rather, it is rooted in errors of
human psychology.

In a 2005 study by Thalia Wheatley and Jonathan Haidt,
participants who were susceptible to posthypnotic suggestion
were hypnotized to feel a pang of disgust upon reading a
random word: either "often" or "take."[38] The experimenters
then had participants read a vignette featuring people depicted as committing some moral transgression. For example,

> Congressman Arnold Paxton frequently gives speeches
> condemning corruption and arguing for campaign fi-
> nance reform. But he is just trying to cover up the
> fact that he himself [will *take* bribes from/is *often*
> bribed by] the tobacco lobby, and other special inter-
> ests, to promote their legislation.[39]

Participants who read a version of the vignette featuring
the word that matched their posthypnotic suggestion—and
thus would have felt a pang of disgust upon reading it—
tended to judge the transgression significantly more harshly.

Feeling artificially heightened disgust can thus make us more morally judgmental.[40]

There's more. In a follow-up experiment, the researchers included another vignette as a control, in which a student council representative named Dan was described as either "trying to *take* up" or "*often* picking" topics of widespread mutual interest for discussion at their meetings. This behavior is obviously perfectly benign, even praiseworthy. Despite this fact, participants who read the version of the vignette that matched their posthypnotic suggestion, and thus elicited a pang of disgust, tended to condemn Dan for his innocent behavior. "It just seems like he's up to something," said one of the participants. Dan came across as a "popularity-seeking snob" to another. His behavior "seemed so weird and disgusting" to someone else. "I don't know [why it's wrong], it just is," they concluded, firmly.[41]

The researchers were surprised by these effects (remember, the morally neutral vignette had been included as a control here). Such results turn out to be very robust, though, and have been induced by several other measures—including exposing participants to a bad smell, seating them at a disgusting desk (littered with debris, beside an overflowing trash can), having them recall a physically disgusting experience, and showing them a disgusting video clip (of a dirty toilet). Notably, inducing another negative emotion, sadness, did not produce these effects, showing that they were not driven by negative affect generally.[42]

The lessons are clear: First, people routinely misinterpret their visceral disgust reactions as *moral* disgust, leading them to judge morally bad actions more harshly, and even to deem neutral actions morally problematic. Second, when this occurs, people reach for reasons to justify their moral ill feelings, engaging in post hoc rationalization of a moral verdict already rendered.

It is hence telling that disgust has been shown to be heavily implicated in negative judgments about fat people. In a 2010 study that canvassed both American and Australian participants, disgust toward fat bodies was the strongest predictor of these fatphobic judgments.[43] Fat people were also among the social groups that elicited the most disgusted reactions: we are on a par with politicians and unhoused people, and second only to smokers and drug users, in eliciting revulsion.[44]

If fat people are regularly regarded with visceral disgust, then our bodies are liable to be moralized, even though we have committed no misdeeds. Rather than fat people being seen simply as people, and fat bodies simply as bodies, we will tend to be viewed as moral failures, and our bodies deemed moral problems—urgently in need of solutions, whether cruel or ostensibly concerned and well meaning. Hence the moral panic over fat people being a burden on the healthcare system, despite the general indifference to many other health risks when they are taken by thin people. Compare too the complaint that fat people who do not hide themselves away—and indeed merely exist in public—are "glorifying obesity": a made-up sin surely driven by the need to rationalize disgust reactions.

There are reasons why, despite the advent of fat activism, these reactions and the attendant hand-wringing are likely to be persistent. Disgust is a particularly sticky emotion that, once felt toward an object, is hard to undo. Disgust stains, spreads, and seeps into its objects. If a person feels nauseated by a particular food, say, because it made them sick on one occasion, they will often immediately form a disgust association with that food and be averse to it long afterward. (Disgust is thus the only emotion that is susceptible to what is called "one shot" conditioning.[45]) What's more, disgust is easily learned and socially contagious: if one person demonstrates their disgust toward an object, others who witness this disgust will often come to share it.[46] This makes sense from an evolutionary perspective, given that such social contagion would once have helped people to avoid contaminated food and pathogens.

Moreover, disgust strongly motivates us to avoid interacting closely with what is deemed to be disgusting—while sometimes creating a fascination with looking at it from a distance. Disgust can make its objects beckon, even glitter, tinged with the allure of prurience.[47] In short, it makes us curious. Witness the common reaction to people asking on Facebook if anyone wants to see something disgusting, such as a gnarly wound or bruise, in the comments. There are almost always at least a few takers ready to rubberneck. The popularity of exploitative reality TV shows featuring very fat bodies, such as *My 600-Lb. Life,* may be partly explained by such mechanisms.

Disgust is, finally, the emotion of social rejection. When people are found irredeemably disgusting, they may be marked for "social death," to use the sociologist Orlando Patterson's notion—deemed beyond the pale of many ordinary social relations, including friendship and intimate relationships, as well as in public discourse and privileged professional settings.[48] It's thus unsurprising that fat people routinely face discrimination and bias not only in medical contexts but in our education, employment, and dating and social lives.

The link between disgust and social rejection also explains

the extreme lengths people are frequently willing to go to in order to avoid being judged disgusting by those around us. And so we continue struggling mightily to lose weight through dieting, despite the evidence that this won't work in the long term. We are thereby seeking not only to fit in, by making our bodies smaller, but to garner the moral approval such strenuous efforts may earn even regardless of their success. We are trying to be "good fatties." We are trying to avoid being shunned, shamed, and blamed. And, when it comes to social acceptance, we are hungry for scraps of sustenance.

CHAPTER 5

SOMETHING TO BE DESIRED

The first time I recall a boy commenting on my body was when I was in the fifth grade. I must have been ten. "Fat little Kate-lyn," Jack said, apropos of nothing, during a PE class.[1] Everyone else giggled as I felt frozen in place with shame. It is unlikely to surprise you—and in most ways, it hardly matters—that at the time I was a pretty average weight, barely even chubby. And yet with that comment, my gaze—previously trained outward on the ball, or my classmates, or (most likely) the horizon—turned sharply on myself. I saw myself through the lens of Jack's contempt, even disgust, in that moment. And I felt myself monstrous in size and diminished in social stature. (Note that apparently paradoxical word "little," and the use of the diminutive— "Kate" is my full first name.)

I was a figure of fun. As I grew older and bigger, that would become a routine occurrence.

Another incident remains particularly vivid. I had begun to attend a previously all-boys' school at age sixteen, the year the school integrated, accepting me as one of three girls among a cohort of hundreds of boys. (The point was so I could study for the International Baccalaureate rather than the local high school graduation certificate in Australia.) I became close friends with a boy named Kieran. He used to call me in the evening for long, meandering conversations, even though we were together at school most of the day anyway. Rumor had it that he liked (like, *like*-liked) me. One night—and again, apropos of nothing—he proposed to rate me on an attractiveness scale from 1 to 10. He gave me a 7, which struck me as generous. "Why 7?" I wanted to know. "Well," he said smugly, "you have nice eyes and hair, but your figure leaves something to be desired." The sting of the words did not abate as they echoed in my mind long after we had hung up. I heard them when I stripped down for a shower. I heard them as I tried to go to sleep that night. I heard them when I twisted to peer at myself in the mirror, trying to see myself as he must.

That candid assessment was still salient some months later when I sat, with Kieran and our friend John, at a local Pizza Hut one night, hanging out before debate practice. They ordered and ate normally. I, meanwhile, had nothing. "She's eating light," John explained to the server. I mentally corrected him: I was eating *nothing*. I regularly went all day at school without eating, trying to avoid the cafeteria and the ignominy of being seen, as a now slightly "overweight" teen, to consume anything. I would return home to my daily meal of a few hundred calories. My parents were worried, but I concealed from them the extent of my dieting, often scraping my dinner into the trash, or giving it to the dogs, and pretending I'd eaten.

As a result, I learned to function—more or less—on very little sustenance. Back then, I would frequently rather be hungry than run the risk of weight gain. I was sometimes willing to starve to enjoy the relief of weight loss. And, though my unrelenting hunger might have saved me from a full-blown eating disorder, the toll of trying to shrink myself was nevertheless considerable. I, like many people, was so afraid of being sexually rejected for my fatness that I'd do almost anything to be smaller. This is sexual fatphobia—and it does so much damage.

That little comment, that small quip, that my figure "left something to be desired": it continued to echo for many years. It conspired with other, more horrifying incidents—having "fat bitch" scrawled on my locker, which was also doused with fish oil, to indicate, and cause, olfactory disgust—to leave me not only insecure but, at times, desperate for positive male attention. The high school graduates' last assembly saw a series of the usual superficially lighthearted prizes awarded to students, from "Most likely to succeed in white-collar crime" to "Most likely to have children out of wedlock," and so on. "And Kate Manne receives the prize for being the person"—I waited, trepidatious, bracing myself for the punch line—"most likely to have to pay for sex." The punch line was my sexual unattractiveness. The punch line was my body. The auditorium roared with laughter.

I recognize now, looking back, that the hostile treatment

I faced in high school was likely the result of a complex glut of factors. I was at the top of my class; I was outspoken; and I was sexually unavailable, with a stereotypically "hot" boyfriend who attended another school. ("He must be a face man, not an ass man," one of my school friends opined of him.) There was envy and jealousy and perhaps even attraction, as well as contempt and disgust, in the mix then. Kieran learned of my new relationship over the phone one evening, abruptly hung up, and essentially never spoke to me again.

A therapist once remarked to me, some fifteen years later, "They must have been so scared of you," instinctually sympathizing with the boys whose turf I had encroached on. In some sense, the negging and the harassment and the bullying weren't about me; they were about them and their insecurities, he tried to point out to me. But this is manifestly cold comfort: as I've said before, when your effigy is your body, you burn along with it.[2] And my body, such as it was, made for a crucial point of vulnerability. It gave misogyny an "in." My fatness not only made me a target but, in being a target already, gave them a way to get to me. And get to me they did, much as I might have liked to deny it.

This is how misogyny works: take a hierarchy, any hierarchy, and use it to derogate a girl or woman. We value intelligence: so call her stupid, inane, clueless. We value rationality: so call her crazy and hysterical. We value maturity: so call her childish and irresponsible. We value morality: so call her a bad person. We value thinness: so call her fat and, implicitly or explicitly, ugly. We value sexual attractiveness: so make her out to be the kind of person whom no one could ever want. This despite the fact that not only can fat people be found sexually attractive, it is a *common* sexual preference, at least if porn consumption is any indication.[3] And this jibes with the point that, as we saw earlier, it's not that we downrank fat bodies because we inherently dislike them. Rather, we dislike them because they are often downranked nowadays, following the advent of the fatphobic beauty hierarchies steeped in anti-Black racism.[4]

These various "down girl" moves can affect any girl or woman. You don't have to be particularly fat, or even fat whatsoever, to be called "fat" as a potent form of misogynistic derogation. In the midst of the brutal misogynistic takedown of Australia's first female prime minister—the slim, polished Julia Gillard—the writer Germaine Greer mocked the size of her ass, shamelessly playing to a nation of hooting haters.[5] I could never have forgiven Greer even before learning of her trans-exclusionary politics.[6] When it comes to the sisterhood, some so-called feminists are traitors.

But none of this should obscure from us the way that people who *are* fat, especially very fat, become targets of harassment just because of the size and shape of their bodies. Such harassment can take on a life of its own and rob them of their right to simply exist in public.

In her first book, *What We Don't Talk About When We Talk About Fat*, Aubrey Gordon recounts her experience of walking home from work and being pursued by a stranger. "Excuse me," the stranger shouted. "Are you big enough yet?" She scrutinized Gordon's body—looking her up and down repeatedly, her jaw hanging open—and solicited other people to participate in the harassment. "Is everyone else seeing how fat this bitch is? Look at her!" (Other passersby fortunately declined to join in; but they also didn't defend Gordon or come to her aid in any way.) "How do you let that happen? Can you even hear me? I deserve an answer!"

Obviously, the incident was stressful and upsetting for

Gordon in the moment. (And whenever such harassment occurs, the threat of physical violence is never all that distant.)
But it stayed with her too: robbing her of peace and sleep
that evening, leading her to work from home the next day,
and haunting her long afterward as she simply tried to go
about her business. "For months, I cannot think about what
this stranger said—I can only feel it. I remember her constantly. Shame fills my body like a water balloon, fragile in its
fullness."[7]

Shame is of course a natural human response to being
told, implicitly or explicitly, that you are not sexually
desirable—not just to a particular person, but in general, to
anyone. It marks you as damaged goods, as untouchable, as
unfuckable, even fundamentally unlovable. As the writer
Lindy West puts it, "Denying people access to [sexual] value
is an incredibly insidious form of emotional violence, one
that our culture wields aggressively and liberally to keep marginalized groups small and quiet."[8]

Gordon recounts another instance of street harassment to
which she was subject. She was followed late at night by an
older man, who saw her at a crosswalk. "No one will ever
love you," he said. "Not looking like that." Then more
loudly, twice, for emphasis. "No one will ever love you." He
drew closer, his face twisting into a grimace; she ran from
him. On this occasion, Gordon was not just left humiliated
or shamefaced. More than anything, she was terrified by this
act of raw, unprovoked aggression.[9]

✦ ✦ ✦

After my experiences in high school, I did not initially worry
that no one would ever love me. I was shielded, for a time, by

a variety of factors—being at most a "small fat," having a loving family, and dating a boyfriend who was never anything
but sweet and respectful. But, as time went by, and after our
breakup, those experiences caught up to me. I became desperately afraid that no other man would ever want me. Another man's love seemed quite unthinkable.

And so I entered a period during my college years of
needy and sometimes risky promiscuity. I went out to night-
clubs and raves. I took up smoking to allay my social anxiety
and to have something to do with my hands there. I reverted
to not eating for days at a time, losing a significant amount of
weight in the process. (I gained it back soon afterward.)
Partly to aid my dieting, I took party drugs like speed and
ecstasy. I drank more than I could handle. And I slept with
more or less any conventionally attractive man who approached me.

All of these behaviors, while not necessarily problematic in
themselves, made me feel empty, anxious, and depressed,
given my natural proclivities for order, comfort, and safety.
Most important, they put me at risk and made me vulnerable
to sexual predation.

This is a delicate point. Since Tarana Burke's #MeToo
movement was popularized late in 2017, we've understandably tended to focus on cases that are the most morally
straightforward: where a woman is sexually harassed or assaulted by a man and hence, by definition, does not invite it
or consent or participate voluntarily.

Such a focus is, as I say, understandable: one has to start
somewhere, and the simplest concerns are the easiest to gal-
vanize public support around. (We've also tended, much
more problematically, to focus on rich, white, otherwise privileged Hollywood actresses, which is a betrayal of Burke's

original centering of the Black and brown girls who are especially vulnerable.)

But predation can take complex forms and include dynamics where its subject does participate in, or even invite,
acts that should never have been proposed to begin with. I
remember going home one night with a man named Nick,
some fourteen years my senior—or probably more, I now
recognize. I was nineteen. He was ostensibly thirty-three.
Over drinks at a bar we both frequented, he said I had the
face of an angel, and tilted my chin up sharply to kiss him.
Later, I learned that his cheesy, indeed groan-worthy, pickup
line had been a proxy for a different, and more specific, judgment. He had confided in a friend that he thought I looked
like "a little Elvira," but "more compact" and with "even
bigger boobs." (Inaccurate.) White Australian men not infre-
quently treated me, in my Jewishness, as slightly exotic: opin-
ing that I must have "Spanish blood," or that my Jewish
friend Noa and I must be sisters. (This despite the fact that
she was tall and willowy, and I was quite the opposite.)

When we got back to his place, Nick complimented my
face again. "Do you like my body too?" I asked him, yearning
for validation. He hesitated. "I like how you're so confident
in it." My precarious confidence evaporated. I contemplated
leaving, but I felt too far in at that point. My top was already
off, and both his age and his self-assuredness intimidated me
in the moment. The prospect of making an excuse and finding my way home felt impossible and exhausting and, perhaps, futile. I knew he would try his utmost to make me stay.
Probably I would end up sleeping with him anyway. I did
what I felt I had to.[10]

These forms of bad sex—and I mean "bad" both ethically

and hedonically—are ubiquitous in our culture. Girls and women not only have our refusals, or lack of affirmative consent, ignored. We also say yes when we wish we could say no out of a sense of social and sexual obligation. And, in some cases, we feel starved of positive male attention in a world that has humiliated us and derogated our bodies.

It is crucial not to misunderstand this point. There's an enduring myth that fat women can't be sexually assaulted, because we would have reveled in the attention. This lie does tremendous, demonstrable damage: A 2017 trial for sexual assault in Canada saw the judge opine that the seventeen-year-old victim likely enjoyed a forty-nine-year-old man's sexual advances because he was handsome and she, meanwhile, was "slightly overweight." (She did have a "pretty face," though, the judge acknowledged, thereby paying her the most backhanded compliment known to fat womankind.) This was probably the girl's first experience of seduction, Judge Jean-Paul Braun hence mused, and she must have been at least "a little flattered."[11] A recent study found that when a woman sexually coerced by a man was depicted as fat rather than thin, participants expressed greater sympathy with the perpetrator, had less negative affect toward him, and posited more mitigating factors for his criminal behavior.[12]

In reality, not only can fat women be sexually assaulted, but there is even evidence that this is more likely to happen to us than our thinner counterparts.[13] But the systematic downranking of certain bodies—ones that are fat, as well as trans, nonwhite, or disabled—leaves some of us vulnerable to additional harms. For one, we may consent to sexual and romantic relationships we don't want out of a sense that we're not entitled to say no, or that this is the best we can do. You may well bank the checks you get when you're living with a deficit—however dubious their source, and however paltry their cash value.[14]

We often operate, despite ourselves, with a certain implicit model of sex: he wants it and asks for it; she either consents or refuses. He is the pursuer, the initiator, and the subject who desires, in this picture. She is its object—passive, desired, and, hence, desirable. *Man wants woman; man fucks woman; woman is fucked; he fucked her.*

This picture gets a lot wrong, as the philosopher Quill R Kukla has pointed out. It's sexist; it's heteronormative. And it misses the possibility of sexual negotiations that take a better form, in being an ongoing conversation—which should be had, we might add, between two not only consenting but enthusiastic parties.[15]

It also misses the way that women are *not* always desired, and are in fact routinely derogated by men, and society at large, in terms of our sexual desirability. Consider the dynamics of catcalling: When a man catcalls a woman in a prototypical way, by wolf whistling or calling her "hot," he is not just paying her a crude compliment of the kind she would rather not receive. He is issuing his *judgment*, his stamp of approval, his benediction. He is positioning himself as someone entitled to preside over the sexual, and hence social, value of women at large. It is her job to be attractive; to please, to soothe, to serve him. And his verdict, even if positive, is provisional. If she ignores or rejects him, he may well reverse or negate it, by calling her a bitch, frigid, or, as the case may be, fat and ugly.

Catcalling is about surveillance, then, not appreciative acknowledgment. And it can issue in the sneering rejection as well as leering endorsement that any adequate feminist account of sexual objectification must reckon with.

It is strange in the literature on objectification how little is said about the way some of us are deemed not shiny objects but, rather, tarnished ones—and lackluster compared with others.[16] Consider, for example, the philosopher Martha Nussbaum's famous list of seven ways of objectifying a person, or (on her account, equivalently) treating someone as an object. Namely, objectification may involve the following:

1. treating someone like an *instrument* of one's own purposes;

2. denying their *autonomy,* by treating them as lacking in self-determination;

3. denying their *subjectivity,* by treating them as something whose experiences, if any, need not be taken into account;

4. treating them as *inert*—as lacking in agency or even activity;

5. treating them as *violable*—as something that may be smashed, broken up, or broken into;

6. treating them as *property*—as something that can be owned, bought, sold, and so on;

7. treating them as *fungible*—that is, as interchangeable with other objects of the same type, or different types.[17]

Conspicuously absent from Nussbaum's list, and her subsequent discussion, is attention to the way objectification often involves comparing people with each *other* and positioning them in a hierarchy.[18] Far from treating people as fungible—interchangeable with others of the same type—objectification can hence involve an obsessive interest in evaluating and ranking and making minute distinctions between people. And weight, a changeable and linear and infinitely gradable quantity, provides a basis for so doing that is both expedient and pernicious. Some of us are praised; some of us are put down; some of us are trashed and treated like garbage.

Hence the practice engaged in by some straight men of not only rating individual women's looks but contrasting and grading us. This can involve an element of objectification added to Nussbaum's list by the philosopher Rae Langton: reduction to body parts.[19] I recall a boy I went to school with saying, with a blithe sense of entitlement, that the ideal girl would be Amy's head on Brooke's body. *That* would be a 10, he confidently informed us.

Many straight men have a potent sense of entitlement to "hot" wives and girlfriends too: to female sexual partners who rate highly according to the standards operative in their milieu. To put it simply, such a man is not just interested in what *he* finds attractive; he also cares, or cares more, about how *other* men would rate his choice of partner, which is typically inversely proportional to her weight, among other factors. Whether highly ranked or not, girls and women suffer greatly from this social arrangement—from the shitty men who reject us, to the shitty men who deem us worthy only until we age, sag, or gain weight. In Zadie Smith's novel *On Beauty*, Howard, a white professor of art history, cheats on his Black wife, Kiki, after more than two decades of marriage. She yells at him, during one of their many confrontations, about his choice of lover: "A tiny little white woman I could fit in my pocket. . . . My *leg* weighs more than that woman. What have you made me *look* like in front of everybody in this town? You married a big black bitch and you run off with a fucking leprechaun?"[20] Howard mumbles for a bit until she forces him to speak up: "All I said was . . . Well, I married a slim black woman, actually." "Holy *shit*. You want to sue me for breach of contract, Howard? Product expanded without warning?"[21] And indeed, clauses in prenuptial agreements forbidding a wife's weight gain are far from unheard of. The ugliness of this setup supports whole sectors of late-stage capitalism, in the form of the diet, beauty, and so-called wellness industries.[22] These are upheld by a toxic combination of misogyny, ageism, and fatphobia, often dutifully self-administered to avoid the ignominy of losing our looks, our man, our life force.

Of course, fat boys and men also suffer from the oppressive effects of fatphobia, particularly inasmuch as they occupy other marginalized social positions, in being Black, trans, queer, or disabled, as Da'Shaun L. Harrison has persuasively argued.[23] The impugning of fat male bodies stems partly from the fact that fat is frequently coded as feminine, and fat men may thereby be perceived as insufficiently masculine. They may hence be perceived as incapable of serving as romantic interests, as the story of the fat Black opera singer Limmie Pulliam recently made apparent. A brilliant vocalist, he was nonetheless body-shamed out of the industry in his early twenties and stopped singing—even at home or in church—for more than a decade. He worked as a security guard and a debt collector. Recently, he made his debut at

Carnegie Hall, at the age of forty-seven. "I'm usually the only one who looks like me. . . . There is always a sense of isolation, of not fitting in," he reflected, in a moving interview. "Some in the industry . . . have difficulty in seeing Black males in romantic leads." This is especially true for fat Black men and other masculine people. As Pulliam put it, "It felt like it was OK to make fun of people of size and that we weren't worthy of careers. . . . 'Lose 50 pounds, get in touch with me again, and I'll give you a live audition,'" he recalled being told by more than one opera director.[24]

Still, it is girls, women, and other marginalized genders who are disproportionately likely to face sexual fatphobia and its associated violence. We see this in the fact that, in 2014, parents were around twice as likely to google "Is my daughter overweight?" as "Is my son overweight?" even though boys were slightly likelier to be so classified. (Parents were also nearly three times more likely to google whether their daughter was ugly; how a Google search might turn up the answer to this question remains something of a mystery.)[25] We see this in the fact that as many as 90 percent of so-called obese women in heterosexual relationships have been bullied and belittled for their weight by their male partners; anecdotally, at least, the converse seems to be less common.[26] We see it in the fact that "dad bods" are considered sexy; "mom bods," not so much. And we see it in the noxious practice of "hogging," or a "pig roast," where young men compete with each other to see who can bed the fattest, or heaviest, woman—including, recently, at Cornell University, where I have been teaching for the last decade.[27]

As well as the gross assumption that fat women will be "easy"—again, in being grateful for any male attention—the practice of hogging owes to the ambivalence exhibited by many straight men toward fat women. They may well want us sexually, but they view our sexual worth as minimal or non-existent, and are subsequently loath to take us seriously, let alone publicly acknowledge us, as partners. As the writer Hanne Blank memorably puts it, "Whether someone finds you fuckable and whether someone thinks you're sufficiently high-status to suit their self-image are two different things."[28] As fat women, we may be a cheap, tasty snack, not a proper meal, then: the sexual equivalent of junk food. They'll throw away the wrapper and brush away the crumbs, sated but vaguely disgusted—with both us and themselves—when they are done with us.[29]

I remain ashamed of being treated in this way, often by older men, whose approval I so craved after my experiences in high school. I learned that I would not have to pay for sex, after all—far from it. But my sexual relationships in my late teens were dangerous, exploitative, and deeply unsatisfying. I did not feel entitled to better until I lost a lot of weight, in my early twenties, and fortunately met a man who treated me beautifully even after I regained it all, and then some. His name is Daniel, and he is now my husband.

A straight man's mistreatment of a fat woman he's attracted to doesn't come out of nowhere: if he is open about this attraction, or it is somehow revealed, he is liable to be shamed, scorned, and downranked by other people, including women. This is another way in which men may be affected by fatphobic disgust, which—as we've seen—is directed toward not only fat women but even the men these women are pictured sitting *next* to.[30] In *The Story of the Lost Child*, the fourth and final novel in Elena Ferrante's celebrated Neapolitan series, the narrator, Elena—nicknamed Lenù—harbors decades of unrequited love for the intelligent but feckless cad, Nino. He is a serial philanderer, fathering and then neglecting numerous children; he is arrogant and rude; and he is irredeemably selfish. But Lenù loves Nino madly anyway and leaves her husband for him, eventually conspiring to have his child, Imma, and moving in together. Regardless of Nino's conspicuous faults and continued unfaithfulness, the decisive blow to his image in Lenù's eyes is his fucking their fat, old, deeply unglamorous servant, Silvana. When Lenù walks in on the pair in the bathroom, this is what she sees:

> Nino was in his undershirt and otherwise naked, his long thin legs parted, his feet bare. Silvana, curved forward, with both hands resting on the sink, had her big underpants at her knees and the dark smock pulled up around her waist. He, while he stroked her sex holding her heavy stomach with his arm, was gripping an enormous breast that stuck out of the smock and the bra, and meanwhile was thrusting his flat stomach against her large white buttocks.[31]

Lenù flees the apartment with baby Imma, upon which she "discovered that I had no tears, I wasn't suffering, I was only frozen with horror." She continues:

> Was it possible that that Nino whom I had discovered as he was thrusting his taut sex inside the sex of a mature woman—a woman who cleaned my house, did my shopping, cooked, took care of my children; a woman marked by the struggle to survive, large,

worn-out, the absolute opposite of the cultivated, el egant women he brought to dinner—was the boy of my adolescence?[32]

Yes, she finally realizes: this is who he is. But Nino remained untarnished in Lenù's eyes until he marked himself as "alien" and "ugly" in view of not his philandering, or his sexually exploitative behavior, but his choice of sexual partner in a fat, older, working-class woman.[33] Disgust prevails as Lenù felt "a revulsion not different from what I would have felt if I had seen two lizards coupling."[34] Later, she is struck by the ridiculousness of the "scene of sex between that fat woman and skinny Nino."[35] Eventually, Lenù's disgust and horror give way to rage and hatred: "I hated Nino as until that moment I had never hated anyone."[36] It doesn't even dawn on her—or if it does, she doesn't care—that Nino might well have been raping Silvana.

As fat girls and women, we contend with the boys and men who judge us and find us wanting. We leave "something to be desired," in failing to be so. But Lenù's narrative hints at a truth that remains, to me, just as painful: girls and women play a crucial role in perpetuating sexual fatphobia. And they may not only internalize but deliberately weaponize it in policing and pulling rank over other girls and women.

In my own life, for every Jack there was a Jill—the girl one year above me in elementary school who told me about a boy named Mark from another school who supposedly liked (like, *like*-liked) me. When I expressed skepticism, Jill told me, with a cruel smile, that Mark liked his girls "a little chubby."

Ultimately Mark turned out to be an invention, as she eventually admitted in a tone of offhand boredom. Not only did he not like me, he never even existed.

Why did Jill make him up? Just to mess with me, and to have something to joke about with her many male friends. The idea that a boy would like me in *that* way was apparently truly laughable.

For every Nick who called me "a little Elvira," there was an aunt—my own aunt—who described me, in front of my family, as "an intense-looking girl with big boobs." "Don't be offended," she said, smirking, seeing my face turn ashen, "I am too." On other occasions, she suggested I shrink myself—breasts and all—by going on extreme diets. I was furious then; perhaps unfairly, I remain so.

For every Kieran there was a Candice—a girl who attended the boys' school with me, who had forewarned her group of male friends there not to expect to like me (in any sense), because I was somewhat fat. She didn't even have the decency to cover her tracks well. The night before we started at the school, she invited me to sleep over at her house, in a gesture of the incipient friendship that never really materialized. A male friend of hers at the boys' school called her up on her house phone (remember, this was the 1990s), and she told him she was with me. "What's Kate like?" he must have asked, because Candice began to describe me as the smartest person she'd ever met, almost as if I'd swallowed a dictionary. (I blushed with profound embarrassment, beginning to realize that her description was not doing me any favors.) "And she's . . . you know," Candice added to the boy, conspiratorially, casting a sidelong glance at my body. "Not, like, Madeline Davis–level, but . . . yeah." Madeline Davis was the fattest girl at our old school. I flinched in humiliation. And I failed, to my shame, to speak up for her—or for myself, it lately occurred to me.

As girls and women, it's not surprising that we learn to pay such close attention to what boys and men want from us. It may give us a modicum of power to please them. Misogyny distinguishes "good women" and "cool girls" and punishes the remainder. (Of course, being deemed "good" or "cool" by misogynistic standards is a dangerous kind of currency.) And this can make female solidarity something of a challenge. Misogyny, as I've argued, finds in fatphobia a powerful and convenient ally: it constructs a ready-to-hand hierarchy among girls and women based on the infinitely gradable metric of body mass, usefully complicated by body shape, breast size, waist-to-hip ratio, and various markers of privilege.

Some fat activists and advocates say that fatphobia seeks to eliminate fat people: that the prevailing attitude toward fat bodies is essentially genocidal. I'm not denying that this can be the case, but I'm not convinced that it always is. If we didn't exist, there would be significantly fewer people for thinner folks to feel superior to.

Candice told me, later, that her middle-aged father had commented on my body. "She's *very* attractive," he'd apparently said. Candice imitated his leering. "I found it kind of disturbing," she reflected. "I think he wants you, Kate; it's disgusting."

Candice's father wasn't the only older man whose roving eye—or worse—I had to contend with as a teenager. And therein lies the answer to a question I'm often asked, nowadays, when people learn about my high school experience. Why didn't I leave? Why did I stick out two full miserable years at the boys' school? Surely I could have told my loving, attentive parents what it was like, and they would have done something. I could have; they would have. The short answer as to why I didn't is that I was frozen and stubborn. But the full story lies in the heavy, roaming hands of a music teacher at my old school. I didn't want to go back there; I felt that I couldn't. And I didn't have it in me to have that necessary conversation about why I wouldn't. He had left abruptly; perhaps other students spoke up when I didn't. But his smell was still everywhere. It suffused the whole campus. It still comes to me when I think of him, a kind of olfactory hallucination. I still smell his aftershave around corners, in hallways, on stairwells.

When I confided in a trusted male teacher about what had happened, I told him that I couldn't tell anyone else. And I begged him not to report it. "No one else would believe me," I said dully. "I'm not one of the pretty girls. Who would want me? Nobody." I couldn't bring myself to say the words "ugly" or "fat" to him. But that was my real meaning.[37]

For want of a safe school environment as a girl, I got myself into a much worse one. And at the age of fourteen, I'd already intuited an important piece of social knowledge: as a fat girl, I would be deemed not only unfuckable but also unbelievable.

CHAPTER 8

SMALL WONDER

During my first year of college, at the age of eighteen, I fell deeply in love. I fell for philosophy, the discipline that is famously supposed to begin in wonder. (As Plato has his character of Socrates say, "Wonder is the feeling of a philosopher, and philosophy begins in wonder."[1]) But much as I loved—and continue to love—my discipline, it hasn't always loved me back, or even recognized me readily as one of its practitioners. When presenting at philosophy conferences, and simply walking around my own department, I have often been assumed to be a secretary, a care-taker, or, at nearly forty, a student. "You don't look like a philosopher," said a senior male figure, looking me up and down, at one of my first professional workshops. Once, when I was a convocation speaker, a faculty member I found myself chatting with casually beforehand was so surprised to learn that I was the one giving the address that he saw fit to apologize for his startled, perplexed reaction. It probably didn't help that I was seven months pregnant at the time, and hence even fatter than usual—it being one of the few times in my life that I felt not only entitled but obligated for the sake of my baby to routinely eat to the point of satiety.

I took the lectern smiling, but shaking. I felt not just self-conscious but like an impostor. That's the problem with labeling it "impostor syndrome": when one is literally treated as an impostor, it is less a psychological state than an accurate reflection of social reality.

The social reality in philosophy is, well, not pretty. We are not diverse.[2] We are, by far, the most white male–dominated discipline of any humanities field (with history a distant second).[3] Women recently made up just 17 percent of full-time philosophy faculty members in the United States.[4] We are on a par with the least diverse STEM fields, including "pure" mathematics and physics.[5] We have a massive sexual harassment, as well as racism, problem.[6] We are, in my view, increasingly transphobic, as well as classist and ableist.[7] We are also deeply, and systematically, fatphobic.

In writing this book, I've had many occasions to wonder: Where did I learn to hate my fat body? From the culture, of course: from books, movies, and TV, via about a million sources. From the boys who teased me to the men who slept with me and communicated, in ways subtle and not, that my body was a problem. From the girls and women who perpetuated this system, by scrutinizing, policing, and derogating fatness—mine, their own, and others'. From doctor's offices to people on the street to the general awfulness of the internet, fatphobia is everywhere, as we have been seeing.

But in my case, and many others, there's more to the

story too. As a philosopher by trade, I've come to realize that my discipline's fatphobia has affected me deeply. It communicates—again, in ways subtle and not—that not only are fat bodies a moral and sexual problem; they are a sign of *intellectual* failure too. And these messages have implications well beyond the discipline and the academy at large. Philosophers both reflect and inform the broader intellectual culture. We are regarded, for better and worse, and fairly or unfairly, as the premier humanities discipline and a font of intellectual authority. And so an examination of fatphobia in my own field can serve as a lens, indeed a magnifying glass, for something much larger: the way we think the minds housed in fatter bodies are less than, even stupid.

✦ ✦ ✦

Philosophy, with its characteristic emphasis on reason and rationality, implicitly conceives of those qualities as the province of the lean, rich, white men who dominate my discipline. It has been remarked by more than one author that there is a dearth of fat bodies in academia in general.[8] Small wonder, perhaps, when we praise arguments for being muscular and compact, and criticize prose for being "flabby" or flowery (and, implicitly, feminine).[9] When it comes to our metaphysics—our pictures of the world—we pride ourselves on a penchant for austerity or, as the twentieth-century philosopher W. V. O. Quine put it, "desert landscapes."[10] And what is the fat body in the popular imagination but excess, lavishness, redundancy?[11]

Quine, writing in 1948, held that philosophy should be as spare as possible in identifying the objects over which to quantify (or count as distinct entities). He set out to argue against the idea that there are possible objects—which "subsist"—alongside actual, existing ones. And he wrote of this metaphysical picture with palpable disdain: "[Such an] overpopulated universe is in many ways unlovely. It offends the aesthetic sense of us who have a taste for desert land-scapes, but this is not the worst of it. [This] slum of possibles is a breeding ground for disorderly elements." For how would we count the merely possible elements in this "slum"? "Take, for instance, the possible fat man in that doorway; and, again, the possible bald man in that doorway. Are they the same possible man, or two possible men? How do we decide? How many possible men are there in that doorway? Are there more possible thin ones than fat ones?"[12] (Women, seemingly, were not on Quine's horizon.)

Quine's invocation here of classist as well as fatphobic tropes, deployed to comic effect—do fat men take up more space than thin ones, even when they are merely possible?—was clearly in some sense deliberate.[13] This is part of what made Quine a master stylist—and a tastemaker—in the disci-pline. He doesn't only argue against a "bloated universe," in all of its "rank luxuriance."[14] He also invites the reader to share his scorn, which is sometimes more effective than ratio-nal argumentation. Disgust, as we have seen, is easily dis-seminated. Of all the moral emotions, it is the most catching; it seeps, stains, and sticks to its (more or less deserved) ob-jects.

And hence, as a fat philosopher, I have long struggled to reconcile my image of my body with its role in the world as the emissary of my mind. I think of it, tongue in cheek, as my "body-mind" problem.[15] As I confessed in the introduction, I have sometimes been unable to bear the idea of sending out my "soft animal" of a body, in the words of the late poet

Mary Oliver, to represent a discipline that prides itself on sharpness, clarity, and precision. I have felt betrayed by my soft borders.

This false binary exists partly in my own head, yes, but very much in others' too. I was recently apprised of a caption on a portrait of David Hume, the famous eighteenth-century philosopher, in an introductory philosophy textbook: "The lightness and quickness of his mind was entirely hidden by the lumpishness of his appearance."[16] Thus have other fat philosophers been warned that our bodies may similarly mask our intellects. And often, we are treated not as a party to the conversation but, rather, as its object—by turns comic, or expendable, or a problem. No wonder so many fat men—not to mention women and nonbinary people—remain at the doorway of philosophy, or never approach it to begin with.[17]

The fat man has suffered worse fates, and other insults, in philosophy. He is simultaneously a figure of fun and a site of violence in ethics, thanks to the notorious trolley problem. In this imaginative exercise, devised by the twentieth-century philosopher Philippa Foot, a railway trolley is hurtling out of control, about to hit and kill five people haplessly tied to the tracks, for reasons left unspecified. You are positioned at a lever that, if pulled, would divert the trolley onto another track, whereupon it would hit and kill just one luckless soul likewise tied up there (again, for no known reason). The six people involved are supposed to be all, somehow, relevantly, morally equivalent—innocent, good sorts, and solid citizens, neither murderers nor possessed of the cure for cancer, for instance. So ought you to pull the lever?[18] This is one of the first questions frequently posed in introductory ethics courses.

Most students say that you indeed ought to do so (though many also flinch at the prospect). But the question then arises: Suppose that instead of being positioned at a lever ready to divert the trolley to kill the one person, you are standing on a bridge alongside a very fat man, overlooking the trolley heading toward the five. You realize that, if you push him down from the bridge, then his weight will stop the trolley—while your presumptively thin body would not be up to the task. You would kill him in the process. (Somehow, you know all this.) Ought you to push the fat man into the path of the oncoming trolley, in order to save the five people who are presently tied to the tracks?[19] Or, as a book on this subject puts it, more bluntly, as its titular question: Would you kill the fat man?[20]

Students are often more reluctant to say yes to this question, even though the two problems have the same form— ought you to kill the one to save the five?[21] And this is supposed to raise questions about whether it is actually worse to cause harm in an "up close and personal" manner, by directly pushing the fat man off the bridge, rather than causing harm at one remove, by merely pulling the lever such that the trolley runs someone over. Or perhaps we are just more squeamish about the former than the latter.

Whatever one thinks about this rather brutal moral calculus, it is telling that the description of the fat man, and his potential downfall, tends to elicit laughter rather than a sense of sobriety, let alone tragedy. And this thought experiment, as it is called, is hardly alone in treating certain people's bodies in philosophy as dispensable, even disposable—as always ready to be crushed in service of a probative example. Another similarly fatphobic case imagines a fat man who gets stuck in the mouth of a cave that is rapidly filling with water. Those inside will drown unless they blow him up with a stick of dynamite that one of them happily has at the ready. Ought they to do so?[22]

Again, whatever one says about these questions, ought we to *think* in this way? Should we teach our students to consider people's bodies in general, and fat bodies in particular, as props to be exploited not only for comic effect but as bores to drill down insistently in the search for moral principles? The very rational relentlessness—and the relentless rationalism—of philosophy that I once loved now fills me, at times, with a deep, abiding uneasiness.

Still, I stay with it, because I believe in the power of philosophy to arm people with the tools to help fight important battles, including in matters of social justice. As members of a discipline that rarely establishes consensus, and indeed thrives on fruitful, intelligent disagreement, we can also teach students something invaluable by example, in our collective practice. No matter where you are in a social hierarchy, you are entitled to ask questions. You are entitled to disagree with your social superiors, and you may have the better end of the argument if you are sufficiently thoughtful and careful and open-minded. You are even entitled to disagree with figures as venerated and iconic as the ancient Greek philosophers Plato and Aristotle—including, as we'll see, regarding the nature of human appetite.

✦ ✦ ✦

For Plato, the glutton could not be a philosopher. In the *Timaeus*—his most widely read and influential dialogue until

the Middle Ages—he theorizes the human body and its functions in the context of broader questions about the world's
creation. This led him to an interest in the nature of the appetite, and the relationship between it and our faculty for
reason or rationality. He distinguishes between man's mortal
and immortal soul. The latter contains intelligence and reason, whereas the former "contains within it those dreadful
but necessary disturbances," such as pain, pleasure, and the
capacity for passions and emotions. These are things we need
to live in the world, but are dangerous inasmuch as they are
capable of "staining" the immortal, divine soul.[23] As the historian Susan E. Hill puts it, "Justice depends on reason's capacity to control, and not surrender to, emotions and
senses."[24]

The immortal soul—the rational part of us—lives, thought
Plato, in our heads. The mortal soul is located in different
parts of the torso, divided "the way that women's [living]
quarters are divided from men's" within a household. The
superior, masculine part of the mortal soul—the heart and
lungs, in particular—is located above the midriff. As Plato's
character of Timaeus speculates,

> Now the part of the mortal soul that exhibits manli-
> ness and spirit, the ambitious part, they settled nearer
> the neck, so that it might listen to reason and to-
> gether with it restrain by force the part consisting of
> appetites, should the latter at any time refuse outright
> to obey the dictates of reason.[25]

Meanwhile, the inferior part of the mortal soul, the digestive system, is theorized as "something like a trough for the
body's nourishment." Our creators placed it where they did

to keep it as far as possible from our heads, "the part that takes counsel," so that the "clamor and noise" of our stomach, that "wild one," wouldn't interfere with the mind's deliberations.[26] The liver has the job of taking "images and phantoms" sent from the head to frighten the appetites into submission to reason.[27] The intestines, meanwhile, are meant to slow the passage of food through our bodies so that we are capable of satiety. Timaeus holds that "the creators of our race knew that we were going to be undisciplined in matters of food and drink. They knew that our gluttony would lead us to consume much more than the moderate amount we needed." It is thanks to the intestines that our greedy stomachs don't require constant feeding. If they did, "gluttony would make our whole race incapable of philosophy and the arts, and incapable of heeding the most divine part within us."[28] Hence, "among all of the appetites," Hill writes, "gluttony stands, in the *Timaeus,* as the greatest threat to philosophy."[29]

So we see that a theory of hierarchy *within* one human body—with the head supposed to rule over the stomach—could easily serve as a basis for a hierarchy of *different* human bodies, based on our purported degree of rational self-mastery or control over our appetites. And this in turn ultimately rendered fat bodies suspect, since their denizens came over time, as we've seen, to be suspected of lacking such discipline.[30]

Although Plato predominantly focuses on the creation of the male body in the *Timaeus,* he also had a theory about how women came to be. The first generation of men who resisted rationality, for example by being gluttonous, was "reborn in the second generation as women."[31] Femininity, Hill argues, is thus firmly rooted for Plato in the appetites and aligned with that which is unruly and even unjust about human beings.[32]

But for Plato, as we saw earlier, the fat body doesn't seem to come in for criticism as such. True, he was concerned with human proportionality. But he was as worried about the small body of a large-souled man as the large body of a small-souled one. As Hill puts it,

> Plato's focus on proportionality allows for the possi-
> bility that if a large body has the appropriate large
> soul to go with it, balance occurs. Translator Donald
> Zeyl concurs that Plato's reference to large (*mega*)
> bodies may include, but does not necessarily mean,
> the fat body, and that there could certainly be large
> and well-proportioned bodies. From this perspective,
> a fat body is not necessarily out of proportion, it is
> only out of proportion if the body rules the soul.
> Thus, for Plato, a fat person can be a philosopher,
> while the gluttonous man cannot; the *appearance* of
> the fat man carries with it no inevitable moral judg-
> ment.[33]

The upshot is that Plato was against gluttony, not fatness as such. If the body of a great-souled man was fat or other-wise large, and thus body and mind were in harmony, then all was as it should be.

Plato's protégé, Aristotle, was less suspicious of pleasure, but no more sanguine about gluttony. Famously, in his *Nicoma-chean Ethics,* Aristotle developed "the doctrine of the mean,"

which theorizes human virtue as typically being the mean that lies between two extremes or excesses in human behavior.[34] Courage, for example, is the mean between the extremes of cowardice and foolhardiness.[35] Notably, however, there are areas of human life where one extreme is more tempting or common than another.[36] The appetite is one such, where the vice of "intemperance"—which encompasses being oversexed as well as gluttonous[37]—is far more of a problem for us than "unimpressionability" or, as it is sometimes translated, "insensitivity" to pleasure.[38] ("Persons defective in the power to enjoy pleasures are a somewhat rare class, and so have not had a name assigned to them: suppose we call them 'unimpressionable,'" Aristotle proposes.[39]) Overall, the human appetite is construed as a potential impediment not only to the virtue of temperance but ultimately to the flourishing (*eudaimonia*) that depends upon such virtues' proper exercise. And if we flourish, it is partly by wanting what is good for us, rather than harboring rogue appetites.[40]

So perhaps it's unsurprising that food was salient to the philosopher-translator C. D. C. Reeve when he sought to explain Aristotle's theory of virtuous action to a contemporary audience:

> Suppose, for example, that we are faced with a lunch menu. We wish for the good or happiness. We deliberate about which of the actions available to us in the circumstances will best promote it. Should we order the fish . . . or the lasagna?[41]

The ideal here is to recognize the supposedly healthy option, fish, as superior, to want it, and to order it: this embodies the aforementioned virtue of temperance. Next best is self-control (sometimes called "continence"): recognizing that the fish would be preferable, hankering for the lasagna, but ordering the fish manfully. Then there is *akrasia,* or "weakness of the will": still recognizing the rational superiority of the fish, but wanting and ordering the lasagna regardless. Then, worst of all: having the profoundly mistaken worldview that would involve lionizing lasagna—and so, Reeve imagines, ordering it *with extra cheese* followed by a large ice cream sundae, and having the audacity to feel good about having thus gratified one's taste for fat, salt, and sugar.[42]

What explains the alleged viciousness—that is, the vices—of such a person? What explains their supposedly false conception of what is (again, supposedly) good for them? Reeve offers on Aristotle's behalf that bad habits, especially those developed early in life, are the culprit:

> If we had acquired "good eating habits" instead, we would have a different conception of that part of the good that involves diet. We would want and would enjoy the fish and salad and not hanker for the lasagna and ice cream at all. Failing that, we would, as weak-willed or self-controlled people, at least not wish for it.[43]

This is, to my mind, eminently wishful thinking. And the result is an unlikely mash-up of Aristotle and a childhood obesity concern troll.

I have no problem with notions like temperance and self-control—well, in moderation. In many domains in life, we need these qualities to get our work done, stay the course, and care for those around us when various temptations beckon. But when it comes to food, these notions tend to backfire and make us more fixated on food, not less so. Restriction can lead to disordered eating and other physical and mental health problems. This emerged clearly in the—famous, and horribly unethical—Minnesota Starvation Experiment, where men in the 1940s lived for months on "semi-starvation" rations. Most became food obsessed, with some poring over cookbooks and licking the pictures wanly. They dreamed and fantasized about food, and lingered over the meals served to them twice daily.[44] Many became depressed, irritable, anxious—and skeletal. The mental health effects of their diets often persisted even after the "refeeding" process had helped them gain the weight back. Notably, they had subsisted on around fifteen hundred calories a day: more than many people are now allotted by their diet app—or their doctor.

There's also a large body of evidence suggesting that, even in less extreme cases, "restrained eating" can be problematic. People who expend a lot of effort limiting what or how much they eat tend to binge when forced to break their diets.[45]

Moreover, empirical evidence—and clinicians' practical expertise—has shown that teaching children to like and appreciate a wide range of foods is actually healthiest. We have known this for some time now. In the 1920s and 1930s, Clara Davis showed that children left to their own devices to select the food they wanted to eat from a smorgasbord of options intuitively gravitated toward foods that would fulfill their dietary needs as well as satisfy their appetites.[46] A 2006 study showed that, conversely, if you pressure children to finish their vegetable soup, they ultimately eat less of it and comment on it more negatively.[47] Children, it turns out, have a kind of "nutritional wisdom" that would be best trusted and not interfered with.[48] Distinguishing between "good foods" and "bad foods" is harmful, counterproductive, and unnecessary.

But Reeve, channeling Aristotle, is in good company when he demonizes certain foods and regards even occasionally indulging in them as the paradigm of irrationality. The standard example of weakness of the will in contemporary philosophy remains having a piece of cake or a cookie. Thomas Nagel writes, for example, in the opening of his paper "Free Will,"

> Suppose you're going through a cafeteria line and when you come to the desserts, you hesitate between a peach and a big wedge of chocolate cake with creamy icing. The cake looks good, but you know it's fattening. Still, you take it and eat it with pleasure. The next day you look in the mirror or get on the scale and think, "I wish I hadn't eaten that chocolate cake. I could have had a peach instead."[49]

Daring not to eat a peach, and to instead enjoy the chocolate cake, is thus the inaugural and paradigm example of the sort of minor rebellion that sometimes makes us think of ourselves as free—and foolish.[50]

He isn't a philosopher, but the cognitive psychologist Steven Pinker betrays a similar attitude when he bemoans the fact that rationality is no longer considered "phat" (as in, cool).[51] Pinker goes on to chide the irrational doofus who prefers the "small pleasure" of having lasagna now—rather than steamed vegetables—over the "large pleasure of a slim body" in perpetuity. They "succumb" to "myopic discounting": an ableist term for short-term thinking illustrated by a fatphobic example.[52]

Why are lean, white, male academics so up in arms about lasagna, specifically? A question for the ages—or an ethnographer of conference dinner menus.

The philosophical disapproval of indulgence, together with the widespread assumption that fat people eat more and worse than thin people, spills out to the ways that people are treated in academia. Femininity and fatness are an especially dire combination. Fat women are often suspected of being weak-willed. One of my friends in philosophy recalls a colleague saying of her, deliberately within earshot, "If she can't discipline what she eats, how can she discipline how she thinks?" Along similar lines, the psychology professor Geoffrey Miller once saw fit to tweet, "Dear obese PhD applicants: if you didn't have the willpower to stop eating carbs, you won't have the willpower to do a dissertation #truth." Miller was reprimanded by his university.[53] But he is still teaching there. And his fatphobia, while brazen, seems not to be unusual: one study showed that "obese" applicants to a psychology graduate program were significantly less likely to get in if there was an in-person interview. Disaggregating the results by gender revealed that this result held only for women.[54]

Sometimes such fatphobia takes the form of concern trolling about a budding academic's career prospects. Another friend confided that she was repeatedly told during graduate school for English literature that her body shape would make her unemployable, "because only thin women are seen as in-telligent." She later spoke to several other graduates from her program (which she describes as "otherwise extremely sup-portive and cozy") who had been told the same thing by the same few professors—"lose weight and look smarter." This message was apparently extolled regardless of the student's body type, and conveyed to some men as well as women. But there's no such thing as too smart or too thin, seemingly, for women in academia.[55]

These oppressive body norms intersect powerfully with another frequent site of prejudice: pregnancy. One professor recalls teaching a class in logic while pregnant: "Students openly ridiculed me, imitated me when my back was turned to get laughs, put insulting notes on my desk and, at the end of the semester, collaborated to give me the worst course evaluations of my life. They made it clear that they thought I was a freak and a buffoon, and that I had no business teach-ing at their university." Later, it emerged that the bullying had an at least partly bodily basis: one of the students in the class, whom the professor encountered socially, was flustered to find out that she'd been pregnant at the time. He now saw fit to apologize. "I'm sorry," he said, "we all thought you were just built like that." And what if she had been?[56]

Fatness and femininity remain a liability. I am flooded with a painful memory of one of the first friends I made in graduate school mocking a brilliant fat female philosopher for wearing too much makeup ("to compensate for her weight," he opined) and keeping diet shakes in her office. Could these judgments be related to the fact that some years later, at a conference dinner, the organizer proposed in all seriousness to take a vote about whether this same brilliant woman was actually a charlatan? It is difficult to know. But it is not any one incident that makes the difference here: collectively, and cumulatively, they do their predictable damage.

At the time of this incident, I was quite fat too. When I returned to the same conference the next year, I was some fifty pounds thinner, due to a combination of starvation and diet pills. I had started my job as a philosophy professor in the interim, and though nobody had said anything explicitly, the pressure I felt to lose weight before presenting myself as an intellectual authority figure had been all consuming. I had internalized the message: shrink, or be belittled.

The intellectual biases against fat people extend well beyond philosophy and even academia. Not only are they rampant in education, as we've seen, they extend to any so-called thinking profession. And they loom large in cultural depictions of fat people. From Homer Simpson to Peter Griffin to Miss Piggy to Fat Amy to Jerry Gergich to Ralph Kramden of *The Honeymooners,* the stereotype that fat people are stupid and oblivious and incompetent is everywhere.[57]

Often, we're represented as ignorant to the point of not even knowing what we look like. I grew up watching *The Simpsons,* in which a well-known scene has Marge anxiously imagining who her son, Bart, might grow up to be if he isn't subject to more discipline. She envisions him as "Bang Bang Bart," a sleazy male stripper wielding two fake guns as props, a cigarette dangling from his mouth, working in a seedy nightclub. He also has a large gut that hangs over his holster. "You're fat," complains one patron—herself not a small woman. "Just more of me to love, honey," says the glassy-eyed, oblivious Bart. The women begin to boo, throwing things at him onstage and eventually knocking him over. "My poor baby!" Marge exclaims, coming to from this waking nightmare. She can hardly imagine a worse prospect for her son's future—or a more natural result of not punishing him sufficiently.[58]

We see a similar dynamic play out in the recent, critically acclaimed HBO comedy series *Hacks*. The character of Kayla is an assistant to Jimmy, a talent manager in Hollywood. Kayla is a fat woman, which is supposed to make her flirtatious behavior toward Jimmy funny—and pathetic. When he (justly) accuses her of sexual harassment, she chalks the conflict up to the simmering sexual tension between them. The joke is on her, of course. Not only is the idea that her thin, white, handsome male boss would find her attractive humorous in itself, but we're invited to scoff that Kayla *doesn't even know how fat she is.*

In *I Feel Pretty*, Amy Schumer's character is borderline fat and brims with self-confidence for much of the movie. The explanation? She hit her head hard, resulting in literal brain damage that makes her painfully oblivious to her physical inadequacy.[59]

In the recent film *The Whale*, Brendan Fraser's character, Charlie, is all too aware of his fatness. Fraser dons a fat suit to play the six-hundred-pound man, who is depicted as a pitiable, tragic figure, eating himself into an early grave partly because of the supposed unbearability of living in such a body. His death wish makes him avoid going to the hospital when his blood pressure skyrockets. He is held to be a prisoner of his fatness—Fraser explicitly compared the fat suit to a "straitjacket"—rather than constrained by a hostile social world, not to mention a grossly fatphobic healthcare system.

The straitjacket of fatphobia remains troublingly invisible throughout the film's two-hour running time. And the possibility that there might be good parts of Charlie's life regardless seems not to have occurred to the filmmaker, Darren Aronofsky, or the playwright, Samuel Hunter, who wrote the script as well as the play the film is based on.

The Whale is fatphobic many times over. Its title could hardly be more derogatory. The suit makes fatness into a costume. Charlie's eating habits are an invitation to moralizing, even horror. We are encouraged to gawk at his attempts to simply move his body—or, in the opening sequence, masturbate to gay pornography, in a particularly prurient and intrusive moment. But perhaps worst of all, the film is premised on the idea that it's surprising, even miraculous, that a man with this body should have an agile, subtle mind, which sees him working as an expository writing professor at an online college. (He keeps his camera off while lecturing so no one will have to look at him, reinforcing the film's sense of claustrophobic voyeurism.)

"Since Charlie is mostly a sedentary lump, you might expect him to have a lumpish personality too," wrote the film critic Owen Gleiberman, glibly swallowing its fatphobic premise. "But Fraser doesn't play him with a heavy, glum, downbeat vibe. He's gentle and spry, with a quick temperament—you might even say there's something light about him—and this allows us, from the start, to see the man buried in the fat."[60] Remarkable. We are expected to be wowed by the adept mind housed within this very fat body, and to congratulate ourselves for recognizing this, in Aronofsky's mawkish parody of empathy.

But there's nothing inevitable about the idea that the

brightest minds tend to be housed in thin, male bodies. As
Carmen Maria Machado—a self-identified fat woman, not to
mention one of the most gifted writers working today—has
shown, we could choose our metaphors differently. We might
celebrate minds that are ample, broad, deep, expansive,
abundant, overflowing with ideas: *fat*, even, where that is
held to be a good thing. Machado recounts her childhood
reverence for the character of Ursula from *The Little Mer-
maid*, in all of her exuberant villainy and unapologetic agency:
and her sheer fatness. "And even though she had the power
to be thin—literal magical power, the sort the weight loss
industry would sell its soul to her to obtain—her fat mind
chose her fat body."[61] Ursula's mind is enviable in its ampli-
tude, its capaciousness, its unshrinking flair for conquest.[62]
And she knows that her body, to paraphrase Sonya Renee
Taylor, needs no apology—or amendment.[63]

What explains the sense that a film like *The Whale*—written
and directed by two currently thin white men—needed making?[64] What explains the sense on the part of the audience
that this is where to turn for insight into the subject? As Ash
Nischuk points out, creators living in very fat bodies could
provide much more illumination on the nature of life within
them. "So many fat people are out here writing, creating, and
telling real stories," she said in an interview in 2018. "We just
need people to listen."[65] That we don't is the result of testimonial injustice—a notion explored by the philosopher Miranda Fricker.[66] Often, when fat people speak, and testify to
their lived experience, we discount what they say because of

the aforementioned social stereotypes about their lack of competence and acumen. Sometimes, as the philosopher Kristie Dotson explores through the concept of testimonial quieting, we don't hear them in the first place.[67]

Nischuk created *The Fat Lip* podcast—which she describes as by, about, and for fat people—to help rectify this injustice.[68] And in it, she explains that it's not her very fat body that primarily makes her life worse. It's the way bodies like hers are derogated, erased, and systematically exploited. She is in most ways a happy and flourishing person—who recently described her life as "full of joy and kindness and loving people and swimming and dogs and laughing with friends and enjoying myself . . . on this wild planet"[69]—despite the fatphobic world which she has to navigate. Yes, she sometimes requires a mobility aid to travel longer distances, such as when moving through an airport; but this is not a basis for judgment or fear or pity, as disability activists have long taught us.[70] Yes, she sometimes prefers to sit rather than stand during routine activities, such as showering and meal preparation; fortunately, seats exist.[71] And yes, she may require a good-size seat; but that is a logistical problem, not an existential one—and the world's problem, not her body's.[72]

Nischuk recalls a casting assistant writing her an unsolicited email after seeing her photos on Instagram, under the #infinifat hashtag she created. The assistant wanted to gauge her interest in appearing on the TLC reality show *My 600-Lb. Life,* in which bodies like hers are presented as spectacles for the purposes of entertaining and reassuring audience members that at least they're not *that* fat. (A cynic might say that *The Whale* is just *My 600-Lb. Life* adapted for a morally aspirational, self-consciously liberal audience.) The show also effectively serves as an advertisement for the weight-loss surgeries most participants receive—a booming, lucrative industry. Nischuk writes, movingly,

> The producers of this show will take great care to show the parts of you that the audience will find the most horrifying. They want you to seem grotesque. Monstrous. It is very important that your very existence seem as shocking and tragic as possible. . . .
>
> But you must subject yourself to this—to being made a gruesome spectacle and cautionary tale—to *live*.
>
> These compassionate heroes will save your *life* for the low, low price of your actual human dignity.[73]

But human—and bodily—dignity is, or ought to be, unconditional. It's your birthright. A crucial part of such dignity is being free from the assumption that you *must* be unhappy or unhealthy or otherwise pitiable just by glancing in your general direction. So is being free from the assumption that your fat body is good evidence that your mind is somehow lacking.[74]

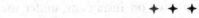

The flip side of testimonial injustice and quieting is what I've called *epistemic entitlement:* a socially dominant group member's sense that they are entitled to hold forth, to say what they think they know, to condescendingly *explain* to us. Men often do this to women, as the writer Rebecca Solnit has famously shown—hence the coinage "mansplaining."[75] White people often do this to nonwhite people, in what gets called "whitesplaining," And thin people often do this to fat people—in what has been termed, aptly enough, "thinsplaining." (Have you tried diet and exercise? No, those concepts are wholly unfamiliar to me, a fat, rock-sheltered Martian.)

Nowhere is such thinsplaining more evident than in the work of certain bioethicists, those moral philosophers tasked with answering questions about our rights and responsibilities with regard to human and other bodies. In his piece "Weigh More, Pay More," the Australian philosopher Peter Singer opines that fat people should pay more for their airplane travel. Singer writes from an airport, with the air of a man looking around and feeling disgusted by the bodies he is encountering. He opens: "MELBOURNE—We are getting fatter. In Australia, the United States, and many other countries, it has become commonplace to see people so fat that they waddle rather than walk." Singer observes that a "slight Asian woman" (whose race is mentioned despite its complete irrelevance) has checked in with perhaps ninety pounds of baggage, which she will pay to transport. But why shouldn't the man in line behind her, whom Singer eyeballs as weighing at least ninety pounds more than her, similarly pay for his "excess" baggage in the form of his own person? "In terms of the airplane's fuel consumption, it is all the same whether the extra weight is baggage or body fat," Singer notes. Fat people are explicitly theorized as a burden—on the planet, on the healthcare system, and on other people. "Obesity is an ethical issue, because an increase in weight by some imposes costs on others." It is noteworthy that Singer targets fat people rather than simply heavy ones—including those who are, say, tall and muscular. This despite his officially disavowing the idea that fat people are to be penalized because of our sinfulness or supposed choice to have let ourselves get this way. He writes, "The point of a surcharge for extra weight is not to punish a sin, whether it is levied on baggage or on bodies. It is a way of recouping from you the true cost of flying you to your destination, rather than imposing it on your fellow passengers."[76]

These costs are in fact minimal. Many fat people pay more already, as we've seen, in having to buy two seats to accommodate their one body. Others pay more for the privilege of being even remotely comfortable by purchasing first-class tickets. Moreover, a detailed calculation undertaken by one pilot suggests that a passenger will cost an airline approximately 1 cent per kilogram per hour on an A320 aircraft, compared with their seat remaining empty. So, for a five-hour flight from Melbourne to Darwin, it would cost around $2 extra to transport the fat man Singer targets in his article compared with the "slight" woman, based purely on their body weight.[77] Airlines charge a premium for excess baggage (in the order of hundreds of dollars for ninety pounds of luggage) not because they have to, but simply because they can. Their pricing model involves making ticket prices as low as possible and then imposing outrageous surcharges for anything "extra" people might need, including food, Wi-Fi, or more legroom.

As for the idea that we should pay for any "burden" we impose on other people, this does not pass muster either. Recalling our earlier discussion, we might wonder: Should we impose a fee on adventurous mountaineers who end up needing help from search and rescue? Should we impose a tax on chronically ill people who take on a heavy workload and become stressed, and thus have their symptoms worsen? We should not be in the business of policing people in this way.

And, to a large extent, we aren't, which makes this focus on fatter bodies telling—and, plausibly, discriminatory.

If Singer had asked a fat person, he might have been impressed by the most obvious and important reason why fat people should not be charged more for flying: stigmatization. Or maybe not, since he notes that friends of his did indeed raise this objection when he mooted his modest proposal. But Singer dismisses this risk in one sentence, on the grounds that flying, unlike healthcare, is not a human right. Perhaps not as such, but the idea that fat people are not entitled to visit their families or do their jobs, both of which often require airplane travel, is eyebrow raising. Fat people may even be entitled, much like anyone, to move across the country or take the occasional vacation.

What is striking about Singer's argument here is not just that it is inhumane; it is also not very clever. It makes manifestly false assumptions; it traffics in bad analogies; it misses obvious objections; and it acknowledges key objections only to ignore them. Singer is one of the most celebrated (if by turns controversial) ethicists in the world; but his prejudice against fat people leads him to be irrational, or at least rationally disappointing.[78]

If Singer talks over fat people, and ignores the import of our testimony, other philosophers see fit to engage with us directly. In his piece "Obesity: Chasing an Elusive Epidemic," the bioethicist Daniel Callahan argues that an "edgier" strategy is needed to combat the supposed problem of fatness: shaming (or "stigmatization lite," as he calls it). We need to "find ways to bring social pressure to bear on individuals, going beyond anodyne education and low-key exhortation. It will be imperative, first, to persuade [fat people] that they ought to want a good diet and exercise for themselves and for their neighbor and, second, that excessive weight and outright obesity are not socially accepted any longer."[79] (When were they, this past century?) Fat people have become complacent about our fatness: we need, says Callahan, the "shock of recognition."[80] He goes on to opine that "obesity is in great part a reflection of the kind of culture we have, one that is permissive about how people take care of their bodies and accepts many if not most of the features of our society that contribute to the problem."[81] Among these, Callahan identifies modern conveniences such as cars, elevators, escalators—and the electric can opener.[82]

I am moderately sure that electric can openers are not responsible for the so-called obesity epidemic.[83] It's bad enough that Callahan moots these implausible diagnoses and such a cruel solution to this supposed problem. But it only gets worse when he shifts from speaking *about* fat people to talking to us directly, in posing and suggesting we be asked the following sorts of questions:

If you are overweight or obese, are you pleased with the way you look?

Are you happy that your added weight has made many ordinary activities, such as walking up a long flight of stairs, harder?

Would you prefer to lessen your risk of heart disease and diabetes?

Are you aware that, once you gain a significant

amount of weight, your chances of taking that weight back off and keeping it off are poor?

Are you pleased when your obese children are called "fatty" or otherwise teased at school?

Fair or not, do you know that many people look down upon those excessively overweight or obese, often in fact discriminating against them and making fun of them or calling them lazy and lacking in self-control?[84]

This is thinsplaining at its most obnoxious. And it is characteristically, by turns, either redundant or wrongheaded.

For, as fat people, we of course know all too well that we are looked down upon for our weight and that, far from making us smaller, stigmatization frequently leads to further weight gain.

We are also the ones who know that while living in a fat body may be hard, it is fatphobia, not our fatness, that primarily takes a toll on us.

We are the ones who know that fatness is not a death sentence and that depriving oneself routinely, as diets demand, is not trivial.

We are the ones who know that far from being undisciplined, fat people are often extremely disciplined; a lifetime of dieting will make some people's will *iron*.

We are among those who know that an iron will is about as much good as bootstraps, in a world that hates you and wants to shrink you.

And we are among those who know the most about certain facets of the human condition. For example, we can help dispel the fantasy that bodies are *reasonable*—by which I

mean, subject to rational control and capable of being wres-
tled into submission via that suspect thing called mastery.

For bodies are *not* reasonable. They bend, they sag, they
break. They get fat. They get old. They get ill. They become
disabled. They die, ultimately, and we die with them. That is
of course frightening. ("Doesn't everything die at last, and
too soon?" in the words of Mary Oliver.)

But our bodies are ourselves, as the feminist slogan has it.
We are not separate from our bodies, nor are our bodies divided up between the better and the worse parts of our mortal souls, *pace* Plato. And when it comes to our appetites, we
are all in the end wild ones. So we will have to learn to live
with, and in, our physical selves in all of their glorious and
infuriating vulnerability and intransigence. The body's resistance to weight loss is only the beginning.

CHAPTER 7

DINNER BY GASLIGHT

You already know that diets don't work. For the vast majority of dieters, initial weight loss is reliably followed by weight regain over the next few years. Many people end up heavier than they started. And diets, or the process of losing and regaining weight, do reliable damage to many bodily systems. It is subsequently unlikely that diets make us any healthier in the long run. It is very well established that they do not typically make us thinner.[1]

And yet America is still on a diet. Every year, an estimated forty-five million Americans undertake to lose weight in this way;[2] we also spend more than $50 billion annually on weight-loss products and programs.[3] In the process, we make ourselves hungry, weak, irritable, and, often, sicker and fatter.

Why? Why do we keep doing this to ourselves, when we know better—or ought to?

I suggest: we are gaslit.

In the 1938 play *Gas Light*, by Patrick Hamilton, Bella Manningham is a young wife who sees the gas light in her bedroom flicker every night. She knows that this is happening, and she knows what it means: that another gas light must have been switched on somewhere else in the house, since the gas pressure from one would siphon off gas pressure from the other. She also has strong suspicions about who is doing this (though not, as yet, why): she believes her husband is creeping about upstairs, in the attic, after he ostensibly goes out for the evening. Adding to her suspicion is the fact that shortly before he returns—again, ostensibly from outside— the light regains its former, full flame, suggesting the gas light upstairs in the attic must have been switched off again. (Interestingly, there's no indication that Mr. Manningham has ever thought about the fact that his turning on the lights in the attic—for nefarious purposes of his own that will soon become apparent—will affect the lights in his wife's bedroom.)

Notice that this setup in the play is thus subtler than in the film, where the husband actually denies the wife's perceptions of the gas light flickering. In the play, she knows what she sees, and she knows what it means, at least deep down, or at a certain level. She suspects who is behind it too. This is an important difference: the film version invited the parody of a recent *Saturday Night Live* skit, where the husband, Gregory, bids his wife, Paula, to enjoy her steak, having actually presented her with a pineapple. Paula responds, drily, "Dude, I don't care how crazy I am. This is a pineapple." "No, ma'am, it's a rib eye, just like the one he's eating," replies Gregory's co-conspirator, their servant: "*Dig in!*" "Okay, I feel like maybe you're, like, *trying* to drive me mad," responds Paula, played by Kate McKinnon. She eventually unearths a book: *How to Gaslight Your Wife,* by Gregory.[4]

The point of the sketch is that there's actually a strict limit to how implausible a gaslighter's claims can be, at least initially; one cannot typically gaslight someone by beginning with claims that are ludicrous on their face. The target will simply disbelieve him, rather than suspecting *herself* of being delusional or otherwise defective. But in the play version of *Gas Light,* Bella's beliefs are effectively undermined by her husband's subtler domineering tactics. And she is prevented from articulating her suspicions, even to herself, by her growing state of confusion, agitation, and downright fear of him. She fears that she is the one to blame for the increasingly fraught state of their marriage too—for he accuses her of imagining things, and of not trying hard enough to restore her sanity, of not "pulling herself together" and working to "get better."[5] (In reality, he is hiding their possessions around the house and holding her responsible for their disappearance, among other manipulations designed to drive her to the madhouse.)

Eventually, thanks to a detective who shows up unannounced to talk to her, Bella discovers her husband's secret: he is really the diabolical Sydney Power, who slit the throat of their house's former owner, Alice Barlow, in order to steal her rubies some fifteen years prior. But Power never managed to find the rubies, and thus prevailed on Bella to buy this house so that he could resume his search for the jewels in the attic every evening. The following dialogue makes it clear that Bella knew on some level what her husband was doing all along, if not why he was doing it:

BELLA MANNINGHAM: It all sounds so incredible [but] . . . when I'm alone at night[,] I get the idea that—somebody's walking about up there—[Looking up.] Up there—At night, when my husband's out— I hear noises, from my bedroom, but I'm too afraid to go up—

DETECTIVE ROUGH: Have you told your husband about this?

BELLA MANNINGHAM: No. I'm afraid to. He gets angry. He says I imagine things which don't exist—

DETECTIVE ROUGH: It never struck you, did it, that it might be your own husband walking about up there?

BELLA MANNINGHAM: Yes—that is what I thought— but I thought I must be mad. Tell me how you know.

DETECTIVE ROUGH: Why not tell me first how you knew, Mrs. Manningham.

BELLA MANNINGHAM: It's true, then! It's true. I knew it. I knew it![6]

But, as I wrote in my book *Entitled,* Bella didn't dare to mentally "go there," despite her warranted misgivings, despite her cognizance, even despite her *knowledge.* She was so busy struggling to correct her own supposed faults and sins, and so in the grip of her husband's overall domination, that she never questioned his movements, let alone his motives.[7]

Her suspicions remain unaired until it is almost too late for her—and only then because of a gallant detective's intervention.

For Bella is told, either implicitly or explicitly, that she cannot trust her own judgments and that her mind is playing tricks on her. She is told—again, either implicitly or explicitly—that she is weak-minded, irrational, and feeble. She is told that she is sick, that she needs to take her medicine, and that she will have to see several doctors if she does not rally. She is told that she is pasty and unattractive, and compared unfavorably by her husband with their "saucy" younger servant, in a humiliating encounter. She is told, perhaps most painfully of all, that her moral character is doubtful—that she is mischievous, even wicked, as well as feckless and irresponsible (for supposedly stealing and hiding some of their possessions, as well as losing others). A final, fatal blow to Bella's self-image: she is told she is harming others. Her husband claims that she has deliberately hurt their pet dog, whom Bella loves dearly. His paw injury is all her fault.[8] And if she does not admit to these myriad failures and sins, she will be locked up in a madhouse—and wind up dying alone, a cautionary tale for the ages.

Gaslighting thus works on victims to make them scramble for a foothold. They may be derogated with regard to more or less any value that human beings seek to embody: rationality, intelligence, health, beauty, morality, and so on. As a result, the gaslit person may lack the wherewithal and self-confidence to question the prevailing narrative, or to challenge an authority figure, even if they know it, and him, to be a false one. They are disoriented and confused. They are often depressed and anxious. They are not delusional or "crazy"—or not to begin with, at any rate.[9] They have been systematically deprived of the resources to assert what they know, despite their indeed knowing it, deep down, to be the case. But they struggle to act on their knowledge and to muster effective resistance to the pernicious forces facing them.

It is important for our purposes to notice that gaslighting needn't depict us as, or aim to drive us, mad. Rather, I propose, gaslighting should be understood as a systematic process that works to make us feel *defective* in some way for the beliefs, thoughts, feelings, desires, and appetites to which we are, in reality, entitled.[10] We are made to feel guilty, sinful, shameful, irrational, oversensitive, or paranoid—as well as, sometimes, downright crazy—for harboring these mental states. Gaslighting attacks a person's mental freedom, her capacity for independent thought. If gaslighting succeeds, then the victim winds up mentally being colonized.

Notice too that few if any of these effects on a target or victim require that the perpetrator be malicious—or even that there be an individual perpetrator whatsoever.[11] As several authors have argued, gaslighting can encompass purely *structural* or collective cases, as well as subtler interpersonal ones.[12] There need be no Mr. Manningham in the room—or even outside it—to make gaslighting possible. Instead, gaslighting can work to hamstring someone's mental life via prevalent cultural forces, practices, institutions, and whole groups of people in dominant social positions.

The example of rape culture helps to bring this out. Victims are routinely made to feel hysterical, unstable, and confused, and hence unreliable witnesses to the crimes committed against them. They are attacked for their appearance: If they are deemed too attractive, they were asking for it. If they are deemed not attractive enough, it never happened. It is all their own fault regardless. They were giving mixed signals, they were in the wrong place at the wrong time; they failed to scream; they failed to struggle; they drank too much. And what were they wearing?

We are similarly gaslit by diet culture. We are told, either implicitly or explicitly, that we cannot trust our own bodies and that our appetites are misleading us. ("You're not hungry, you're thirsty." "You don't want that [bad food] really." "You're an emotional overeater.") We are told—again, either implicitly or explicitly—that *this* diet will work, that this time is different. When it is not, we are told that we are weak-willed, irrational, and feeble for succumbing to our appetites. We are told that if we are fat, we cannot be healthy—so we must pull ourselves together and redouble our weight-loss efforts or suffer dire consequences. We are told we are pudgy and unattractive, and that nobody will ever love us looking like this. We are told we are morally lax. We are told it is all our own fault. We are told we are harming our children and placing a burden on society. We are told we will end up like any number of cautionary examples.

Much of this is the work of vested capitalist interests and the resulting piecemeal profiteering, not some grand, unified conspiracy. That does not make it innocent. Much as in cases of interpersonal gaslighting, the victim of diet culture experiences a severance of the cord of trust that should run between her agency and her thoughts, feelings, appetites, and other, more diffuse mental states, such as her sense of bodily worth and well-being. Increasingly, we know better than to diet or try to shrink ourselves down to size. But gaslighting makes us feel guilty, unworthy, unhealthy, ugly, and, yes, fat—understood as a pejorative, not a neutral descriptor—for refusing to diet. We are not just told what to do. Nor are we merely complicit. We are actively recruited, made agents, in our own oppressive lifestyles.

Diet culture also gaslights us in subtler ways. This dry rice cake is so satisfying. This delicious, fatty food is actually nasty, even disgusting. Nothing tastes as good as thin feels (even though thinness not only is elusive but feels like nothing whatsoever). We just need this one new supplement. We just need this meal kit service. We just need this exorbitantly expensive piece of exercise equipment. Other people have succeeded* where we have failed (*results not typical). This isn't a diet; it's a lifestyle—or a cleanse, or a detox. (Our bodies, by implication, when left to their own devices, are dirty and contaminated.) This isn't a diet; it's about *wellness*. This isn't about being thin; it's about being *strong*—and, sotto voce, thin enough to showcase one's newly developed, rippling muscles. This is about your health, including your mental health. This is about self-care; this is for *you*.

I call bullshit.

But it's understandable that despite knowing better, at least at some level, we often succumb to this messaging. It is constant. And it is everywhere. These messages are often voiced or backed, moreover, by powerful authority figures—including, of course, within the medical establishment. As we saw earlier, fat people who are unwell go to see the doctor about more or less any issue and are told we just need to lose weight (sometimes with tragic results, because our real problems go undiagnosed). Fat people who are healthy go to see the doctor and are told we can't possibly be as healthy as we seem by every standard metric. Fat, active people are assumed to be sedentary, and those of us who report otherwise are assumed to be lying. (Meanwhile, our thin, sedentary counterparts are assumed to be fit and active, as well as hale and hearty generally.) Fat people who experience dramatic, unexplained weight loss are praised and congratulated and deemed a "good fatty," even when this is a symptom of a serious underlying illness. Fat people who gain weight inexplicably are assumed to be overeating and under-exercising, even when we testify that our habits haven't changed.

Fat people are trusted so little, in fact, that some enterprising scientists in the U.K. and New Zealand, at the University of Otago, recently engineered a device that uses custom-made magnets to forcibly bolt our mouths shut. It leaves just a tiny opening—some two millimeters—to allow for the passage of liquids, breath, and speech. It is called, ominously, the DentalSlim Diet Control. We so lack control over our own food consumption, they reasoned, that we need to be kept on a liquid diet by this twenty-first-century torture device.[13]

Such messages are further backed by our education system and echoed in many families before their recipients are old enough to question them. Children are told, more or less explicitly, by their parents and their teachers that they need to diet and lose weight well before they have reached physical maturity. When Weight Watchers fell into financial trouble recently, it attempted to regroup by marketing a diet app, creepily named Kurbo, to children aged eight to seventeen.[14] As the psychologist Lisa Du Breuil has pointed out, there's something particularly insidious about teaching young girls both to curb their food intake and to not trust their sense of hunger. As she put it in conversation with Virginia Sole-Smith,

> When we train children in diet culture to not trust their bellies, it's a very bad message to send, especially

for girls—don't trust your gut, don't listen to your body. That moves out into other ways that they're supposed to be paying attention to what their gut tells them.[15]

True, some of the measures that target children's weight are ostensibly friendly and certainly well meaning, as with Michelle Obama's campaign to promote healthy eating and movement in schools. But some of them are deliberately shaming. Many of us have horror stories about being mistreated by our gym teachers—from being on the receiving end of cutting remarks to being forced to run laps until we vomited to being stripped down and having our errant flesh poked and prodded and measured.

In February 2020, the high school basketball coach Aaron Thomas was declared Rhode Island's "Schoolboy Coach of the Year." One year later, his career was over, after it emerged that he'd been conducting "fat tests" on his charges using calipers in close quarters, one-on-one, for a decade. These boys were often naked. "It would be private, just me and him. He would do length, height, start to do body fat, and he would kneel down [measuring] my quad and saying are you comfortable . . . if you aren't shy, you can take down your boxers. I had to move my privates out of the way because he was so freaking close," one former student athlete told *The Boston Globe* recently.[16] Even if the "fat tests" were simply a pretext for this blatant sexual abuse, the cover worked because of our culture of pediatric fatphobia.

Da'Shaun L. Harrison has also written wrenchingly of the plight of Gina Score, a fourteen-year-old girl who had been convicted of shoplifting and sent to a South Dakota boot camp in 1999. Score, who weighed 226 pounds, was forced to do a 2.7-mile run, during which she collapsed of heat-stroke. The girl was then left in the sun for three hours without treatment because the staff all thought she was faking it. They drank soda and made fun of her. Meanwhile, she had a seizure, wet herself, and eventually died of organ failure. Her death was the product of the horrific child abuse, cruelty, and neglect that many fat children face in some measure.[17] As Harrison writes,

> [Score] was neglected, at least in part, because she was fat. The nearly three-mile run she was forced to do, the idea that she was faking what would be her own death to avoid exercise, the fact that her instructors left her to lie in the sun while they drank sodas—a beverage people have long shamed fat people for drinking—were all a targeted response to her fatness. And it killed her. She was murdered by a culture designed to punish fat people at the behest of "health" itself.[18]

Harrison has subsequently spoken of being forced to run laps around the neighborhood as a fat kid, wearing a trash bag, in their mother's desperate attempt to get their weight down. They had asthma and frequently couldn't breathe for gasping.[19] They don't blame their mother, though, who was just trying to follow doctor's orders. She was scared her fat child would die without such a harsh intervention.[20]

Some parents *are* cruel, though. One woman recalls her mother sitting her down when she was ten and asking her, snidely, "Do you realize your bottom is now bigger than mine is?" before giving her a lecture about how she needed to get her weight under control. Again, this girl was ten. The kicker? To accompany the lecture, her mother had given her a snack: a large bag of potato chips—precisely the kind of food she said her daughter must cut back on. There's only one word to describe this behavior: a mindfuck.[21]

✦ ✦ ✦

So: we are gaslit out of telling ourselves what we know, responding to our own desires, and even having the wherewithal to pursue our own hunger. We are not just gaslit in this way by other people and society at large. We gaslight *ourselves* sometimes, by treating ourselves as defective for aspects of our mental life—beliefs, desires, intentions, and feelings—that don't conform to the dictates of a white supremacist, ableist, ageist, and fatphobic patriarchy. We feel like failures for no longer believing that the next diet is the answer. We feel like losers for not even really *wanting* to lose weight anymore. And we feel like greedy fat gluttons (in the pejorative senses) for normal human appetite.

I have long been subject to this gaslighting myself. I have failed, and refused, to listen to my own sense of what my body wanted and needed to be. I have failed, and refused, to listen to the voice of my own hunger, in going on one diet after another. And I have even tried to silence my hunger using diet pills.

For about a decade, starting in my mid-twenties, I took endless over-the-counter "supplements" procured on the sly from GNC, with ugly names like Hydroxycut, smelling of iodine or sulfur. I bought pills that claimed to be bitter orange—reputedly an appetite suppressant—from dubious third-party sellers on Amazon. The closet of my tiny attic office, which I cherished during my time at Harvard as a postdoc, was stuffed with the empty bottles. These drugs did approximately nothing. I then graduated to using the prescription stimulant Adderall.

It started with a visit to a psychiatrist at Harvard, to discuss the antidepressant I'd been taking for some time. I said I wasn't sure it was working any longer; I felt easily distracted and was having trouble maintaining my focus, among many other symptoms of depression. She asked me a series of questions that made me realize with surprise that she suspected I had ADHD. Even though I was skeptical, I leaned into the diagnosis. And so, shortly afterward, I found myself with a prescription for those bright pink little round pills I would soon come to rely on.

I had heard Adderall was a powerful appetite suppressant, but I was not prepared for just how powerful it would be for me. I could go days without food. I was suddenly working around the clock. I was losing weight rapidly. I felt like I was soaring.

Then, all too predictably, this wonder drug turned out to be not so wonderful after all. My lower back muscles became so tight and sore from clenching them that a massage therapist I booked an appointment with said she'd never felt anything like it; the pain just under my rib cage was so intense that she could barely touch me. I became extremely lethargic on the rare day when I didn't take the medication that summer. I was growing increasingly irritable, even prone to bouts of uncharacteristic anger. I was going down rabbit holes in my work. My marriage was suffering. I needed to stop taking it.

Instead, I upped the prescription.

And up and up and up. When I changed doctors upon moving to Ithaca, they never questioned my diagnosis and didn't blink when I asked for ever-higher doses. And although I was careful to eschew the drug in any context where it could spark my social anxiety—teaching, giving talks, having meetings, and so on—I was usually on it in my own time. Those times became much darker: I would pull all-nighters in my office, furiously writing thousands of disorganized words that never saw the light of day. On one of those occasions, I had been simply trying to write a one-thousand-word blog post summarizing some of my work—a task that today would take me about an hour. But Adderall made me so anxious and frenetic and wild with rage that, somehow, I couldn't do it. I spun my wheels for hours and hours, going around and around in frenzied mental circles. I lost the kind of agency that is hard-won for me on a good day.

I took Adderall on and off for five years, all told, hoping to recapture something of that original magic of productivity—and, truth be told, weight loss. The weight loss didn't last: I was fatter than ever by the end of it. I was more tired than I can describe, possibly suffering from something called "adrenal fatigue." I would often sleep for sixteen hours, given the opportunity. I was deeply depressed. I was chasing an illusion.

To be clear, for those who need it, and at the appropriate dosage, Adderall and similar drugs can be lifesavers. But they can be ruinous for people like me who have untreated anxiety, among other issues. I should have realized that in short order. I should have abandoned my pipe dream of untold efficiency and unprecedented thinness. Yet somehow I gaslit myself into believing that the Adderall wasn't the problem; rather, the problem was my mind and, especially, my body.

✦ ✦ ✦

Gaslighting operates not only with sticks but also with carrots. In the opening of *Gas Light*, Mr. Manningham praises Bella for being "very good lately" and offers to bring her to the theater for a little diversion, "to take her out of herself."[22] Bella is ecstatic at the prospect of going out; she is virtually a shut-in, partly since her husband has deliberately isolated her from all of her friends and relatives. She is all the more thrilled by the occasion for her husband's offer: "Oh, Jack, I'd be better—I could really try to be better . . . if only I could get *out* of myself a little more." Her husband is immediately filled with suspicion that she is not taking her "illness" seriously. As Bella scrambles to explain ("I *have* been better—even in the last week . . . because you have stayed in, and been kind to me"), he assumes a skeptical air, chalking up the improvement in her mental state to the nasty medicine he has forced on her.[23] Nevertheless, he asks her to choose whether she would prefer to see a comedy or a tragedy. (Does she want to laugh or cry? "It matters so wonderfully little!" Bella effuses.[24])

Then all is lost: or, rather, it is taken away. Mr. Manningham fixates on the wall behind them. He speaks in a tone that is calm and menacing: "I have just observed something very much amiss. Will you please rectify it at once, while I am not looking, and we will assume that it has not happened."[25] The picture that belongs on the wall there has disappeared, and Bella is held responsible for its absence. What follows is a dreadful scene—the servants are summoned and made to swear on the Bible that they did not remove the picture—and Bella is tricked into guessing its whereabouts behind the stairs (where it has turned up twice before). This is subsequently invoked as proof positive that she took it. Bella is left hysterical—all the more so when her husband revokes his offer to take her out to the theater. He fumes: "It is now for you to control yourself, or take the consequences. . . . If we are going to be enemies, you and I, you will not prosper, believe me."[26] (Of course, it was all a setup: Bella's husband was the one who took down and hid the picture to flummox her.)

This scene captures in heartbreaking fashion a common abusive dynamic: A victim is briefly made to feel good about herself, and promised emotional and material rewards, before it all comes crashing down again. She is made to blame herself and told that she must learn to control her wayward behavior.

A similar dynamic attends dieting, even in the absence of an abusive individual who is intending to harm us. We lose a little weight and feel proud, better, optimistic. We look forward to fitting into our "skinny jeans"; other people praise us—including the women who, by policing other women's bodies, or simply participating in diet culture themselves, do such untold damage. "I guess I didn't realize how big I was until I saw it on your faces," says Samantha to her three girlfriends in *Sex and the City: The Movie,* released in 2008. She has gained perhaps ten pounds at the age of nearly fifty. "How—and I say this with love—how could you not realize it?" Carrie asks Samantha, incredulous.[27]

And then, before we know it, our supposed progress is undone: When we regain the weight, we are told that we have only ourselves to blame and that we have failed due to a lack of willpower. We must get ahold of ourselves; we must learn to control our appetites. We hear these messages from our own inner voice, oftentimes, dripping with shame and self-censure.

✦ ✦ ✦

In this way, dieting keeps many of us on a perpetual tread mill. We fall off periodically. But we keep getting back on. Perhaps we are hoping to be the exception to the rule that dieting does not make us thinner in the long run.

And this is not, in itself, necessarily irrational. True, the high failure rates for diets should make us pessimistic about our prospects for success. But there are some things in life we may attempt even when the success rate is very low: climbing Mount Everest, publishing a bestseller, or, for that matter, getting a tenured job in philosophy.

But the difference is that these low-success-rate endeavors plausibly have a claim to make our lives better even in the absence of ultimate satisfaction. The mountain climber becomes fit and skilled and gets to enjoy incredible views. The writer may manage to at least pen their novel, and even get published and reach some people, despite its not landing on the bestseller list. The aspiring philosopher who enters a funded PhD program gets to pursue their intellectual passion and deepen their love of the subject even if they are unable to make a career of it. And, inasmuch as even these more modest goals fail, or make people reliably unhappy in the process, these pursuits deserve close scrutiny and perhaps to be abandoned.

Is dieting a practice that we benefit from, somehow, even if it does not tend to work in the long term for the vast majority of people? The answer is no. It makes us hungry, irritable, and fixated on the foods we can no longer enjoy or must at least restrict severely. It disposes many people to mental health problems such as anxiety, depression, and, troublingly, eating disorders.[28] It comes with all of the negative health consequences that are linked not to being fat per se but to weight cycling. It does not get us closer to our goals, and in fact it often makes us fatter in the long run.

Dieting also takes up valuable mental bandwidth that could be devoted to other projects, including creative and altruistic ones. It makes socializing more difficult, as we avoid certain social occasions or are preoccupied with avoiding food when we get there. It can make us, frankly, boring. (Nobody except, perhaps, another dieter wants to hear about our new "eating plan" or the dangers of sugar alcohols.)

And even for that rare person who loses weight and keeps most of it off—and thus counts as a success story by the standards of the industry—the work required to stay at their new size is frequently herculean. One woman who has maintained a fifty-five-pound weight loss for eleven years now consumes eighteen hundred calories a day, restricts her carbohydrate intake, and works out daily after strapping twenty-five to thirty pounds to herself using a vest and ankle weights. Thus shackled, she performs a fifty-minute exercise video at double the speed of the instructor. (She used to run for an hour but had to stop, following a foot injury.) She is constantly plagued by what she describes as "intrusive thoughts and food preoccupations." And she describes her efforts to maintain her weight not as a lifestyle but as a job. It sounds like an exhausting, and not terribly rewarding, one.[29]

Similar weight maintenance war stories are common, and involve instilling the kind of minute self-surveillance in people that Mr. Manningham could only dream of. Many fat or formerly fat people will dutifully weigh themselves daily and feel slightly better or worse about themselves on this basis, constructing a hierarchy of selves derived from their morning weigh-in. One weight-loss doctor's greatest success stories include a man who continues to weigh not just himself but every morsel of food he consumes, including when out at restaurants. (The staff are often willing to do it for him.)[30] A female patient, now herself a specialist in obesity medicine at the VA, lost more than one hundred pounds as a contestant on *The Biggest Loser.* After regaining some of the weight, she now keeps what she describes as an "iron grip" on her diet—bringing her own food to work every day, counting her calories on an app, and preventing herself from gaining too much weight during her pregnancy. She does not allow chocolate or desserts to enter her household. "I am hyper-aware of everything I eat," she said. "It is an active effort." She works out vigorously nine days out of ten. And still, her weight fluctuates: each time she lets down her guard, the pounds begin to return. It never gets any easier, she told a reporter.[31]

Another weight-loss doctor was asked why some people succeed on certain diets, at least temporarily, and others fail repeatedly. "Beats me!" the doctor said, cheerfully. This is apparently the million-dollar question.[32]

And it is also in the interests of some heavy hitters in the diet—and now so-called wellness—industry not to furnish it with an answer. In 2007, a study showed that of even Weight Watchers' most successful, "lifetime" members, only 16 percent maintained their target weight over a five-year period. (The study, notably, was funded by Weight Watchers and was thus prone, if anything, to be too flattering to the program.) Richard Samber, the former finance director of Weight Watchers, saw that result as a good thing. He said of the company, "It's successful because the other 84% have to come back and do it again. That's where your business comes from."[33]

Not everyone at Weight Watchers approved of Samber's blithely profiteering message. The company's chief scientific officer at the time, Karen Miller-Kovach, tried to put a more positive spin on the data. "We cannot sustain a business on failure. There's a reason why we have been around

50 years . . . because people come to us time and time again to help them with their chronic condition of weight management." That's one way of reframing things: dieting, and weight loss, ought not to be sustainable but, rather, sustained indefinitely. Regarding the finding that only 16 percent of even their most successful members reached and maintained their goal weight, Miller-Kovach demurred: "Is it everything we would want? No. But then what's the alternative? The alternative is doing nothing."[34] Well, exactly.

Meanwhile, Dr. Carl Heneghan, director of the Centre for Evidence-Based Medicine at Oxford University, was scathing about these findings: "So basically you pick the best people, the lifelong members and actually even they struggle, with the majority of people not obtaining their long-term goal weight. After 40 years . . . when are people going to wake up and say this is not the answer?"[35]

It is difficult to know. Gaslighting robs us of lucidity and keeps us going through the motions—even when the oscillation of our weight, much like the flickering of the gas light, suggests a serious problem with our situation.

In the final act of *Gas Light*, Mr. Manningham says to his wife, "Do you know what you remind me of, Bella, as you walk across the room? . . . A somnambulist, Bella. Have you ever seen such a person? [You have] that funny, glazed, dazed look of the wandering mind—the body that acts without the soul to guide it."[36]

But, contrary to Mr. Manningham's view, the gaslit person's problem is not that our bodies are out of control or that our wits have deserted us. Rather, our minds, under too-tight control, forestall our body's bid for freedom—from, among other things, chronic hunger.

CHAPTER 8

THE AUTHORITY OF HUNGER

My daughter, at twenty months, became fascinated with her belly button. At every chance she got, she began lifting her T-shirt to joyfully point it out. The inference that Mommy and Daddy had belly buttons too was not far behind, and neither were further exploration efforts. But when she lifted my shirt, I found myself instinctively sucking in my stomach. I felt shame, and ashamed of my shame. And that's when it hit me: I had to sort my head out, regarding my body, for the sake of my daughter.[1]

This realization came shortly after perhaps my most extreme diet to date—and one to which, I am sad to say, my daughter had borne witness. I had gone low carb again shortly after the pandemic began, and experienced six months of making zero progress. And so, without really deciding to,

I simply stopped eating. I didn't eat for more days than not during the month that followed.

I was moved by a vague residual sense of obligation—despite all my feminist, fat activist leanings—to do what women do after having a baby. We shrink ourselves back down to size. I was already tipping the scales into the "severely obese" category of the BMI charts even before getting pregnant. Having gotten off the Adderall once and for all before trying to conceive, my weight had rebounded. Although I didn't gain that much weight during pregnancy, afterward my body felt even softer: a behemoth, shapeless, formless. I wanted to again "be good," to be visually recognizable as obedient. I dreamed of muscle and sinew and leanness and hollows.

And I came to hate not only my body but my hunger, my appetite.

I am hardly alone in this. In a fatphobic society, we all too often learn to view hunger as the enemy. The idea that we are obligated to diet, even to the point of being chronically hungry, is everywhere. "Intermittent fasting" is very much the watchword of contemporary diet culture. In the first episode of the 2021 Fox reboot of the 1970s TV show *Fantasy Island,* a morning news anchor named Christine pays a small fortune to stay on an island where her wishes can come true. Her fantasy is being able to eat—"and eat and eat and eat"—without gaining an ounce. For, she declares, she has been hungry for the duration of her television career. (Her storyline is called "Hungry Christine" in the episode's title.) And she is presented as the everywoman, released from sensible if stringent dietary restraint for a brief, wild, magical period—which sees her eventually indulging in a little light cannibalism.[2]

But the widespread idea that we should learn to live with chronic hunger can, and should, be challenged. Not only are we not obligated to lose weight, for reasons canvassed earlier in this book, but there is something deeply immoral about the dictates of diet culture that posit and impose on us these pseudo-obligations. They often leave us perpetually hungry, and thus experiencing bodily discomfort—and sometimes suffering, even torment. We all deserve to be free from this, since it serves no valid purpose.

In the very first lecture of my introductory ethics course, I begin with a simple observation: Pain and suffering are bad, and are the kinds of things that we ought to prevent and to end, if possible, in the name of morality. Pleasure and enjoyment, moreover, are surely good—the kinds of things that we ought to promote and to foster, at least if no one gets hurt in the process.

These ideas, as simple as they are, provide the basis for one of the first systematic ethical theories, known as utilitarianism. According to this doctrine, developed by Jeremy Bentham and John Stuart Mill, we should assess any possible action by considering the amount of pain and suffering it would cause, and the amount of pleasure and joy it would bring to everyone in the world. This gives any course of action a measure called "net utility," calculated by subtracting the prospective pains from the prospective pleasures. We should act, according to utilitarianism, so as to maximize net utility added up for every member of the moral community, both human and nonhuman. In other words, we should act so as to maximize pleasure and minimize pain, taking into account the pleasures and pains of everybody—ourselves very much included.

Few philosophers now believe that utilitarianism is the whole of the truth in ethics. Famously, it has counterintuitive and even cruel implications in cases like the "fat man" variant of the trolley case canvassed earlier, where it bids us to callously sacrifice one person to save a larger number.[3] Still, there's something about the basic idea that utilitarianism tries unsuccessfully to capture which remains undeniably attractive. Peter Singer, whom we met at his least convincing and most inhumane previously in these pages, attempted to get at this idea too in what is now perhaps the most widely taught and celebrated ethics paper in the world, "Famine, Affluence, and Morality." In it, he proposed the suffering prevention principle, according to which, if it is within our power to prevent bad outcomes, like pain, suffering, and hunger, without sacrificing anything morally important, then we ought, morally, to do it.[4] Singer uses this principle to argue that we—the presumptively affluent—have demanding duties to address the hunger of needy others around the world, by giving much more of our incomes to charity than we do customarily. Singer has also argued that similar considerations make a powerful moral case for vegetarianism. For, eating meat contributes to the pain and suffering of all of the nonhuman animals who are not only slaughtered for our tables but often grossly mistreated in the process, as in factory farming.[5]

Whatever one thinks about these specific arguments, it's hard to disagree that a social practice that causes serious pain and suffering, and has no significant upside, is morally problematic. But curiously, this point has not been widely noticed to have implications for another common social practice: dieting.

✦ ✦ ✦

Does dieting really cause suffering? I can assure you that it does, on the basis of my own experience. Contrary to the hopeful thought that losing weight just requires cutting back on sweets, or avoiding overeating, I am among the many people who has to eat almost nothing in order to see the scales move.[6]

And so sometimes I wound up eating nothing whatsoever. At first I would go one day and feel cold and a little foggy. I felt hungry, of course, and was consumed by thoughts of food. But at that point, on day one, I was still relatively clearheaded. That would change on day two or three, by which time I wasn't thinking well enough to decide to resume eating. By day four or five, when I lasted that long, I wasn't thinking at all. I would cease to be an agent.

I managed, in some sense, to keep functioning for the duration: fulfilling basic professional responsibilities, caring for my daughter, returning urgent emails. But I would get colder and colder, and less and less efficacious. My mouth became dry and puckered, as if I had just imbibed strong tannins. My stomach churned constantly, almost painful in its hollowness. Sleep was my only respite, but I was often too hungry to manage it. The hunger gnawed away at me— determined, relentless. It felt like not an emptiness but an active, sapping mandate. My body was telling me to eat. And, churlishly, I ignored it. Then I lost the capacity to listen altogether.

On and on it went. I became less and less able to reason myself out of the fugue I'd fallen into. The brain fog that descended by day three cast a thick pall over everything around me and everyone in my sightlines. In the end, I felt utterly disconnected from my young daughter, who needed me, and even my husband, who was asking me in increasingly urgent tones whether everything was all right with me.

It wasn't, of course. But I hid the extent of my fasting from him and from everyone. I couldn't help myself. I couldn't ask for help from other people. I literally couldn't—I no longer had the energy.

I came to, during the worst of these episodes, because of a doctor who failed to help me. I was seeing him for a follow-up appointment, and the room was hot and airless. I was double masking (it was *that* stage in the pandemic), and I was on day seven of my fast with no specific plans to break it. I had consumed only plain sparkling water—devoid not only of calories but even of flavor—for that whole time. I had never gone this long before. I was too frozen to be frightened.

Sitting on the exam table, sticking faintly but ineluctably to the medical paper, I felt the edges of my vision start to go fuzzy, then brown, then black. I realized I was about to pass out. I felt more embarrassed than anything, and figured I should warn my doctor before I just keeled over. He assumed my two masks had gotten to me. "Don't worry," he said cheerfully. "We were just about done here anyway." He gave a little wave and left me to my own devices.

Earlier, he had complimented me on my rapid weight loss.

It was anger that woke me up that day. He could have, should have, asked me if I was okay. Ideally, he would have inquired as to whether I was eating properly—as in, enough. Was I eating enough to sustain myself? What was I doing to lose the weight? Was I going hungry? It would have been so easy to ask me these basic questions: instead, I received approval, silence, absence.

So I got home that day—nursing my precious, lucid anger—and ate. My simple meal tasted weepingly, achingly delicious. As the sugar rushed into my bloodstream, I had a moment of painful clarity: I couldn't do this anymore. I couldn't simply ignore my hunger.

Pain has been construed by some philosophers not as a sensation but as an imperative: a "make it stop" mandate that we hear inwardly.[7] According to this theory, pain whispers—or shouts—in our ear, "Get off that limb! You are injured." Hunger similarly bids us to eat, to assuage its characteristic gnawing. "Eat something! Do it," it urges us firmly.

Such states of pain and hunger and need are what I have long theorized as *bodily imperatives:* they tell us, for example, to go to sleep or quench our thirst. They tell us to pull our hand away from a flame, or gasp for air when we are starved of oxygen. They speak to us, almost literally.

In my view, bodily imperatives constitute our most important *moral* imperatives. They tell us what we are called upon to do for other people and creatures, and ourselves, conceived as subjects.[8]

What, then, are the limits of these bodily imperatives? I certainly would not want to say that every desire we have fits into this category. Bodily imperatives are distinguished by a number of key features. First, many are universal, or nearly so: almost everyone experiences states like hunger, and for those who temporarily do not, it is generally a sign that something else has gone wrong with the body, such as a serious illness or state of grief that robs us of our appetite.[9] Second, bodily imperatives go *deep* in a particular way: although a mere desire for a new iPhone may be intense, it is hardly the first thing one would wish for if one were stranded, say, on a desert island. Much as with the general idea behind Maslow's famous hierarchy of needs, bodily imperatives like the yen for oxygen, food, water, sleep, warmth, and—I would add—some modicum of control over one's surroundings, plus a measure of social dignity, afford us with some of our most basic priorities in life. They are thus the kind of thing that torturers know all too well how to use against their victims: for, when the body is protesting, people can be broken.[10]

Finally, bodily imperatives are not up to us in an important sense. While one can, with effort, curtail one's desire for a new iPhone, or not develop such a consumerist urge in the first place, hunger is not the kind of thing that we can directly control or even distract ourselves from for long. We can and often do ignore it, of course. But we typically cannot help but feel it—frequently, despite ourselves.[11]

The idea of bodily imperatives as moral imperatives has plausible ethical implications. Consider someone struggling to breathe—whose body cries out for air, who is veritably gasping. Such a state constitutes a demand on us all to try to get this person help, and to prevent such a state of bodily need and panic from arising to begin with. This abstract moral imperative in turn gives rise to numerous more specific ethical duties and prohibitions.[12] It helps to explain the gross ethical wrong that is constituted by strangulation—deliberately cutting off someone's air supply being one of the most evil actions one can take against a person, inasmuch as it is not only very dangerous, and inherently controlling, but also a form of torture.[13] Such an imperative also compels us to do what we can to stop the spread of potentially severe respiratory illnesses, like COVID-19, by wearing masks and getting vaccinated. It makes the medical practitioners who attend to these patients, despite the risks to themselves, all the more clearly heroic. They are not only saving lives and staving off long-term health problems; they are helping to assuage the terrible suffering that comes with breathing difficulties.[14]

Being chronically very hungry is its own kind of torment—and one that many of us impose on ourselves, albeit under the influence of potent social forces. For, as this book has repeatedly shown, the oppressive forces of fatphobia play a coercive role in making people feel a false sense of obligation to go on extreme diets. This is the essence of diet culture. If I am right about the moral significance of bodily imperatives, then these pseudo-obligations are in fact morally pernicious: they tell us to ignore states of visceral need and hence inflict serious suffering upon us.

Maybe you're still skeptical. So I want you to imagine a practice that tells people to resist *sleeping* as much as possible. (Arguably, there is a practice that approaches this at the moment, in the form of "grind culture."[15]) Forget naps, of course. Forget getting seven or eight or nine hours of sleep a night, even if you need it. Ideally, people should go for days and nights at a time without succumbing to their urge to sleep altogether. We could come up with a fancy name for this ideology, like "intermittent sleeplessness." We could lie and tell people that there are huge benefits to living in this way—mental clarity, clearer skin, a longer life span, and a more attractive physique—despite the ample empirical evidence that they're just making themselves more and more tired and desperate for rest. Their body is telling them to sleep. We tell them to ignore it.

Now add a few more facts. This system targets some people more than others—girls and women, in particular, along with people of color. (Again, in the case of grind culture, this is plausibly a reality, as work by Tricia Hersey of the Nap Ministry has brilliantly highlighted.[16]) It also costs us a lot of money, as we pursue increasingly extreme means—pharmaceutical and surgical—to keep ourselves from sleeping regularly.

What would you conclude about the morality of this system? And, if you are opposed to it, ask yourself how, if at all, diet culture is any different.

Why did I tell you about my most extreme diet? Is this just a flex? When I began to write this chapter, in the aftermath of that episode, I had to conclude that it was. It felt like a veiled way of performing the role of the good fatty—who, yes, may be fat, but had tried as hard as anyone to shrink my body dutifully.

And so I stopped writing.

Then I tried again, more recently. I felt the need to tell you how very wrong I had been. How complicit I had been with diet culture, for all my grand talk of resisting patriarchal strictures.

But, ultimately, it felt like a confession of a sin that was less mine than a completely predictable product of the social world I lived in. It felt like an admission of guilt when what was needed was self-compassion—and trenchant social criticism.

And then I started to write that story: the one you have been reading. The one that I hope warns others just how easy it is to be gaslit by diet culture—and how sad, bad, and dangerous the results can end up being. I can see now that I was neither strong nor weak for my efforts. I was simply in the grip of insidious social forces that harm so many people— vulnerable ones especially. Sometimes they even kill us.

For dieting is a gateway to eating disorders for a significant number of people: one important meta-analysis showed that more than one-third of people classified as "normal dieters" became "pathological dieters" within the next two years, with restrictive eating habits that were demonstrably unhealthy. Moreover, around a quarter of "pathological dieters" progressed to partial or full-syndrome eating disorders over the same time period.[17] And while we should be careful not to confuse correlation with causation here—it's possible that dieting, rather than causing eating disorders, is an early warning sign or symptom—these findings are nonetheless suggestive. They suggest that any attempt to neatly disentangle ordinary, "healthy" dieting from disordered eating and even full-blown eating disorders will be difficult if not impossible for a considerable portion of the population. For many people, dieting has always been, or eventually becomes, dangerous. We should not forget that of all mental illnesses, certain eating disorders, like anorexia nervosa, carry the highest risks of mortality.[18] And, of course, they involve terrible suffering by their very definition.

I came close, I now believe, to developing an illness known as atypical anorexia—very much a misnomer, since there are more patients with this condition than the "typical" variety. Moreover, atypical anorexia is disturbingly prevalent in the populations most vulnerable to eating disorders, affecting nearly 3 percent of adolescent girls and young women in one representative study.[19] So-called atypical anorexia is characterized by the same symptoms as anorexia nervosa—including a hyper-focus on weight, a distorted body image, an intense fear of weight gain, a prolonged refusal to eat, and difficulty thinking clearly and focusing—with one major difference. These patients are not underweight. And because of this, their struggles often go undetected, even unsuspected, despite immense bodily and psychic suffering. Their skin yellows, becomes papery; they experience abdominal pain and gastrointestinal symptoms, including vomiting blood; their immune system worsens; and they have no energy to speak of. They may not be able to stand upright, or go from sitting to standing without fainting, due to a condition known as orthostatic hypotension.[20] One-third of patients with this condition experience amenorrhea (the cessation of their menstrual period); one-quarter present with bradycardia (a slow heart rate); at least 40 percent will require hospitalization.[21]

I was spared the worst of this, to my immense relief. But I now know I was in danger.

And as fat people, in particular, we're simply not asked by doctors if we might be suffering from these symptoms or experiencing the warning signs. If a person who has exhibited dramatic weight loss over a one-month period can nearly faint at her doctor's office and not get asked a single relevant question, how hard might you have to battle to get diagnosed with this illness?

This is not a rhetorical question. Research by the eating disorders researcher Erin Harrop has shed crucial light on its answer. They have shown that patients with atypical anorexia are routinely denied care on the grounds that they're too fat to have an eating disorder—even when they are exhibiting all of the above physiological symptoms, and great psychologi-

cal distress as well. On average, a patient with atypical anorexia will suffer for well over a decade between onset and
diagnosis.[22]

✦ ✦ ✦

I engaged in an extreme form of dieting that involves being
chronically hungry. But what about less drastic measures that
instead involve restricting certain types of food, or eating
them in very limited quantities, for the purposes of weight
loss?

It is important to be careful here. Food is highly constrained for many if not most of us. I certainly don't mean to
suggest that we are necessarily the victims of diet culture if
we don't eat with abandon. People have illnesses and diseases
and food allergies and intolerances; they have special nutritional needs, including those that help to stave off future pain
and suffering; they are on a tight budget; they have little time
or energy for food preparation. They have moral or religious
scruples that keep them from eating certain food groups, either alone or in combination.[23] They may live in a so-called
food desert. They may be poor or otherwise subject to food
insecurity. They may have other priorities and be an "eat to
live" person, rather than the converse. For all these reasons
and more, being a pleasure-seeking, unfettered gourmand is
simply not on the table for many people.

But there is a case to be made for not having one's food
intake restricted by the goal of weight loss specifically, And
there is value in an *anti*-diet culture—which many, like me,
have found in the practice of "intuitive eating"—that en-
courages us to take what pleasure and comfort and joy we
can from food.[24] In some cases, this is considerable. The sim-

ple pleasures of well-buttered toast, a slice of watermelon made extra juicy with a judicious sprinkle of salt, or a bowl of steaming white rice anointed with hot sauce, may provide real solace. The comfort is arguably just as important as the pleasure here: as many people discovered during the pandemic, there are few things that soothe us as adults as well as good food does. And good food does not have to be expensive or elaborate, as many cookbook authors and food writers have long taught us.

It's commonly assumed that as long as our meals fulfill our basic nutritional needs, then the extent to which they satisfy us and please our palates is more or less a moot point. This may be true for some people, but it is quite false for others. Recall Steven Pinker's offhand remark that it is irrational to prefer the lasagna to the steamed vegetables, because the "small pleasure" of the rich dish today is outweighed by the larger pleasure of having a slim body in the future.[25] I wonder: Has he considered how drab it is to eat low-fat food every day? How tired one gets of steamed vegetables? How many such ultimately depressing choices people make in service of getting or staying thin? How much we might long for lasagna?

There's also an individualistic—and, arguably, masculinist—assumption at work in diet culture, which minimizes the role of food in *shared* pleasures, both daily and during special celebrations. But there is something immensely valuable about being tied to the world, and our bodies, and each other, by the thrice-or-so daily practice of satisfying our hunger, frequently in the company of loved ones. It is both a protest against and a protection from the bodily alienation engendered by diet culture.[26] And there is something similarly valuable in engaging in special feasts together, often with dishes

that have a particular familial or cultural or religious significance, consumed for so much more than the sake of sheer
nutrition. Diet culture forbids, or at least interferes with, all
of this.

Finally, even if dieting doesn't bring suffering on ourselves, but merely a vague sense of deprivation, it can put
other people in danger: most notably, our children. In the
United States, nearly half of girls aged three to six worry
about being fat,[27] and some 80 percent of girls aged ten have
already been on a diet.[28] Around the world, more than
20 percent of all children studied exhibited disordered eating, according to a recent meta-analysis—with girls, again,
being disproportionately affected.[29] Moreover, a key predictor of bodily dissatisfaction among girls aged six to eight is
their perception of their mother's dissatisfaction with her
body—which, in practice, will often be evidenced by her
dieting.[30] And lest we let fathers off the hook here, another
study showed that a father's body dissatisfaction and "drive
for thinness"—which, again, is closely linked with dieting
behaviors—is likewise fraught: it was identified as a key risk
factor for his prepubescent daughter developing the early
warning signs of an eating disorder.[31]

It will inevitably be asked: But isn't overeating very much
a problem too? It depends how you define "overeating." If
you mean consuming what is supposedly too many calories
for your body, in order to satisfy your hunger, then I would
dispute this definition. It is just *eating*. It may lead to a fatter
body than is deemed socially acceptable, but which ought to
be embraced as a normal and valuable part of human diversity. On the other hand, if by "overeating" you mean continuing to eat past the point of fullness, to the point of
discomfort or even nausea, then I would agree that this is a

problem inasmuch as it causes bodily distress and is more than an occasional choice (to overindulge on Thanksgiving, say, in order to fit in more pie tastings). But then my hedonic arguments in this section would not extend to endorsing this practice, since it brings more pain than pleasure by definition. Theorizing the phenomenon of overeating in this sense is well beyond the scope of this chapter.[32] But I would just add that it seems to me the most understandable thing in the world that some people's bodies, long accustomed to being denied or ignored, not only tell them to eat but yell, even scream, at them to do so—and do not let up even after they have been sated. When it is a constant threat, our bodies grow afraid of deprivation.

Whatever you think about the goal of weight loss, dieting typically doesn't get us there, as this book has now amply demonstrated. As such, dieting, even in its more superficially benign forms, leads to decreased pleasure and increased suffering with no real payoff; it is hence a morally bankrupt practice. But what about certain practices that are demonstrably or arguably more effective in inducing weight loss? This brings me to two possibilities that both work, in various ways, to hijack our hunger cues and our ability to eat to achieve satiety: bariatric surgery and appetite suppressants.

Bariatric surgery works partly by making someone unable to eat much without experiencing pain and suffering—imposing, in effect, a bodily imperative on them not to eat more than a very modest amount of food in one sitting. Otherwise, they may be subject to stomach pain, cramping, bloating, nausea, vomiting, diarrhea, and an effect aptly named "dumping" (where food moves too rapidly from the stomach to the small intestine after eating, leading to the above symptoms, plus dizziness, light-headedness, and a rapid heart rate, in some cases). Bariatric surgery tends, at least in the short term, to reduce hunger and cause other metabolic and hormonal changes that are not yet fully understood. Together, these effects typically produce rapid weight loss, leading to the average patient ultimately losing around half of their so-called excess weight, according to the American Society for Metabolic and Bariatric Surgery.[33] This is, obviously, a much more pronounced effect than dieting.

There are many drawbacks of bariatric surgery, though. The more extreme versions of the procedure effectively amputate a large part (up to 80 percent) of the stomach despite its functioning normally.[34] Given its recent advent, the long-term effects of such interventions haven't yet been determined, making the practice an unfolding human experiment whose scale is ever increasing. The number of bariatric surgeries performed annually in the United States increased by more than 50 percent between 2011 and 2020.[35] And this is presumably related to the fact that bariatric surgeries turn a tidy profit in this country, among others.

The surgeries themselves can be dangerous. An estimated one in two hundred patients die after the most common bariatric procedure, gastric bypass surgery,[36] due to complications like bleeding, infection, and blood clots.[37] And although this mortality rate is often compared favorably by industry insiders with the mortality rates for other operations, like gallbladder surgery, it is a significant risk for an elective procedure.[38]

As well as the risk, pain, and expense of bariatric surgery (which is sometimes but by no means always covered by health insurance), many patients experience serious problems in the aftermath. Opioid addictions are a common issue.[39] It frequently becomes difficult for the person to eat or enjoy food without dire consequences afterward. And many subsequently experience nutritional deficiencies (including anemia and scurvy), gallstones,[40] hernias, intestinal leakage,[41] bowel obstructions,[42] and serious bone loss.[43] Many people—around one-third—gain a significant amount of weight back regardless.[44] Even some weight-loss doctors are hence willing to admit that "cutting your stomach in half isn't an ideal solution" to the supposed problem of obesity.[45]

Bariatric surgery also requires follow-up interventions, including other surgeries and hospitalizations, with notable regularity: around one-third of patients will require some such within five years of their original surgery.[46]

Perhaps most disturbingly of all, studies show that people who undergo bariatric surgery are at least twice as likely to commit suicide as their counterparts who do not.[47] True, correlation is not causation, and we should be careful about extrapolating a causal direction here. But these findings remain deeply troubling, and anyone contemplating such operations ought to be apprised of them. As the psychologist Kasey Goodpaster put it, "For many, bariatric surgery is considered the 'last resort,' and if it does not result in the quality of life improvements one expected, it could lead to despair."[48]

To be clear, I am deeply sympathetic to the people who undergo bariatric surgery to help their bodies better fit the world, just as I am sympathetic to people who are perpetually on a diet. Plausibly, one of my arguments earlier in this book implies that individuals are entitled to take on the health risks that come with attempting weight loss in these ways, just as they have the right to let themselves be fatter if they choose to. But, at the level of the social practices I'm primarily interested in criticizing in this book, there is ample room for concern here. The weight-loss-surgery industry is preying on vulnerable people by making them feel they are not only entitled but *obligated* to subject themselves to these risky measures, and often without a compelling medical justification. There is no such obligation. Moreover, as the fat activist and writer Ragen Chastain has argued, there's good reason to think that many fat people would *not* want these surgeries if the world was less fatphobic:

> Our acceptance of the idea that fat people should have their digestive systems mutilated and risk death for thinness brings a couple of things into sharp relief, [including] just how horrific weight stigma is in our culture. I wonder if thin people can imagine being treated so poorly with such regularity—not just by bigoted people, but by a world that isn't built to accommodate them (and blames them for that)—that they would be willing to have a healthy vital organ amputated in a way that will be, at best, life-altering and at worst, fatal. We need to wrap our heads around the fact that in our current society, weight-based stigma is so horrific that doctors recommend surgical intervention. Think about that for a minute—we're not just giving bullies our lunch money anymore, we're giving them our perfectly healthy stomachs.[49]

I share Chastain's worries about bariatric surgery as a growing social practice, one that has the potential to worsen fat stigma and dangle a tempting solution to a state of physical being that, for many bodies, is actually a nonproblem. I long for a world in which every body fits, and believe that this is what we must demand, morally and politically—along with a world in which nobody goes hungry for no good reason, including for the sake of weight loss.

As well as ignoring our hunger, and making it difficult to satisfy, some of us try to silence it. We take diet pills—specifically, appetite suppressants. As discussed in the last chapter, I have done this myself. I have done this with a frequency and an alacrity that embarrasses me immensely.

Most of these pills, purchased over the counter, are snake oil. Others were effective for some, but so dangerous that they had to be pulled off the market. The prescription drugs fen-phen (fenfluramine plus phentermine) and Redux (dexfenfluramine, often prescribed alongside phentermine) led to serious heart valve damage that now appears to be irreversible.[50] And they caused tens of thousands of people to develop primary pulmonary hypertension, a thickening of capillaries in the lungs that makes breathing increasingly difficult and ultimately leads to heart failure.[51] The journalist Alicia Mundy describes the result in the worst cases as "death by slow suffocation."[52]

Phentermine, a stimulant, remains available on its own. It routinely produces modest weight loss—for the low, low price of hypertension, heart palpitations, shortness of breath, chest pain, and insomnia, among numerous other common side effects.[53]

Adderall and other stimulants can induce weight loss too. Although it is difficult to obtain good data on their efficacy, seeing as they are rarely prescribed even off-label for this purpose, I can tell you from my personal experience that it did take the weight off.

It also left me anxious, frantic, sleepless, and, briefly, suicidal. To say that it was a bad idea is a massive understatement. And that is even before the weight came back, inexorably.

Although some will be shocked by what I did, the practice is pretty widespread. One study showed that nearly 5 percent of college students reported taking illicit prescription stimulant medications, including Ritalin as well as Adderall, for the express purposes of weight loss.[54] (Notably, this did not include students who had a prescription, which can be obtained with relative ease from unscrupulous doctors even in the absence of a credible ADHD diagnosis.) Another study showed that of drug-using, college-age women, more than 15 percent reported taking illicit substances, predominantly stimulants like cocaine, amphetamine, methamphetamine, and ecstasy, in order to lose weight. "Women engaging in more extreme weight loss behaviors are at high risk for initiating and maintaining illicit stimulant use for weight-related reasons," the researchers added.[55]

Such drugs have significant side effects: mental health symptoms including anxiety, panic, paranoia, and psychosis. Depression is common too, especially following discontinuation. They can cause dry mouth, nausea, stomach pain, and vomiting. They make certain people act in a grandiose way and even feel invincible—which can be not only annoying but dangerous in some cases, for both themselves and others. These drugs cause sleep difficulties and disturbances, headaches, and shakiness. And they are even associated in extreme cases with cardiovascular problems, such as strokes and heart attacks. Stimulant abuse sometimes proves fatal.[56]

The price of thinness, as we see time and time again, is the violation of basic bodily imperatives—if not in the form of hunger, then in the form of a desperate need for oxygen. Or sleep. Or peace and respite.

And the simple fact remains that our bodies need nourishment, whether or not we feel hungry. (News just in: we need food to live. Surely worth this book's cover price.) Appetite suppressants make it far too easy to push ourselves into risky territory, on this score among others.

So, even for those who would maintain, contrary to my own view, that there is some value in weight loss, neither of the two main current alternatives to dieting—weight-loss surgery and diet pills—is worth the significant risks it poses to the many understandably desperate people whom the relevant industries exploit and prey upon. And the upshot of this is considerable. There is currently no morally acceptable practice that serves to reliably make fat people thin. Even if you—again, unlike me—worry about some people's fatness, there is nothing to recommend to them within the bounds of ethics.

But here's a thought experiment: What if there were a simple, painless way, devoid of side effects, to make fat people thin? A new generation of weight-loss drugs—most prominently, semaglutide (marketed as Wegovy and Ozempic, weekly injections)—are touted by some as at least coming close to that. Their claims may be overblown with respect to efficacy and misleading with respect to a purported lack of side effects. (These drugs may lead to thyroid cancer, according to the boxed warning;[57] they induce nausea, vomiting, and digestive distress in many people who take them, and they are currently very expensive, costing well over $1,000 per month unless covered by health insurance, which remains unusual at the time of writing.[58]) But we can certainly *imagine* such a drug being better, and being distributed free of charge to anyone who wants it. What then? What should we think about this social practice?

I can imagine many readers hesitating at this juncture. So consider, by way of an analogy, the practices of using skin-lightening creams to make darker-skinned people paler, rhinoplasty—colloquially called a "nose job"—to minimize the evidence of a supposedly Jewish nose (like mine, for the record), or Botox to smooth out lined or wrinkled skin (mine is certainly heading in that direction). Even if these interventions were perfectly safe and costless and painless—which they're currently far from being—I would still find them objectionable at a social level of analysis. For they flatten out difference, in the form of human bodily diversity, which I believe we ought to value. They flatten out such difference not at random, moreover, but in a way that upholds white supremacist, anti-Semitic, misogynistic, and ageist beauty standards.[59] Inasmuch as these practices become widespread, then, there's something regrettable going on. And I think that these practices are, well, in a word, creepy.[60]

I believe that fat bodies are part of the same kind of valuable human, bodily diversity. I believe not only that fat people should be respected, and treated with dignity, and given access to adequate healthcare, and so on. I believe that our *fatness* contributes something worth having. We add something to the world with our size and shape and sheer existence. As Roxane Gay put it, "I have presence. . . . I take up space. I intimidate."[61]

Fatness can be beautiful, sure, but I think that is the least of it. It can be arresting, provocative, comforting, protective, and deeply countercultural. It is a vast blank canvas for interesting artistic and creative possibilities. Fatness makes for dazzling burlesque performance and dramatic designs in fashion.[62] "You can mold fat, lift it, move it around into fantastical forms, you can make a truly radical silhouette because there's just more body there to work with," as one Twitter user, @isocrime, put it recently.[63]

Fatness can nurture pregnancy and support breast-feeding and the growth of our children. Fatness is a baby's deliciously fat wrists—sometimes called "fat bracelets"—and round little bellies. Fatness is the thrilling undulation of a fat opera singer's belly, and Nicole Byer's gorgeous bikini poses. Fatness is ample and fluid and luscious and irrepressible. It can inspire love, awe, reverence. It can instill a sense of solidarity, of shared vulnerability, a common fate in spite of all of our differently sized and shaped bodies. And fatness can elicit fear and repel just the right people, whose intolerance for wayward flesh makes them the wrong ones to get close to. A woman's fatness in particular will work to "alienate small, bitter men who dared to presume that women exist for their consumption," as Lindy West writes, thus "lay[ing] bare their cowardice in recoiling at something as literally fundamental as a woman's real body."[64]

Fatness, in other words, is something to *value*. If all or even most fat people took the magic weight-loss pill we're imagining, something important would be lost. We would lose, to again quote @isocrime, "the luxury of softness and lushness, the freedom to take up space . . . to be more than what people expect, to live wreathed in the gravity and physicality of flesh."[65] We would be collectively diminished inasmuch as fatness was eliminated or even rendered a rarity.

But even while acknowledging the social harms of the magic pill, you might still wonder, as a lone fat individual: Should *you* take it?

As before, we should distinguish two questions: whether you are *entitled* to take it, and whether you are *obligated*. I think you are entitled as an individual to do most things you want to do to your body, as long as it isn't egregiously imprudent (like riding a motorcycle without a helmet—or, arguably, taking amphetamines to lose weight), and as long as it doesn't directly harm other people (like smoking indoors around young children). It is, in the end, your body. And, if you want to make your body smaller—or your skin lighter, or your nose straighter, or your "frown lines" smoother—then I believe you have the right to. Life is hard, and the world's racism, colorism, anti-Semitism, sexism, misogyny, ageism, and fatphobia, among many other forms of bigotry, can make it so much harder to live with the stigmatized features. I certainly don't think you should be blamed or shamed or criticized for taking an easier path, or doing what you may need to do to make your life bearable or even livable in some cases.

But I want you to know you're not obligated to make any of these choices. In particular, you're not obligated to shrink yourself to please others, or society, or even to appease your own internalized sense of what you ought to look like. The fact that a notional pill could make you thin without cost— either medical or financial, we're imagining—might shorten the list of cons. But it doesn't make the pros decisive for you, or indeed ensure there are any whatsoever.

In fact, I would go further. While I think you're entitled

to take the magic weight-loss pill we're imagining, there would also be something good—cool, gutsy, admirable—in *refusing* to do so.[66] (I think the same, for the record, about refusing to lighten your skin or alter your facial features via surgery or Botox, notwithstanding the social pressure.[67]) You'd thereby be putting your body on the line for the sake, in part, of fat representation in particular and body diversity more broadly. You'd be showing up in the world in a way that resists narrow and, frankly, fascist body norms and ideals and values. You'd be standing in solidarity with people othered and marginalized on account of their fatness. You'd be standing with the younger me who was bullied. You'd be standing with Aubrey Gordon when she was harassed. You'd be standing with Da'Shaun L. Harrison as they were forced, as a fat kid with asthma, to run laps wearing a trash bag until they couldn't breathe for gasping.

You would stand, moreover, with countless silent others who are yet to tell their stories, or whose stories are yet to unfold, within a fatphobic social world that we have the collective power to make so much better.

You aren't obligated to do any of this. But good for you if you manage it. And good for all of us, ultimately.

Of course, you can't refuse this magic pill now and thus demonstrate your solidarity and resistance to fatphobia in the way that I've outlined; that pill doesn't exist yet, and it may never. But you *can* refuse to diet—or to take Ozempic. Those of us with the privilege and the means—financial, psychological, and social—can choose to honor our hunger and even our more specific cravings, vesting them and our bodies with a measure of authority. We can thereby stand up to the exploitative, capitalist, gaslighting nightmare that is diet culture. We can thereby lessen the loneliness of having a body that looks like *most* of our bodies in America today, but that is nonetheless frequently a basis for guilt and shame and self-hatred. We can thereby resist fatphobia in its potent intersections with misogyny, racism (particularly anti-Blackness), classism, transphobia, homophobia, ageism, and ableism. And we may thereby become, in more ways than one, *unshrinking*: reclaiming space in a way that is unapologetic, fearless, graceful.

And so these days, most days, I manage to say "fuck you" to diet culture. I eat when I am hungry. I eat what sounds good to me. Sometimes, even often, I have the goddamn lasagna. I share it with my daughter. I know that she is watching me, taking in everything.

CONCLUSION: NOT SORRY

On May 16, 2022, *Sports Illustrated* released the cover of its annual swimsuit issue. It featured Yumi Nu, the plus-size model, in a strappy black one-piece with large cutouts. Nu, it should be noted, conforms to conventional beauty ideals in all but two respects. One, she is not white (she is Asian American). Two, she is not thin—though still only a "small fat" woman.

The reactionary Canadian psychologist Jordan B. Peterson saw fit to tweet about it. "Sorry. Not beautiful. And no amount of authoritarian tolerance is going to change that," he opined.[1] Plenty agreed, though the tweet drew a lot of heated criticism, leading Peterson to withdraw from social media. For about five minutes.

One month later, Peterson retweeted another image: the *New York Post*'s story about the woman named "Sexiest

Woman Alive" by Maxim Hot 100, Paige Spiranac. The triptych featured the—thin, white, blond—Spiranac posing in high heels and a bikini and displaying her cleavage in an open button-up shirt. "Ok. She might be beautiful :)" tweeted Peterson, hornily.[2] (He didn't weigh in when Spiranac made tabloid headlines a few months later, after she was fat-shamed on Instagram for negligible weight gain.[3])

Such attitudes and the practices they give rise to are, of course, distressingly common. And the way that Peterson gives voice to them is unwittingly revealing. "Sorry," he offers, and of course he's not sorry. But the high-handed tone suggests a man rejecting something offered to him, meant for him, personally. It's not just that it's not for him. It's *for* him, but not up to his definitive, exacting standards. When it comes to beauty, he is the arbiter, and his pleasure is the measure. And, sadly, the world often agrees and grants such privileged men this false authority.

At the end of this book, you may be wondering how I now feel about my body. What follows will not be, I'm afraid, a triumphant conclusion. In part this is because my story is still very much being written. And in part it is because it is not in bodily self-love, but rather a shift in perspective, in which I have found my freedom.

The thought that has helped me the most, in navigating all of this, is that *my body is for me.* Your body is for you. My body is not decoration. Your body is not decoration.[4] Our bodies are our homes, as the slogan has it.

It goes without saying that you can have a reaction to my body. That reaction may be positive or negative or neutral—

and good, bad, objectionable, non-objectionable. Contrary to what Peterson and his ilk may have you believe, it is not authoritarian to recognize some attitudes toward others' bodies as rude, even obnoxious. You're entitled to your opinion. But I'm entitled to think you an *asshole* for having it, and doubly so for expressing it when nobody asked you.

Of course, it's complicated. The ways I want to express myself bodily will inevitably be informed by the culture in which I live, and by the complex confluence of norms that structure how I'm perceived and received in the world. And I may want to do things with and to other bodies, who may consent, indeed relish the prospect. But still. My body, for all that, is for me. And yours is for you.

This notion—"body reflexivity," as I'll call it—differs from both body positivity and body neutrality.[5] It does not prescribe any particular evaluative stance toward one's form. It is compatible with finding oneself beautiful, or sexy—or not, as the case may be. We may decline to think about our appearance much whatsoever. Body reflexivity prescribes a radical reevaluation of whom we exist in the world *for*, as bodies: ourselves, and no one else. We are not responsible for pleasing others.

A natural corollary: your reaction to my body is not my problem—or the point, or salvation. The body is not an object for correction or colonization or consumption. I am sorry, not sorry, if my body leaves you cold, or you find it to be wanting.

✦ ✦ ✦

Peterson was not satisfied with the two aforementioned tweets detailing his drearily predictable sexual preferences. A third followed on June 20, 2022, during the peak of Pride Month. He retweeted a video commenting disapprovingly on a drag queen event that had recently taken place in Dallas, Texas. "Sorry. Not beautiful. And also damnably pathological," Peterson intoned.[6] The language was almost quaint; the sentiments were noxious.

The text accompanying the original video read in part, "If I were to bring a toddler or infant into a strip club I would be arrested immediately and CPS would take my child. A hyper-sexual show is no place for children."[7] Meanwhile, the footage showed nothing more racy than one drag queen doing the splits in a white bodysuit, and others being fat, dancing mildly suggestively, in public. Just two children are viewable in the footage—one of them an infant who is unlikely to yet know where their nose is. And both of whose parents are solely responsible for deciding which Pride events to take them to, if any.

Body panics, like moral panics, often focus on the children. If children's bodies are themselves the basis for a moral panic, then so much the better, seemingly. Currently in this country, trans kids are being targeted along with their parents. In Texas, the parents of children who receive gender-affirming care are subject to investigation by the state and potential charges of child abuse. Nine investigations are ongoing at the time of writing, and could result in children being removed from their supportive, loving families.[8]

The panic over fat kids, and the people who raise them, is a crucial precedent for these developments. For many years, fat people's bodies have been policed and denied access to reproductive technologies, including egg freezing[9] and IVF procedures, as we've seen.[10] Patients struggling with infertility are routinely told to lose weight. A recent study of nearly four hundred so-called obese women showed that doing so made no difference to whether they eventually got pregnant.[11] Meanwhile, parents raising fat children have been threatened with action from child protective or social services, and even had their children taken away from them in some cases.[12]

The American Academy of Pediatrics currently recommends gender-affirming care for trans children.[13] It also (independently) recommends bariatric surgery for "severely obese" children as young as thirteen.[14] The former measure enables trans kids to flourish and be who they are, bodily. And it demonstrably reduces their risk of depression and even suicide.[15] Whereas bariatric surgery sets fat kids up for a lifetime of being unable to meet their basic nutritional needs or satisfy their hunger without suffering, as we saw in the previous chapter. It also seems likely to increase suicide risks, if adult patients are any guide to pediatric ones. Yet it is the prospect of trans kids receiving gender-affirming care that has attracted the bulk of the public outcry. Clearly, when it comes to performing supposedly irreversible surgeries on children (which gender-affirming care may but need not involve), the hand-wringing is highly selective—and prejudiced. And, as one might expect in a transphobic as well as fatphobic society, it gets things precisely backward.

We are yet to get comfortable, as a society, with the fact that bodies are a diverse lot, and children's bodies are no exception. When it comes to fatness, this obvious conclusion remains frustratingly elusive, even despite the rise of intuitive eating and anti-diet discourses within some parenting circles. Indeed, these ideas often serve to subtly reinscribe the very fatphobic logic they were originally designed to combat. There is a sotto voce insistence that if you don't restrict your children's eating unduly, or emphasize "good foods" versus "bad foods" too much, they won't get fat. This is as opposed to the more radical and salutary message that some people, children included, *just are fat* and there is absolutely nothing wrong with that.[16]

A post of an impeccably organized lunch box on Instagram, featuring hummus and carrot sticks and strawberries and three lone M&M's—#intuitiveeating #antidietculture #bodypositivity—is not going to do much to address our culture of pediatric fatphobia, as Virginia Sole-Smith has argued.[17] Neither is a bunch of rainbow-emblazoned merchandise going to help the trans children whose bodies, and identities, need protection from rising fascism.

What is called for is a thoroughgoing political reckoning and subsequent moral recognition: being fat, like being trans, is a valid and indeed valuable way of being in the world. Human diversity in size and shape and body type is something to be embraced. It should not be used as the basis for invidious social distinctions—or the insistence that, as fat people, we punish and starve and shrink ourselves down to size. We are who we are. And we have nothing to be ashamed of. We are wronged bodies, not wrong ones.

So, even in the depths of lockdown during the pandemic, when our family barely saw another living soul due to my husband's immunocompromised status, I pulled up Instagram on my phone and showed my daughter bodies. I showed her fat bodies and Black and brown bodies and trans bodies and the bodies of people who are disabled and have skin and limb and facial differences and more. I showed her pictures of the fat authors whom I so admire and have drawn on in these writings. I showed her the bodies of other people viewed through the lens not of judgment—not even a generic positive evaluation—but of respect and kindness, of gratitude and gladness that they are here in the world among us. I showed her that the world is not meant to be populated by people who look just one way or another. And I taught her what we call the denizen of any such body: a *person*. (She pronounced it "per" to begin with.)

People say, already, that my beautiful daughter looks just like me. Some days, I can even see it. I do so with trepidation.

✦ ✦ ✦

What do I mean when I say that someone's body is for them and no one else? In the first instance, I mean that they are its sole intended beneficiary. Intended by whom? By us, as a political collective, if we are thinking and acting properly.

The notion of who something is *for* in this way can also have important political implications. LGBTQIA+ events, for example, are not *meant* to be for children. They can be a valuable and fun experience for children, to be sure, and the concern about kink at Pride is typically little more than con-servative concern trolling. I myself do not share it, and would take my kid to see a drag queen dancing joyfully in a heart-beat. But many white, cis, straight, middle-class parents falsely think that the *point* of Pride is to provide a learning opportunity for their offspring. Such a sanitized, self-centered conception of Pride is of a piece with corporate rainbow washing, which cynically treats Pride as a chance to sell more products. Both make the mistake of failing to center the peo-ple by and for whom Pride was created—namely, people in the LGBTQIA+ community.

And the point of Pride, originally, was to provide an antidote to the shame visited on these folks by mainstream social forces, especially during the height of the AIDS epidemic, when gay people were even more stigmatized than they are today. (Though Florida's "Don't Say Gay" law, which forbids any discussion of sexuality or gender identity in the classroom from kindergarten until third grade, seems one ominous sign among many that the tides are sadly turning.[18]) Pride says, despite the way we are treated, we have no reason to feel ashamed. We can lift our heads up high. Pride says, in a nutshell, fuck the haters. Kink is an integral part of Pride because of the role that kink-shaming has played—and continues to play—in oppressing queer people.[19] This also explains why "white pride" movements and the like are so pernicious and mistaken; nobody is making white people feel ashamed of their whiteness, notwithstanding conservative caterwauling. As the philosopher Elizabeth Barnes puts it,

> Pride, in the context of social marginalization, isn't the demand that we recognize that the marginalized group is somehow inherently blessed or special. It is, instead, better thought of as something like permission to celebrate. We often celebrate things without thinking they're something that makes us better or superior; we can be proud (in some sense) of having red hair, of being weirdly good at Settlers of Catan, of having an enormous comic book collection, of having a good 10k time, etc. These are things we can celebrate about ourselves without thinking they make us better than people who lack such features. Pride, in the context of social marginalization, can then be thought of as the claim that it's permissible to celebrate a marginalized feature in this way. Some

feature—race, sexuality, disability, etc.—that dominant norms tell you that you should be ashamed of or apologetic about is, in fact, something it makes sense to celebrate.[20]

And so it is with fat pride as well as disabled, queer, trans, and Black pride, and similar. Each of these movements is specific and should not be reduced to an exercise in generic body positivity—nor, for that matter, glossed as advocating anything as anodyne as tolerance. Fat pride is for fat people, in particular, not for the thin white women who have been known to co-opt the body positivity movement that has its roots in Black feminism.[21] Fat pride is for those who have been pushed to the margins by the size of their bodies—and who need to emerge from the periphery and say, "My fat body is for me. And I will celebrate it without apology."

Body reflexivity doesn't require one monolithic attitude toward our own body or that of others. And feeling uniformly positive about one's own body as it is does not seem to me realistic. It is never going to work for all trans people, for example, some of whom need or want to change their bodies in significant ways, and should be supported and celebrated in the process. It is also never going to work for some of the chronically ill and disabled people who may feel, at least at moments, that their bodies have betrayed them, by causing them pain or not having certain functions that can be important to some people. They are allowed to have these kinds of self-doubts and fears and frustrations. We should not be in the business of policing such thoughts any more than we should be policing bodies, or restricting who has access to the resource of bodily freedom.

Recent research jibes with these observations. The researchers set out to investigate the possibility that body positive messaging can be actively counterproductive when it has features of *toxic* positivity. As they explain,

> Recently, popular psychology has coined the term toxic positivity to refer to the expectation that people should experience positive emotions (e.g., satisfaction, gratitude, contentment, joy) and reject negative emotions (e.g., stress, doubt, frustration), which ignores or undermines genuine feelings of distress. . . . Much like with general "toxic positivity," we suggest that many women experience "toxic body positivity," where they are expected and pressured to show body confidence and acceptance, and failure to achieve body positivity is considered weakness.[22]

The researchers thus crafted messages that they classified as body positive and autonomy-supportive ("You are the author of your own happiness. It's up to YOU to be YOU") versus body positive and controlling ("You MUST accept your body or you will never be happy"). Each of these messages was accompanied by a picture of a model whose body they describe as average-sized, wearing jeans and a white tank top. They found that the autonomy-supportive message elicited significantly higher self-evaluation and body satisfaction among participants than the controlling one. Moreover, body shame and body surveillance were significantly decreased following the autonomy-supportive message; no such changes were produced by the controlling one.[23]

It's hard to see how the general mandate to be positive about our bodies could avoid the features that can make positivity curdle into something toxic. True, such positivity isn't *necessarily* toxic, considered at an individual level. But the documented propensity for it to turn toxic when it is billed as obligatory and socially enforced is a huge problem for body positivity writ large. As the researchers put it,

> When body positivity is forced or feels controlling, it can thwart feelings of agency and autonomy and therefore backfire. . . . Placing emphasis on positivity while ignoring negative feelings and experiences exerts a cost to authenticity and self-integration—or, the need to feel true to (and congruent with) oneself.[24]

At the same time, the idea of feeling merely neutral toward one's body strikes me as lackluster. Faint praise is bad enough; *no* praise is dispiriting.

A truly neutral attitude is hard to maintain, moreover, with some psychologists disputing whether it is so much as possible, and others holding that it is at least a rarity. The words still others suggest to capture a neutral affect are, tellingly, quite variable, with some—feeling "meh" or "so-so"—seemingly tinged with negativity.[25] Others, like "feeling nothing in particular," imply a kind of blankness that is surely hard to conjure routinely about a subject matter as fraught as our own bodies. All in all, body neutrality seems at best a precarious retreat from judgment, not a stable resting place. It's like offering a zero instead of a positive or negative number, when what is needed is dispensing with numbers altogether.[26]

Body reflexivity offers an escape from the apparently exhaustive options of positivity, negativity, or neutrality, by proposing a different focus. Rather than changing how bodies are assessed, it urges us to transcend the mode of assessment entirely. ("I don't look at you with a critical eye," is something often said to me by my husband—which means more to me, in the end, than his also telling me I'm beautiful.) A body is not something good or bad or neutral for people generally, but rather something that may suit and work better or worse for its denizen—in other words, the person who inhabits it. And her perspective on her body is the only one that matters.

The idea of body reflexivity is tied, as body positivity and body neutrality are not, to a political ethos—a radical politics of autonomy that would vindicate the right to be fat, or trans, or nonbinary, or queer, or disabled.[27] Moreover, by not requiring any particular attitude toward our bodies, body reflexivity can recognize the psychological consequences of our current political predicament. As Da'Shaun L. Harrison has pointed out, feeling insecure makes sense in a world set up to undermine you. We *feel* insecure because, in being fat or trans or queer or disabled or otherwise nonnormative in a bodily dimension—that which Harrison calls "Ugly"—we are *made* to be insecure in our very embodiment. They write,

> Insecurity . . . must be political. If the politicization of Ugly leads to the social, political, economic, and physical death of a person, they are bound to feel unprotected, uncared for, and unconfident. To that point, Insecurities are valid. It is okay for us to be insecure in bodies that are constantly beat on and berated. Those Insecurities don't change the reality [of]

what anti-fatness, or overall Ugliness, is and what it does. . . . You can't beat people down forever and expect that they never feel the effects of that continued beating. Insecurities are not a personal indictment; they are an indictment of the World.[28]

Body reflexivity need not, and does not, try to paper over this truth. Your body is for you, and the ways it has been impugned stem from the many people and practices and structures that have missed this fundamental idea, instead perpetuating the lie that your body is meant to please or serve or placate others. You may well feel insecure in a society structured around this lie—and that, as Harrison says, is not a moral or personal failing.[29] The world has to be remade; it has to serve you better. In particular, it must cease to enter you automatically into the most pointless yet prevalent of contests: beauty.

The relatively few philosophers who have taken up the question of how to challenge fat oppression have leaned heavily, in various ways, on the idea of reforming beauty standards. A. W. Eaton advocates trying to change our collective taste in bodies, in part by contemplating fat bodies depicted in art in ways that are arresting, pleasing, beautiful.[30] More recently, Cheryl Frazier has drawn suggested lessons from the "fuck flattering" movement, in which fat fashion bloggers wear "unflattering" silhouettes as a form of what Frazier terms "beauty labor as resistance." Fat people thereby "redefine and reimagine beauty, creating space for themselves and other fat people," Frazier argues.[31]

These discussions are subtle and important, and my own suggestion here is, I admit, blunter and less nuanced. Fuck beauty culture, along with diet culture. Burn it down. Raze it. For, as Tressie McMillan Cottom has persuasively argued, in discussing the anti-Blackness of beauty norms, beauty is never just a reflection of mainstream aesthetic preferences. Rather, "beauty is the preferences that reproduce the existing social order"[32]—and excludes people based on body type and skin color not by accident but by design, for profit. We cannot, I believe, modify this system to make it incrementally more just. Injustice is its point, its function, its raison d'être. As McMillan Cottom puts it, "To coerce, beauty must exclude. . . . It cannot be universal."[33]

I hence hold out hope for a future in which our current relentless beauty pageant has no more judges—and not a single entrant. It is not that everybody wins or gets a participation trophy in the form of our collective studied neutrality. There should be *nothing* in its place. There ought to be no contest. And that there is no contest, no judgment, does not mean there can be no appreciation. Go for a walk sometime: you can appreciate a leaf, a sunset, a dog, without ranking it against others or pronouncing it superior. There can be self-expression too; we may feel the most ourselves in particular incarnations. But dress and look how you want not in the name of any kind of beauty but for the sake of being the most yourself that you can presently imagine. Know that your imagination on this score may stretch and rupture. (Or not: bury me in my uniform of black skinny jeans and a shapeless stretchy tunic.)

True, we're a long way off from the total divestment from beauty and diet culture that I envisage. Many people will continue to wish in the meantime that their bodies conformed more closely to dominant, oppressive aesthetic standards. But there are real limits to the bodily changes one can make without serious repercussions, as this book has shown for the case of weight loss in particular. We only have one body. So we will have to learn to live with it—through both unintended shifts and deliberate alterations. Moreover, in living in our changing, aging bodies unapologetically, we set a personal example with political implications. We help to embody bodily diversity and demonstrate its value.

So I am sorry, not sorry, to be someone who is fat and thinks for a living—as a moral philosopher, specifically.

I am sorry, not sorry, to be a fat parent, and one who is raising my daughter to believe in the equality of all bodies.

I am sorry, not sorry, to be teaching my daughter to be unafraid of her own appetite, indeed to embrace her hunger.

I am sorry, not sorry, to have just bought my first swimsuit in more than twenty years. I plan to take my daughter to the pool. I am not going to wear a cover-up. I am not going to think too much about it.

And that feels like a minor miracle—even a happy ending.

ACKNOWLEDGMENTS

It takes a village to write a book, and this one is surely no exception. Indeed, this book—such as it is—feels so much like a community effort that I despair of ever thanking everyone whom I owe in these acknowledgments.

I first encountered fat activism through the lively Fatshionista community and Kate Harding's galvanizing *Shapely Prose* website in the early aughts. And although it took nearly twenty years for me to begin to apply these lessons to my own case, the seeds of fat positivity were thereby planted early—and, I'm glad to say, deeply.

More recently, I've benefited immensely from the philosophical and social justice communities I'm lucky to count myself a part of, both at Cornell University and virtually, via my online circles. I am especially grateful to the many simpatico people I have been able to get to know and keep in touch with, and whose wisdom and courage I've learned from, even throughout this often isolating pandemic. For comments on this manuscript for which I'm particularly grateful, I thank Michael Hobbes, Dr. Susan Hata, Dr. Gregory Dodell, Dr. Evan Rosen, Natasha Wiebe, Matthew Desmond, Elizabeth Barnes, Sherri Irwin, Nicky Drake (who is behind the title of chapter 7—an inspired suggestion), Rachana Kamtekar, W. Starr, and Chelle Parker. For brilliant research assistance, and her astute contributions more broadly, I am extremely thankful to Emily Park, who is on to great things. I'm also indebted to readers of my Substack newsletter, *More to Hate,* for their comments, support, and readership on this topic, among others.

To my agent, Lucy Cleland, I am indebted to you for your incredible instincts, fine attention to detail, and your heartening faith in me and this project. To my editorial team at Crown, Amanda Cook and Katie Berry, I am deeply grateful for your sharp insights, endless patience, and truly brilliant editorial vision. I am also tremendously grateful to my editor at Penguin UK, Casiana Ionita, for her generosity, flair, and faith that I could see this project through to its fruition. And without the interest, insights, and beautifully light touch of Alicia Wittmeyer, my editor for a piece on fatness and philosophy published in *The New York Times* in January 2022, I doubt I would have followed through with it.

While working on this project, I have benefited immensely from the comments and feedback of audiences at Stanford University, the University of California Berkeley, the University of Southern California, Fairleigh Dickinson University, Bergen Community College, Rutgers University, Radboud University (in the Netherlands), Tilburg University (also in the Netherlands), the College of the Holy Cross, St. Lawrence University, the University of Calgary Institute for the Humanities, Miami University, Illinois State University, the Aristotelian Society (based in London, U.K.), and Cornell University, among others. I've also immensely valued the contributions of students and other faculty members at several seminars I've given on these themes at Cornell since 2020.

To my parents, to whom this book is dedicated, thank you again for letting me be—in every sense—and for your keen sensitivity, deep sense of social justice, and unfailing moral seriousness in raising me and my beloved sister, Lucy. To Daniel, my husband, my sine qua non: I could not imagine getting beyond the self-consciousness and self-scrutiny the world taught me were it not for your love and conspicuous lack of a scrutinizing gaze toward not only me but other people. And I could not imagine a better partner, friend, or now, co-parent to our darling daughter. Ultimately, I write in the hopes that she will come to inhabit a world in which she as well as everyone else can flourish and be safe, regardless of their gender, gender expression, race, ethnicity, class, age, neurotype, disabilities, sexuality, body type, or body size. A simple enough goal, which remains frighteningly elusive. We will keep fighting for it together, in community with countless others.

NOTES

INTRODUCTION: FIGHTING WEIGHT

1. The BMI, which stands for "body mass index," is defined as a person's weight in kilograms divided by the square of their height in meters. More on this methodologically flawed and racially problematic—and arguably downright racist—metric will follow in chapter 3.

2. Some important fat activists, and feminist or antiracist authors offering crucial insights about fatness, are J Aprileo, Jes Baker, Hanne Blank, Susan Bordo, Nicole Byer, Sophia Carter-Kahn, Ragen Chastain, Charlotte Cooper, Evette Dionne, Lisa Du Breuil, Amy Erdman Farrell, Laura Fraser, Jeannine A. Gailey, Roxane Gay, Linda Gerhardt, Aubrey Gordon, Brian Guffey, Sofie Hagen, Kate Harding, Da'Shaun L. Harrison, Lesley Kinzel, Marianne Kirby, Kiese Laymon, Kathleen LeBesco, Caleb Luna, Tressie McMillan Cottom, Marquisele Mercedes, Ash Nischuk, Susie Orbach, Cat Pausé, April Quioh, Shira Rosenbluth, Esther Rothblum, Ashleigh Shackleford, Jess Sims, Virginia Sole-Smith, Sondra Solovay, Hortense J. Spillers, Jessamyn Stanley, Sonya Renee Taylor, Virgie Tovar, Jordan Underwood, Leah Vernon, Marilyn Wann, Lindy West, and Rachel Wiley, among many others; this list is far from exhaustive.

3. For a different but related idea, see Da'Shaun L. Harrison on destroying the World and ushering in the Beyond—"a place in which we live without qualifiers, conditions, or labels meant to harm and subjugate our being"—in their brilliant recent book, *Belly of the Beast: The Politics of Anti-Fatness as Anti-Blackness* (Berkeley, Calif.: North Atlantic Books, 2021), 6, and see chaps. 1 and 7 more broadly.

4. Moreover, while many other forms of explicit bias decreased dramatically, explicit anti-fatness decreased only slowly over this time period. For a good lay overview of these findings and their likely meaning and explanation, see Carey

Goldberg, "Study: Bias Drops Dramatically for Sexual Orientation and Race—but Not Weight," WBUR, Jan. 11, 2019, www.wbur.org/news/2019/01/11/implicit-bias-gay-black-weight. For the study itself, see Tessa E. S. Charlesworth and Mahzarin R. Banaji, "Patterns of Implicit and Explicit Attitudes: I. Long-Term Change and Stability from 2007 to 2016," *Psychological Science* 30, no. 2 (2019): 174–92. Note that the researchers did not include gender bias in their analysis, because it was not included in the original Project Implicit website that they used as their data source.

5. See, for example, National Center for Health Statistics, "Obesity and Overweight," www.cdc.gov/nchs/fastats/obesity-overweight.htm.

6. The modest uptick in fatness in this country is real but has often been exaggerated, due partly to lowering standards for the classifications of being "overweight" and "obese" just before the turn of the millennium. The uptick itself likely has multiple complex explanations, such as food access, the built environment, health-care inequities (including with regard to mental health), stress (including that caused by oppression), the microbiome, and even the weight gain caused by perpetual dieting, as will be discussed at length later. See Aubrey Gordon, *"You Just Need to Lose Weight": And 19 Other Myths About Fat People* (Boston: Beacon Press, 2023), 106, for discussion.

7. Ash, "Beyond Superfat: Rethinking the Farthest End of the Fat Spectrum," *The Fat Lip* (blog), Dec. 20, 2016, thefatlip.com/2016/12/20/beyond-superfat-rethinking-the-farthest-end-of-the-fat-spectrum/.

8. Definitions of these terms vary within various fat activist communities and other spaces. But, according to one recent blog post by the writer and activist Linda Gerhardt, a "small fat" person may range from the upper end of "straight sizes" in some clothing brands up to a women's size 18. ("Think entry-level fat," as she puts it; Ash mentions size 12 as a reasonable, if small, entry point; ibid.) A "mid fat" person is, roughly, a size 18–24; a "large fat" is—again, roughly—a size 26–32; and an "infinifat" or "superfat" person (the latter being a term coined in 2008 at the NOLOSE conference) is typically a size 32 and upward. See Linda Gerhardt, "Fategories: Understanding the Fat Spectrum," *Fluffy Kitten Party* (blog), June 1, 2021, fluffykittenparty.com/2021/06/01/fategories-understanding-smallfat-fragility-the-fat-spectrum/. In her post, Gerhardt also notes the term "death fat," created by Lesley Kinzel, which can have an important reclaiming usage within fat communities. Finally, there is the concept of being "Lane Bryant fat"—which encompasses people who are fat but not too fat to buy clothes at this popular plus-size women's clothing store—coined by Roxane Gay in her book *Hunger: A Memoir of (My) Body* (New York: HarperCollins, 2017), 111. Admittedly, all of these categories are both femme-centric and United States focused, so

they are intended as a rough guideline and starting point in self definition, not a universal, definitive metric.

9. The food writer Julia Turshen recently wrote, in a moving essay, of her realization that in her life she had felt either happy or fat: "It hit me one day like a splash of cold water in the face. I had only ever felt two things in my life: happy or fat. . . . Not only had I equated 'fat' with 'anything other than happy,' I had set up a tidy, miserable binary for all of my feelings to fit into." Julia Turshen, "How Writing a Cookbook Helped Me Break Free from Diet Culture," *Bon Appétit,* March 2, 2021, www.bonappetit.com/story/simply-julia-diet-culture.

10. Note that the label "obese" comes from the Latin term for "having eaten oneself fat," *obesus,* which is frequently misleading. People get and stay fat for a large variety of reasons, or no reason whatsoever, as we will be seeing.

11. Notice that this definition encompasses aspects analogous to my definitions of both sexism and misogyny, since the term "fatphobia" has to do more work than this linguistic division of labor makes possible. See my book *Down Girl: The Logic of Misogyny* (New York: Oxford University Press, 2018), chaps. 1–3, as a point of comparison here. And note that for a comparable distinction in this arena we could similarly distinguish between "scientistic fatphobia" and "punitive fatphobia," say.

12. For two classic and groundbreaking pieces on intersectionality, see Kimberlé Crenshaw's "Mapping the Margins: Intersectionality, Identity Politics, and Violence Against Women of Color," *Stanford Law Review* 43, no. 6 (1991): 1241–99, and her "Beyond Race and Misogyny: Black Feminism and 2 Live Crew," in *Words That Wound,* ed. Mari J. Matsuda et al. (Boulder, Colo.: Westview Press, 1993), 111–32.

13. See Ragen Chastain, "Good Fatty Bad Fatty BS," *Dances with Fat* (blog), March 15, 2016, danceswithfat.org/2016/03/15/good-fatty-bad-fatty-bs/, for commentary on the notion of a "good fatty," originally theorized on Harding's *Shapely Prose* blog.

14. In this way, fatphobia differs from racism, in particular, since racial categorizations are usually fairly stable. And while some people's gender and class do change over their lifetimes, of course, a much higher proportion of people can expect to undergo significant weight fluctuations. See Alison Reiheld, "Microaggressions as a Disciplinary Technique for Actual and Possible Fat Bodies," in *Microaggressions and Philosophy,* ed. Lauren Freeman and Jeanine Weekes Schroer (New York: Routledge, 2020), 221.

15. Despite the subsequent danger of the label "fatphobia" being misleading, I think it remains suggestive, and usefully parallel to terms like "homophobia" and

"transphobia," and so adopt it for these reasons. Some people in this space understandably prefer terms like "anti-fatness," "fatmisia," "fat hate," "fat stigma," "fatism," and "sizeism," though, which I regard as loosely synonymous.

CHAPTER 1: THE STRAITJACKET OF FATPHOBIA

1. Jen Curran, "My Doctor Prescribed Me Weight Loss—I Actually Had Cancer," *Glamour,* Sept. 11, 2019, www.glamour.com/story/my-doctor-prescribed-me-weight-loss-i-actually-had-cancer.

2. Laura Fraser, "My Sister's Cancer Might Have Been Diagnosed Sooner—If Doctors Could Have Seen Beyond Her Weight," *Stat,* Aug. 15, 2017, www.statnews.com/2017/08/15/cancer-diagnosis-weight-doctors/.

3. Rebecca M. Puhl et al., "Weight-Based Victimization Toward Overweight Adolescents: Observations and Reactions of Peers," *Journal of School Health* 81 (2011): 698.

4. Rebecca M. Puhl and Kelly M. King, "Weight Discrimination and Bullying," *Best Practice and Research Clinical Endocrinology and Metabolism* 27, no. 2 (2013): 123.

5. Ibid., 119.

6. Sarah Nutter et al., "Weight Bias in Educational Settings: A Systematic Review," *Current Obesity Reports* 8 (2019): 194.

7. Rebecca M. Puhl and Joerg Luedicke, "Weight-Based Victimization Among Adolescents in the School Setting: Emotional Reactions and Coping Behaviors," *Journal of Youth and Adolescence* 41 (2012): 27–40.

8. Puhl and King, "Weight Discrimination and Bullying," 123.

9. See Virginia Sole-Smith's excellent recent book, *Fat Talk: Parenting in the Age of Diet Culture* (New York: Henry Holt, 2023), for more on this and related issues pertaining to the mistreatment of fat children.

10. E. L. Kenney et al., "The Academic Penalty for Gaining Weight: A Longitudinal, Change-in-Change Analysis of BMI and Perceived Academic Ability in Middle School Students," *International Journal of Obesity* 39 (2015): 1408–9.

11. Puhl and King, "Weight Discrimination and Bullying," 119.

12. Christian S. Crandall, "Do Parents Discriminate Against Their Heavyweight Daughters?," *Personality and Social Psychology Bulletin* 21, no. 7 (1995): 724–35. Note that the same pattern was found by this researcher in a smaller, earlier (1991) study.

13. Katrin Elisabeth Giel et al., "Weight Bias in Work Settings—a Qualitative Review," *Obesity Facts* 3, no. 1 (2010): 33–40.

14. Emma E. Levine and Maurice E. Schweitzer, "The Affective and Interpersonal Consequences of Obesity," *Organizational Behavior and Human Decision Processes* 127 (2015): 66–84.

15. Michelle R. Hebl and Laura M. Mannix, "The Weight of Obesity in Evaluating Others: A Mere Proximity Effect," *Personality and Social Psychology Bulletin* 29 (2003): 28–38. As the researchers' second experiment showed, male applicants seated next to the heavy (roughly, size 22) woman were more negatively judged even when she was depicted as a stranger to him rather than his girlfriend, and regardless of whether positive information was presented about her—for example, that she'd won a prestigious award on campus. (Unfortunately, they did not compare the results of seating prospective employees next to people of other genders.) They described the anti-fat bias thus revealed as a "profound" one.

16. See, for example, Giel et al., "Weight Bias in Work Settings"; Lynn K. Bartels and Cynthia R. Nordstrom, "Too Big to Hire: Factors Impacting Weight Discrimination," *Management Research Review* 36, no. 9 (2013): 868–81; and Stuart W. Flint et al., "Obesity Discrimination in the Recruitment Process: 'You're Not Hired!,'" *Frontiers in Psychology* 7, art. no. 647 (2016): 1–9.

17. Flint et al., "Obesity Discrimination in the Recruitment Process."

18. Note that the CVs were randomly allocated by one of the available gender/ weight combinations for each individual participant, so these results cannot be due to the non-obese man's CV having accidentally been more impressive; even if one CV *had* stood out, it was equally likely to have been attributed to the obese man, the obese woman, the non-obese man, and the non-obese woman, for any given participant. Ibid., 4.

19. The extra expense we have to go through as fat people, simply in order to clothe ourselves, is aptly termed a "fat tax." This is best understood as encompassing both the higher price some retailers charge for larger sizes and the fact that some brands don't stock our sizes at all, or carry them only online, meaning we often have to pay more in shipping and returns, among other sources of inequity and inconvenience. See user @marielle.elizabeth's Instagram reel, Oct. 3, 2022, www.instagram.com/reel/CjQonmJJo8T/?igshid=NmY1MzVkODY%3D.

20. See, for example, Josh Eidelson, "Yes, You Can Still Be Fired for Being Fat," New York State Senate, March 15, 2022, www.nysenate.gov/newsroom/in-the -news/brad-hoylman/yes-you-can-still-be-fired-being-fat; and Gordon, *"You Just Need to Lose Weight,"* 109–10, for discussion. Another common form of perfectly legal discrimination against fat people: charging them up to 30 percent more for

health insurance via their employer, due to their not qualifying for special "bonuses" because of their BMI or for not meeting certain weight-loss "goals" prescribed to them. See Aubrey Gordon and Michael Hobbes, "Workplace Wellness," Dec. 20, 2022, in *Maintenance Phase,* podcast, player.fm/series/maintenance -phase/workplace-wellness. The podcast is named for the magical, fictional forever during which people who lose weight are supposed to maintain their initial weight loss, following the diets and "wellness plans" the hosts expertly debunk, among many other topics covered. Thanks to my research assistant Emily Park for excellent discussion on this point and numerous others.

21. Giel et al., "Weight Bias in Work Settings," 35–36.

22. Ibid., 36.

23. Ibid.

24. Christian Brown and P. Wesley Routon, "On the Distributional and Evolutionary Nature of the Obesity Wage Penalty," *Economics and Human Biology* 28 (2018): 165.

25. Ibid.

26. Brown and Routon summarize their findings here thus: "The wage effects of obesity are more prevalent for members of the 1997 cohort [born from 1979 to 1985]. . . . The 5th [wage] percentile is associated with wage penalties of 2–7%, median wage effects of 4–8%, and 95th [wage] percentile effects of 13–27%." Ibid., 166.

27. Ibid., 170.

28. Moreover, in this study, very thin women earned $22,000 *more* annually than their "average" weight counterparts. See Lesley Kinzel, "New Study Finds That Weight Discrimination in the Workplace Is Just as Horrible and Depressing as Ever," *Time,* Nov. 28, 2014, time.com/3606031/weight-discrimination-workplace/. And for the original research, see Timothy A. Judge and Daniel M. Cable, "When It Comes to Pay, Do the Thin Win? The Effect of Weight on Pay for Men and Women," *Journal of Applied Psychology* 96, no. 1 (2011): 95–112. Note that these researchers were using the same data set as Brown and Routon used for their 1997 cohort.

29. Brown and Routon, "On the Distributional and Evolutionary Nature of the Obesity Wage Penalty," 170.

30. Emily Rella, "'Completely Absurd': The Average US Male Can't Fit into Universal Studio's New 'Blatantly Fatphobic' Mario Kart Ride," *Entrepreneur,* Feb. 6, 2023, www.entrepreneur.com/business-news/universal-studios-under-fire -for-fatphobic-mario-kart-ride/444427.

31. Rachel Moss, "Model Confronts Man for Fat-Shaming Her on Plane," *Huffington Post,* July 3, 2017, www.huffpost.com/archive/au/entry/plus-size-model-natalie-hage-perfectly-calls-out-man-who-fat-shamed-her-on-a-plane_a_23013599.

32. Gina Kolata, "Why Do Obese Patients Get Worse Care? Many Doctors Don't See Past the Fat," *New York Times,* Sept. 25, 2016, www.nytimes.com/2016/09/26/health/obese-patients-health-care.html.

33. See Gretchen's story, in Ragen Chastain, "The Fat Misdiagnosis Epidemic," *Glamour,* Aug. 29, 2019, www.glamour.com/story/weight-stigma-is-keeping-patients-from-getting-the-care-they-need.

34. See, for example, "Obese MRI Scans," Newcastle Clinic, newcastleclinic.co.uk/obese-mri-scans/, for some basic information about machines of different sizes, and their comparative rarity.

35. Laura Sharkey, "Yes, Plan B Has a Weight Limit—Here's What It Means for You," *Healthline,* Nov. 18, 2020, www.healthline.com/health/healthy-sex/plan-b-weight-limit#other-factors. Another option, it should be noted, is the insertion of a copper IUD within five days of sex. However, this is a much more invasive, expensive, and often painful procedure than emergency contraceptive medication, and is otherwise a lot less accessible than Plan B, Ella, or other drug combinations sometimes used off-label for this purpose. It's also one of the forms of contraception currently under attack in America, despite strong recent evidence that it prevents fertilization, not implantation, and is hence not an abortifacient. See "Study: Copper IUDs Do Not Appear to Prevent Implantation or Increase HIV Risk," Relias Media, July 1, 2020, www.reliasmedia.com/articles/146320-study-copper-iuds-do-not-appear-to-prevent-implantation-or-increase-hiv-risk.

36. I discuss the connections between these attacks on reproductive rights and misogyny in both *Down Girl,* chap. 3, and *Entitled: How Male Privilege Hurts Women* (New York: Crown, 2020), chap. 6.

37. See, for example, Mikaela Conley, "Some Ob-Gyns Say Obese Patients Too High-Risk," ABC News, May 17, 2011, abcnews.go.com/Health/poll-finds-florida-ob-gyns-turn-obese-patients/story?id=13622579, for reports of weight limits of 250 pounds being implemented by several ob-gyns in Florida in 2011. For a more recent case of a hospital in Canada that imposed a BMI limit of 40 for pregnant patients—while being prepared to handle other "high risk" deliveries—see Moira Wyton, "Mom Files Rights Complaint Alleging Hospital 'Fat Shaming,' " *Tyee,* July 13, 2022, thetyee.ca/News/2022/07/13/Mom-Files-Rights-Complaint-Hospital-Fat-Shaming/. For yet more evidence of this and related forms of mistreatment, see Raina Delisle, "We Need to Stop Discriminating Against Plus-Size Pregnant Women," *Today's Parent,* Nov. 7, 2017, www.todays

parent.com/pregnancy/pregnancy-health/we-need-to-stop-discriminating-against
-plus-size-pregnant-women/. In 2019, the American College of Obstetricians
and Gynecologists issued a statement decrying the practice of turning away pregnant patients on the basis of their body mass.

38. S. M. Phelan et al., "Impact of Weight Bias and Stigma on Quality of Care and
Outcomes for Patients with Obesity," *Obesity Review* 16, no. 4 (2015): 321.

39. Kimberly A. Gudzune et al., "Physicians Build Less Rapport with Obese Patients," *Obesity* 21, no. 10 (2013): 2146–52.

40. Specifically, 24 percent of nurses felt repulsed by, and 12 percent did not want
to touch, fat patients. C. R. Bagley et al., "Attitudes of Nurses Toward Obesity
and Obese Patients," *Perceptual and Motor Skills* 68, no. 3 (1989): 954. And
while this is admittedly an older study, we saw evidence in the introduction that
anti-fat bias has improved little over the past few decades; it is actually getting
worse, by some measures.

41. Phelan et al., "Impact of Weight Bias and Stigma on Quality of Care and
Outcomes for Patients with Obesity," 321.

42. M. R. Hebl and J. Xu, "Weighing the Care: Physicians' Reactions to the Size
of a Patient," *International Journal of Obesity* 25 (2001): 1250.

43. The only item where no statistically significant difference was found in this
study was the physician's rating of the "seriousness of the patient's health problem." Ibid., 1249.

44. Ibid., 1250.

45. See Phelan et al., "Impact of Weight Bias and Stigma on Quality of Care and
Outcomes for Patients with Obesity"; and A. Janet Tomiyama et al., "How and
Why Weight Stigma Drives the Obesity 'Epidemic' and Harms Health," *BMC
Medicine* 16, art. no. 123 (2018).

46. Phelan et al., "Impact of Weight Bias and Stigma on Quality of Care and
Outcomes for Patients with Obesity," 321.

47. "Fat Shaming in the Doctor's Office Can Be Mentally and Physically Harmful," American Psychological Association, Aug. 3, 2017, www.apa.org/news/
press/releases/2017/08/fat-shaming.

48. Jess Sims, "Medicine Has a Problem with Fat Phobia—and It Stops People
from Getting the Care They Deserve," *Well and Good,* Nov. 13, 2020, www
.wellandgood.com/fat-shaming-medicine/.

49. Allison Shelley, "Women's Heart Health Hindered by Social Stigma About
Weight," *Medscape,* April 3, 2016, www.medscape.com/viewarticle/861382.

50. Christine Aramburu Alegria Drury and Margaret Louis, "Exploring the Association Between Body Weight, Stigma of Obesity, and Health Care Avoidance," *Journal of the American Academy of Nurse Practitioners* 14, no. 12 (Dec. 2002).

51. Janell L. Mensinger et al., "Mechanisms Underlying Weight Status and Healthcare Avoidance in Women: A Study of Weight Stigma, Body-Related Shame and Guilt, and Healthcare Stress," *Body Image* 25 (2018): 139–47.

52. Sarah Wells, "Fatphobia and Medical Biases Follow People After Death," *Pop Sci,* Aug. 18, 2022, www.popsci.com/health/medical-fatphobia-body-donations/. Among the reasons cited for not wanting to deal with fat bodies donated to science include the very fact that they are heavier, and therefore require more labor to transport and handle—hardly an insurmountable problem—together with the alarming idea that they are not suitable for first-year medical students to learn about the human body by examining and dissecting. "In a perfect world, they'd like to have a perfect body with perfect anatomy" for these purposes, offered Ronn Wade, director of the Anatomical Services Division of the University of Maryland School of Medicine. This of course raises the question: What, pray tell, is "perfect," and why are medical students only being trained to understand "perfect" bodies? Moreover, for fat people prevented from donating their bodies posthumously, "it's another kind of stigma" and can be "devastating," Wade acknowledged. JoNel Aleccia, "Donating Your Body to Science? Nobody Wants a Chubby Corpse," NBC News, Jan. 9, 2012, www.nbcnews.com/healthmain/donating-your-body-science-nobody-wants-chubby-corpse-1c6436539.

53. This and all subsequent references in the next three paragraphs are to Jackson King, "Fat Trans People Are Having Their Lives Put on Hold Because of Devastating Medical Fatphobia," *Pink News,* Nov. 19, 2021, www.pinknews.co.uk/2021/11/19/fat-trans-medical-fatphobia/, unless otherwise stated.

54. Tyler G. Martinson et al., "High Body Mass Index Is a Significant Barrier to Gender-Confirmation Surgery for Transgender and Gender-Nonbinary Individuals," *Endocrinology Practice* 26, no. 1 (2020): 7. Note that I use the terminology now preferred in the trans community, "gender-affirming surgery," throughout these pages.

55. See Jody L. Herman et al., "Suicide Thoughts and Attempts Among Transgender Adults," Williams Institute, UCLA School of Law, Sept. 2019, williamsinstitute.law.ucla.edu/publications/suicidality-transgender-adults/.

56. Martinson et al., "High Body Mass Index Is a Significant Barrier to Gender-Confirmation Surgery," 6–15.

57. Ibid., 12.

58. Ibid., 13.

59. Moreover, gatekeeping heavier people from getting vital surgeries—including back and knee operations—is a widespread practice, for both cis and trans people. See Kevin Rawlinson and Chris Johnston, "Decision to Deny Surgery to Obese Patients Is Like 'Racial Discrimination,'" *Guardian,* Sept. 3, 2016, www.the guardian.com/society/2016/sep/03/hospitals-to-cut-costs-by-denying-surgery-to-smokers-and-the-obese.

60. See, for example, Virginia Sole-Smith, "When You're Told You're Too Fat to Get Pregnant," *New York Times Magazine,* June 18, 2019, www.nytimes.com/2019/06/18/magazine/fertility-weight-obesity-ivf.html, for discussion.

61. See, for example, Emily Friedman, "Obese Face Obstacles in Adoption Process," ABC News, July 31, 2007, abcnews.go.com/Health/story?id=3429655&page=1. For a more recent account of such obstacles in the U.K., see Anonymous, "We Were Turned Down for Adoption for Being Obese," *Metro,* Oct. 23, 2021, metro.co.uk/2021/10/23/we-were-turned-down-for-adoption-for-being-overweight-2-15462005/. I'll come back to fatphobia in relation to parental rights in this book's conclusion.

62. Denette Wilford, "'Fatphobic' Shelter Worker Refused to Let 'Morbidly Obese' Woman Adopt Dog," *Toronto Sun,* July 26, 2022, torontosun.com/health/diet-fitness/fatphobic-shelter-worker-refused-to-let-morbidly-obese-woman-adopt-dog.

63. Devanshi Patel et al., "Parents of Children with High Weight Are Viewed as Responsible for Child Weight and Thus Stigmatized," *Psychological Science* 34, no. 1 (2023): 35–46.

64. G. M. Eller, "On Fat Oppression," *Kennedy Institute of Ethics Journal* 24, no. 3 (2014): 231–32.

65. Puhl and King, "Weight Discrimination and Bullying," 118.

66. Harrison, *Belly of the Beast,* 15. Note that Harrison capitalizes "Ugliness" to recognize its reality as a political structure (12). And see also the large literature on the biasing effects of physical attractiveness—often called the "halo effect"—for cases of positive discrimination in favor of the conventionally good-looking. See Sean N. Talamas et al., "Blinded by Beauty: Attractiveness Bias and Accurate Perceptions of Academic Performance," *PLOS ONE* 11, no. 2 (2016): e0148284, for one representative treatment of the influence of someone's perceived attractiveness on judgments about their academic performance.

CHAPTER 2: SHRINKING SHOTS

1. Katherine M. Flegal et al., "Excess Deaths Associated with Underweight, Overweight, and Obesity," *Journal of the American Medical Association* 293, no. 15 (2005): 1861–67. Note that Flegal et al. were considering "all-cause mortality" here, which is exactly what it sounds like—death from all causes—as opposed to death due to a particular disease or other reason.

2. In their landmark article (ibid.), Flegal et al. actually found more excess deaths for people in the "underweight" category (nearly thirty-four thousand) than in the "overweight" and "obese" categories combined, even though the former category accounted for less than 3 percent of the population studied, whereas the latter categories made up more than half of it. See also, for example, Alan Mozes, "Underweight Even Deadlier Than Overweight, Study Says: Death Risk Nearly Doubled for Excessively Thin People," *HealthDay News*, March 28, 2014, consumer.healthday.com/senior-citizen-information-31/misc-death-and-dying-news-172/underweight-even-deadlier-than-overweight-study-says-686240.html, for a brief overview of subsequent research by Sissi Cao et al., "J-Shapedness: An Often Missed, Often Miscalculated Relation: The Example of Weight and Mortality," *Journal of Epidemiology and Community Health* 68, no. 7 (2014): 683–90, on this topic.

3. Katherine M. Flegal et al., "Association of All-Cause Mortality with Overweight and Obesity Using Standard Body Mass Index Categories: A Systematic Review and Meta-analysis," *Journal of the American Medical Association* 309, no. 1 (2013): 71–82. Note that this meta-analysis canvassed ninety-seven separate studies and almost three million participants, providing strong further evidence for Flegal's 2005 research.

4. Ali H. Mokdad et al., "Actual Causes of Death in the United States, 2000," *Journal of the American Medical Association* 291, no. 10 (2004): 1238–45.

5. For Saguy's comparison of the above study by Mokdad et al. (which she terms the "eating-to-death" study) and Flegal's (which she terms the "fat-OK" study), see Abigail C. Saguy, *What's Wrong with Fat?* (Oxford: Oxford University Press, 2013), 120.

6. See Aubrey Gordon and Michael Hobbes, "Is Being Fat Bad for You?," Nov. 16, 2021, in *Maintenance Phase*, podcast, 25:30–27:30, player.fm/series/maintenance-phase/is-being-fat-bad-for-you.

7. Saguy, *What's Wrong with Fat?*, 120–21.

8. Ibid., 123–26.

9. Moreover, people in the "overweight" and "mildly obese" categories combined were found to have virtually the same risk profile for COVID-19 as people in the so-called normal-weight category in the same major study. See Paul Campos, "COVID and the Moral Panic over Obesity," *Lawyers, Guns, and Money,* Sept. 16, 2021, www.lawyersgunsmoneyblog.com/2021/09/covid-and-the-moral-panic -over-obesity.

10. Rosie Mestel, "Weighty Death Toll Downplayed," *Los Angeles Times,* April 20, 2005, www.latimes.com/archives/la-xpm-2005-apr-20-sci-overweight20-story .html.

11. Amy Crawford, "The Obesity Research That Blew Up," *Boston Globe,* July 16, 2021, www.bostonglobe.com/2021/07/16/opinion/obesity-research-that-blew -up/. Willett and others' main substantive criticism of Flegal's research was that she failed to exclude everyone who had ever smoked and all people with a preexisting illness in calculating the mortality risks associated with being in the underweight category. But, setting aside real questions about whether this would in fact be appropriate, she and her collaborators later showed that running the numbers in this way made very little difference. Katherine M. Flegal et al., "Impact of Smoking and Pre-existing Illness on Estimates of the Fractions of Deaths Associated with Underweight, Overweight, and Obesity in the US Population," *American Journal of Epidemiology* 166, no. 8 (2007): 975–82.

12. Allison Aubrey, "Research: A Little Extra Fat May Help You Live Longer," NPR, Jan. 2, 2013, www.npr.org/sections/health-shots/2013/01/02/168437030/ research-a-little-extra-fat-may-help-you-live-longer. And for Flegal's meta-analysis itself, see Flegal et al., "Association of All-Cause Mortality with Overweight and Obesity."

13. For a good introduction to the debate between Willett and Flegal, see Crawford, "The Obesity Research That Blew Up." For a more in-depth discussion, see Gordon and Hobbes, "Is Being Fat Bad for You?"

14. For a recent, representative article on this topic, see Glenn A. Gaesser and Steven N. Blair, "The Health Risks of Obesity Have Been Exaggerated," *Medicine and Science in Sports and Exercise* 51, no. 1 (2019): 218–21. The researchers base their titular conclusion on the following four points: "1) a moderate-to-high level of cardiorespiratory fitness (CRF) attenuates, or eliminates, mortality risk associated with high body mass index (BMI); 2) a metabolically healthy obese (MHO) phenotype diminishes risk associated with high BMI; 3) removal of body fat does not improve cardiometabolic health; and 4) data on intentional weight loss and mortality do not support the conventional wisdom that high BMI itself is the primary cause of obesity-related health conditions" (218). More on these points will follow in this chapter.

15. Flegal et al., "Excess Deaths Associated with Underweight, Overweight and Obesity."

16. Note that in this chapter I'm bracketing difficult theoretical questions about what health *is,* exactly, as well as how it is valuable (for example, whether it is intrinsically or merely instrumentally important to our well-being). For important perspectives on these issues, see Elizabeth Barnes, *Health Problems* (Oxford: Oxford University Press, 2023); Quill Kukla (writing as Rebecca Kukla), "Medicalization, 'Normal Function,' and the Definition of Health," in *The Routledge Companion to Bioethics,* ed. John D. Arras, Elizabeth Fenton, and Kukla (New York: Routledge, 2014), 515–30; and Jennifer A. Lee and Cat J. Pausé, "Stigma in Practice: Barriers to Health for Fat Women," *Frontiers in Psychology* 7, art. no. 2063 (2016): 1–15, a work of collaborative autoethnography, among many other relevant pieces of scholarship.

17. The quotations here and below are taken from Stuart Wolpert, "Dieting Does Not Work, UCLA Researchers Report," UCLA Newsroom, April 3, 2007, newsroom.ucla.edu/releases/Dieting-Does-Not-Work-UCLA-Researchers-7832. For the original study, see Traci Mann et al., "Medicare's Search for Effective Obesity Treatments: Diets Are Not the Answer," *American Psychologist* 62, no. 3 (2007): 220–33.

18. One study actually showed that of the people who were followed for at least two years, 83 percent gained back more weight than they lost (Mann et al., "Medicare's Search for Effective Obesity Treatments," 221). Another showed that half of the dieters weighed over eleven pounds more than their starting weight five years after the diet (ibid., 224). And the true numbers may be even worse, Mann argued, since some of these studies relied on self-report measures, where people tend to underestimate or underreport their weight, and people who do regain weight tend to drop out disproportionately and are hence unavailable for follow-ups. "Although the findings reported give a bleak picture of the effectiveness of diets, there are reasons why the actual effectiveness of diets is even worse," Mann summarized. Wolpert, "Dieting Does Not Work."

19. The oft-cited statistic that around 95 percent of diets fail seems to derive from a considerably older study, published in 1959, which nevertheless remains relevant today. The researchers followed one hundred patients treated at the nutrition clinic of a New York hospital who were instructed to follow a low-calorie diet (between eight hundred and fifteen hundred calories daily). Of these, only twelve lost twenty pounds or more and were classified as an initial "success." One year later, just six of these patients had maintained this loss; two years later, only two had. The remaining cases were classified as "failures" (along with a considerable number of people who dropped out of the study). Only one person studied lost

more than forty pounds: fifty-one pounds, to be exact. He reported that dieting contributed to a severe mental health crisis—and ceasing to diet before seeking treatment led to his thirty-five-pound weight regain. A. Stunkard and M. McLaren-Hume, "The Results of Treatment for Obesity: A Review of the Literature and Report of a Series," *AMA Archives of Internal Medicine* 103, no. 1 (1959): 79–85; and see Ragen Chastain, "The Validation and Frustration of Stunkard et al.," *Weight and Healthcare,* Substack, Feb. 11, 2023, weightandhealthcare.substack .com/p/the-validation-and-frustration-of, for discussion.

Another notable study, published in 1989, showed that less than 3 percent of subjects met the demanding standard of being at or below their post-treatment weight on all follow-up visits for the next four to five years, following their enrollment in a fifteen-week behavioral weight-loss program. F. M. Kramer et al., "Long-Term Follow-Up of Behavioral Treatment for Obesity: Patterns of Weight Regain Among Men and Women," *International Journal of Obesity* 13, no. 2 (1989): 123–36.

Also telling is the fact that, according to a 2015 study which followed people for nearly a decade, the chances of a person classified as "obese" *ever* achieving a so-called normal weight are vanishingly small. For a woman like me, for example, who was once classified as "severely" or "morbidly obese" (with a BMI of more than 40), the annual probability of attaining a "normal weight" is 1 in 677 (around 0.15 percent). For men in the same position, the odds are even worse: 1 in 1,290 (around 0.078 percent). Alison Fildes et al., "Probability of an Obese Person Attaining Normal Body Weight: Cohort Study Using Electronic Health Records," *American Journal of Public Health* 105, no. 9 (2015): e54–e59.

20. J. P. Montani et al., "Weight Cycling During Growth and Beyond as a Risk Factor for Later Cardiovascular Diseases: The 'Repeated Overshoot' Theory," *International Journal of Obesity* 30 (2006): S58–S66. See also Kelley Strohacker et al., "Consequences of Weight Cycling: An Increase in Disease Risk?," *International Journal of Exercise Science* 2, no. 3 (2009): 191–201, for further discussion.

21. Matthew A. Cottam et al., "Links Between Immunologic Memory and Metabolic Cycling," *Journal of Immunology* 200, no. 11 (2018): 3681–89.

22. See "Weight Fluctuations and Impact on the Immune System," *US Pharmacist,* Aug. 10, 2022, www.uspharmacist.com/article/weight-fluctuations-and -impact-on-the-immune-system, for a good lay overview. For the original research, see Matthew A. Cottam et al., "Multiomics Reveals Persistence of Obesity-Associated Immune Cell Phenotypes in Adipose Tissue During Weight Loss and Weight Regain in Mice," *Nature Communications* 13, art. no. 2950 (2022).

23. Huajie Zou et al., "Association Between Weight Cycling and Risk of Developing Diabetes in Adults. A Systematic Review and Meta-analysis," *Journal of Diabetes Investigation* 12, no. 4 (2021): 625–32.

24. Wolpert, "Dieting Does Not Work."

25. Moreover, as the fat activist and researcher Ragen Chastain notes, "there is literally NO study that compares formerly fat people who have maintained weight loss to people who were always thin to see if they have similar health outcomes. The study has never been done—partly because there aren't enough fat people who have maintained weight loss." Ragen Chastain, "Is There a Connection Between Fat and Cancer?," *Dances with Fat* (blog), May 10, 2018, danceswith fat.org/2018/05/10/is-there-a-connection-between-fat-and-cancer/. Chastain's point remains true, to the best of my knowledge, at the time of writing, in late 2022.

26. Long Ge et al., "Comparison of Dietary Macronutrient Patterns of 14 Popular Named Dietary Programmes for Weight and Cardiovascular Risk Factor Reduction in Adults: Systematic Review and Network Meta-analysis of Randomised Trials," *British Medical Journal* 369 (2020): m696.

27. For a good popular overview of the current research consensus on the lack of efficacy of exercise for weight loss, see Julia Belluz and Christophe Haubursin, "The Science Is In: Exercise Won't Help You Lose Much Weight," *Vox,* Jan. 2, 2019, www.vox.com/2018/1/3/16845438/exercise-weight-loss-myth-burn-calories. And for one important meta-analysis on this topic, see D. M. Thomas et al., "Why Do Individuals Not Lose More Weight from an Exercise Intervention at a Defined Dose? An Energy Balance Analysis," *Obesity Review* 13, no. 10 (2012): 835–47.

28. A. Janet Tomiyama et al., "Long-Term Effects of Dieting: Is Weight Loss Related to Health?," *Social and Personality Psychology Compass* 7, no. 12 (2013): 861–77.

29. "Why Do Dieters Regain Weight? Calorie Deprivation Alters Body and Mind, Overwhelming Willpower," *American Psychological Association Science Brief,* May 2018, https://web.archive.org/web/20230226080722/www.apa.org/science/about/psa/2018/05/calorie-deprivation.

30. Ibid. Note that what I am calling "willpower" here and throughout the book, in line with these researchers, might also be termed "resolve" or "persistence": it's the sort of thing that enables us to follow through on our New Year's resolutions and other intentions when the going gets tough. Most philosophers believe that the question of how much people possess this quality (which may vary depending on the circumstances) is independent of venerable metaphysical debates about the existence of free will. The latter debates concern whether human actions—be they undertaken with resolve or no—are determined purely by preexisting causal fac-

tors (and whether this is in turn compatible with free will's existence). Whatever one thinks about the deep philosophical questions—still very much an area of hot controversy in my discipline—we can agree that people exhibit willpower (or, again, resolve or persistence) to varying degrees, and that this has little bearing on their body mass.

31. Ibid.

32. Conversely, people who are healthy but "underweight" have been shown *not* to be more active—as many researchers assumed—but rather to "run hotter," in the sense of having a higher resting metabolic rate than heavier people, due to higher thyroid hormone levels. In fact, they both were 23 percent *less* active than so-called normal-weight people, on average, and appeared to get less hungry— consuming 12 percent fewer calories, again on average, even though the study excluded anyone who had eating problems or who purposefully restricted their eating. (Ill subjects and those who had recently lost weight were also excluded from the study.) See Aakash Molpariya, "Surprise! Thin People Aren't More Active, They Are Just Less Hungry and 'Run Hotter,'" *Revyuh,* July 14, 2022, www .revyuh.com/news/lifestyle/health-and-fitness/surprise-thin-people-arent-more -active-they-are-just-less-hungry-and-run-hotter, for a helpful lay overview of this research.

33. Kathryn Doyle, "6 Years After *The Biggest Loser,* Metabolism Is Slower and Weight Is Back Up," *Scientific American,* May 11, 2016, www.scientificamerican .com/article/6-years-after-the-biggest-loser-metabolism-is-slower-and-weight-is -back-up/.

34. See, for example, "Type 2 Diabetes," Mayo Clinic, www.mayoclinic.org/ diseases-conditions/type-2-diabetes/symptoms-causes/syc-20351193.

35. Honor Whiteman, "Could Mouthwash Be Putting You at Risk of Diabetes?" *Medical News Today,* Nov. 28, 2017, www.medicalnewstoday.com/articles/320199, for a good lay overview. For the original research, see Kaumudi J. Joshipura et al., "Over-the-Counter Mouthwash Use and Risk of Pre-diabetes/Diabetes," *Nitric Oxide* 71 (2017): 14–20. And for a subsequent review article on this finding, see P. M. Preshaw, "Mouthwash Use and Risk of Diabetes," *British Dental Journal* 225, no. 10 (2018): 923–26.

36. Some people working in this space hold "prediabetes" to be something of a misnomer since, as the anti-diet psychologist Alexis Conason notes, less than 2 percent of people with so-called prediabetes go on to develop diabetes annually. See her *Diet-Free Revolution: 10 Steps to Free Yourself from the Diet Cycle with Mindful Eating and Radical Self-Acceptance* (Berkeley, Calif.: North Atlantic Books, 2021), 134.

37. See, for example, P. Mirmiran et al., "Long-Term Effects of Coffee and Caffeine Intake on the Risk of Pre-diabetes and Type 2 Diabetes: Findings from a Population with Low Coffee Consumption," *Nutrition, Metabolism, and Cardiovascular Diseases* 28, no. 12 (2018): 1261–66. Of course, just because a finding is statistically significant—meaning that there's a high chance that it is non-accidental—doesn't mean that the relevant risk is necessarily a *large* one. In this case, subsequent research found that an increase in daily coffee consumption of more than one cup was associated with an 11 percent lower risk of developing type 2 diabetes (compared with people who did not change their coffee drinking habits). Conversely, a decrease in daily coffee consumption of more than one cup was associated with a 17 percent higher risk of developing type 2 diabetes. See Hubert Kolb et al., "Coffee and Lower Risk of Type 2 Diabetes: Arguments for a Causal Relationship," *Nutrients* 13, no. 4 (2021), art. no. 1144, for an argument that coffee drinking plays a causal role in reducing the risk of type 2 diabetes. But it remains just that: an argument. Researchers' knowledge of the many causal risk factors that contribute to the onset and progression of this illness remains very much in a state of evolution, and will for the foreseeable future.

38. See, for example, Massiell German and Juliana Simonetti, "Diabetes and Obesity—Inextricable Diseases," *Metabolic Disorders* 7, art. no. 036 (2020).

39. See, for example, Natasha Wiebe et al., "Temporal Associations Among Body Mass Index, Fasting Insulin, and Systemic Inflammation: A Systematic Review and Meta-analysis," *JAMA Network Open* 4, no. 3 (2021). For a good lay overview of the findings of this comprehensive meta-analysis, see Bret Scher, "High Insulin Precedes Obesity, a New Study Suggests," Diet Doctor, March 16, 2021, www .dietdoctor.com/high-insulin-precedes-obesity-a-new-study-suggests. And for an earlier discussion of this hypothesis, see Peter Attia's TED Talk, "Is the Obesity Crisis Hiding a Bigger Problem?," TED Media, 2013, www.ted.com/talks/ peter_attia_is_the_obesity_crisis_hiding_a_bigger_problem/transcript.

40. See, for example, Jennifer L. Shea et al., "The Prevalence of Metabolically Healthy Obese Subjects Defined by BMI and Dual-Energy X-Ray Absorptiometry," *Obesity* 19, no. 3 (2011): 624–30. Their research suggested that when going by sophisticated techniques for measuring body fat percentage, about half of the participants classified as "obese" were metabolically healthy.

41. Look AHEAD Research Group, "Eight-Year Weight Losses with an Intensive Lifestyle Intervention: The Look AHEAD Study," *Obesity* 22, no. 1 (2014): 5–13.

42. The numbers were 50.3 percent (ILI) versus 35.7 percent (DSE) for 5+ percent weight loss, and 26.9 percent (ILI) versus 17.2 percent (DSE) for 10+ percent weight loss. The researchers did note, however, that "the lifestyle intervention's strengths are offset by findings that 32% of ILI participants did *not* lose at least 5%

of initial weight in the first year, and only 34.5% of these individuals achieved this goal at year 8." Ibid., 8, my italics.

43. The study showed fairly disappointing results with respect to long-term glucose control too, with initial improvements for ILI participants followed by worsening results every year, returning to and then exceeding their baseline level after around eight years, on average. (Although their levels remained slightly better than for DSE participants.) See Look AHEAD Research Group, "Cardiovascular Effects of Intensive Lifestyle Intervention in Type 2 Diabetes," *New England Journal of Medicine* 369, no. 2 (2013): 149, fig. 1D. Other studies have shown similar trends. One meta-analysis showed that most people with type 2 diabetes who tried to lose weight returned to their starting levels of glucose control within six to nineteen months, even in the rare cases where they maintained their initial weight loss. See D. Ciliska et al., "A Review of Weight Loss Interventions for Obese People with Non-insulin Dependent Diabetes Mellitus," *Canadian Journal of Diabetes Care* 19 (1995): 10–15.

44. Look AHEAD Research Group, "Cardiovascular Effects of Intensive Lifestyle Intervention in Type 2 Diabetes," 152.

45. According to the CDC, a person with diabetes is twice as likely to have heart disease or a stroke as someone who doesn't suffer from this illness. See "Diabetes and Your Heart," Centers for Disease Control, www.cdc.gov/diabetes/library/features/diabetes-and-heart.html. My thanks to Susan R. Hata, M.D., for extremely helpful comments on this point and numerous others.

46. Rasmus Køster-Rasmussen et al., "Intentional Weight Loss and Longevity in Overweight Patients with Type 2 Diabetes: A Population-Based Cohort Study," *PLOS ONE* 11, no. 1 (2016): e0146889.

47. Note that this study also monitored microvascular disease, including neuropathy, "diabetic foot," eye, and kidney complications. For patients with an intention to lose weight, 49 percent had one or more of these issues at diagnosis, which increased to 58 percent at the six-year mark; for patients *without* an intention to lose weight, 60 percent had one or more of these issues at diagnosis, which increased to 63 percent at the six-year mark. Ibid., 8. Note that no statistical analysis of these differences was included in the paper.

48. See the National Weight Control Registry, www.nwcr.ws, for this anecdata of an estimated ten thousand "success stories" of people who lose more than thirty pounds and keep it off for at least a year. As Ragen Chastain points out, though, most dieters regain the weight within *five* years of their initial weight loss. So the bar for a success story here is troubling. Overall, it's not clear what the NWCR proves, then, despite its being commonly cited in discussions about the long-term

feasibility of weight loss. See her post, "National Weight Control Registry—Skydiving Without a Chute," *Dances with Fat* (blog), Dec. 27, 2012, danceswithfat.org/2012/12/27/national-weight-control-registry-skydiving-without-a-chute/.

49. N. G. Boulé et al., "Effects of Exercise on Glycemic Control and Body Mass in Type 2 Diabetes Mellitus: A Meta-analysis of Controlled Clinical Trials," *JAMA* 286, no. 10 (2001): 1218–27.

50. Vaughn W. Barry et al., "Fitness vs. Fatness on All-Cause Mortality: A Meta-analysis," *Progressive Cardiovascular Disease* 56, no. 4 (2014): 382–90.

51. Chantal M. Koolhaas et al., "Impact of Physical Activity on the Association of Overweight and Obesity with Cardiovascular Disease: The Rotterdam Study," *European Journal of Preventative Cardiology* 24, no. 9 (2017): 934–41.

52. Xiaochen Zhang et al., "Physical Activity and Risk of Cardiovascular Disease by Weight Status Among US Adults," *PLOS ONE* 15, no. 5 (2020): e0232893.

53. See Christy Harrison, *Anti-diet: Reclaim Your Time, Money, Well-Being, and Happiness Through Intuitive Eating* (New York: Little, Brown Spark, 2019), 102.

54. Thanks to Elizabeth Barnes for crucial discussion on this point and others.

55. Wiebe et al., "Temporal Associations Among Body Mass Index, Fasting Insulin, and Systemic Inflammation." In a further recent study, Wiebe and her coauthors hypothesize that both hyperinsulinemia—an excess of insulin in the blood, often caused by insulin resistance—and inflammation may be the chief culprits for the increased all-cause mortality of heavier people. These conditions are more common in heavier people, but they likely aren't caused by a higher body weight (rather, increased insulin may drive weight gain). There are also a significant number of thin people who suffer from hyperinsulinemia and inflammation who face even greater health risks when they do so. The researchers argued on this basis that "the increase in mortality that has been attributed to obesity is more likely due to hyperinsulinemia and inflammation." Natasha Wiebe et al., "Associations of Body Mass Index, Fasting Insulin, and Inflammation with Mortality: A Prospective Cohort Study," *International Journal of Obesity* 46 (2022): 2107–13. My thanks to Gregory Dodell, M.D., for extremely helpful discussion of this paragraph and the research summarized in this chapter generally.

56. Admittedly, these findings were drawn from a small study of fifteen patients, seven with type 2 diabetes, each of whom had twenty pounds of fat removed via liposuction. Samuel Klein et al., "Effect of Liposuction on Insulin Action and Risk Factors for Coronary Heart Disease," *New England Journal of Medicine* 350, no. 25 (2004): 2549–57.

57. Francesco Rubino et al., "The Early Effect of the Roux-en-Y Gastric Bypass on Hormones Involved in Body Weight Regulation and Glucose Metabolism," *Annals of Surgery* 240, no. 2 (2004): 236–42.

58. Ildiko Lingvay et al., "Rapid Improvement in Diabetes After Gastric Bypass Surgery: Is It the Diet or Surgery?," *Diabetes Care* 36, no. 9 (2013): 2741–47.

59. Rebecca L. Pearl et al., "Association Between Weight Bias Internalization and Metabolic Syndrome Among Treatment-Seeking Individuals with Obesity," *Obesity* 25, no. 2 (2017): 317–22.

60. "Fat Shaming Linked to Greater Health Risks," *Penn Medicine News*, Jan. 26, 2017, www.pennmedicine.org/news/news-releases/2017/january/fat-shaming-linked-to-greater-health-risks.

61. Virginia Sole-Smith, "In Obesity Research, Fatphobia Is Always the X Factor," *Scientific American*, March 6, 2021, www.scientificamerican.com/article/in-obesity-research-fatphobia-is-always-the-x-factor/.

62. See N. M. Maruthur et al., "The Association of Obesity and Cervical Cancer Screening: A Systematic Review and Meta-analysis," *Obesity* 17, no. 2 (2009): 375–81; Christina C. Wee et al., "Obesity and Breast Cancer Screening," *Journal of General Internal Medicine* 19, no. 4 (2004): 324–31; and Jeanne M. Ferrante et al., "Colorectal Cancer Screening Among Obese Versus Non-obese Patients in Primary Care Practices," *Cancer Detection and Prevention* 30, no. 5 (2006): 459–65.

63. See, for example, "Obesity and Cancer," National Cancer Institute, www.cancer.gov/about-cancer/causes-prevention/risk/obesity/obesity-fact-sheet.

64. Moreover, when it comes to cervical cancer, one study found that even in patients who *did* receive a state-of-the-art screening, "overweight and obese women had an increased risk of cervical cancer, likely because of under-diagnosis of cervical pre-cancer. Improvements in equipment and/or technique to assure adequate sampling and visualization of women with elevated body mass might reduce cervical cancer incidence." Megan A. Clarke et al., "Epidemiologic Evidence That Excess Body Weight Increases Risk of Cervical Cancer by Decreased Detection of Precancer," *Journal of Clinical Oncology* 36, no. 12 (2018): 1184–91.

65. For a good lay introduction to the so-called obesity paradox, see Harriet Brown, "The Obesity Paradox: Scientists Now Think That Being Overweight Can Protect Your Health," *Quartz*, Nov. 17, 2015 (updated Sept. 23, 2019), qz.com/550527/obesity-paradox-scientists-now-think-that-being-overweight-is-sometimes-good-for-your-health/. See also Katherine M. Flegal and John P. A. Ioannidis, "The Obesity Paradox: A Misleading Term That Should Be Aban-

doned," *Obesity* 26, no. 4 (2018): 629–30, for some important worries about this terminology. Note that sometimes the term "the obesity paradox" is used to label the simple fact that fat people *can* be healthy, or even healthier than their thinner counterparts in some cases.

66. See, for example, Lenny R. Vartanian and Jacqueline G. Shaprow, "Effects of Weight Stigma on Exercise Motivation and Behavior: A Preliminary Investigation Among College-Aged Females," *Journal of Health Psychology* 13, no. 1 (2008): 131–38.

67. Interestingly, there's evidence that weight stigma causes people to eat more too. In one study, when so-called overweight women were exposed to weight-stigmatizing media, they consumed over three times more calories than they did after watching a neutral media clip. This effect was significantly less for their (again, so-called) normal-weight counterparts. See Natasha A. Schvey et al., "The Impact of Weight Stigma on Caloric Consumption," *Obesity* 19, no. 10 (2011): 1957–62.

68. Sole-Smith, "In Obesity Research, Fatphobia Is Always the X Factor."

69. Tomoko Udo et al., "Perceived Weight Discrimination and Chronic Medical Conditions in Adults with Overweight and Obesity," *International Journal of Clinical Practice* 70, no. 12 (2016): 1003–11.

70. Tomiyama et al., "How and Why Weight Stigma Drives the Obesity 'Epidemic' and Harms Health."

71. Note that Wiebe et al., in their study summarized in note 55, effectively postulate a more complicated set of causal relationships here, with inflammation and hyperinsulinemia each *confounding* the association between a higher weight and a higher risk of all-cause mortality, as follows:

Inflammation and Hyperinsulinemia → (Even) poorer health

Higher Weight

See their "Associations of Body Mass Index, Fasting Insulin, and Inflammation with Mortality."

72. See, for example, Haris Riaz et al., "Association Between Obesity and Cardio-vascular Outcomes: A Systematic Review and Meta-analysis of Mendelian Randomization Studies," *JAMA Network Open* 7, no. 1 (2018): e183788. For some important worries about the assumptions made by these studies, see Tyler J. VanderWeele et al., "Methodological Challenges in Mendelian Randomization," *Epidemiology* 25, no. 3 (2014): 427–35.

73. Maximilian Kleinert et al., "Animal Models of Obesity and Diabetes Mellitus," *Nature Reviews Endocrinology* 14 (2018): 140–62.

74. Wiebe et al., "Associations of Body Mass Index, Fasting Insulin, and Inflammation with Mortality." Note too that the Council on Scientific Affairs held in 2012 in a report to the American Medical Association (AMA) that "true causality has not been established in the literature [on the correlation between fatness and ill health], as obesity has only been associated with morbidity and mortality." See Sandra A. Fryhofer, "Is Obesity a Disease?," Report of the Council on Science and Public Health, May 16, 2013, CSAPH Report 3-A-13 (Resolution 115-A-12), accessed Jan. 26, 2023, www.ama-assn.org/sites/ama-assn.org/files/corp/media-browser/public/about-ama/councils/Council%20Reports/council-on-science-public-health/a13csaph3.pdf. Unfortunately, the AMA ultimately ignored this council's recommendation that obesity not be classified as a disease on this basis, among others. My thanks to Natasha Wiebe for extremely helpful correspondence on this point and many others.

75. My gratitude to Michael Hobbes for valuable discussion on this point and many others in this chapter.

76. See Jennifer Saul, "Dogwhistles, Political Manipulation, and the Philosophy of Language," in *New Work on Speech Acts,* ed. Daniel Fogal, Daniel W. Harris, and Matt Moss (Oxford: Oxford University Press, 2018), 360–83. See also Jason Stanley, *How Propaganda Works* (Princeton, N.J.: Princeton University Press, 2015), 137–39, for an illuminating related discussion. Saul offers a useful distinction between *overt* versus *covert* and *intentional* versus *unintentional* dog whistles. I suspect that fatphobic dog whistles can and do take all of these forms, which means that fatphobia may be perpetuated unwittingly within discourses about (un)healthiness, healthy living, healthy food, and so on. But, much as in the case of "government spending," which Saul argues can serve as a racist dog whistle in some contexts, there's no getting around the fact that we *do* need to discuss people's health in order to help improve it individually and collectively, for example, by implementing appropriate public policies. See the volume of essays *Against Health: How Health Became the New Morality,* ed. Jonathan M. Metzl and Anna Kirkland (New York: New York University Press, 2010), for some important—both congruent and conflicting—perspectives on this issue.

77. It's important to note, however, that this implication is culturally specific. In some other contexts, people saying someone looked "unhealthy" may imply that they looked too *thin;* similarly, saying that someone is looking "healthy" can actually be a way of adverting to their weight *gain.* Plausibly, these differences have to do with whether weight gain is feared and rued or, alternatively, regarded as a good sign in that someone has had ready access to the food that is in short supply,

either in reality or in the enduring cultural imagination. Thanks to Anna Milioni and Uma Chakrabarty for intel on the Greek and Indian contexts, respectively.

78. Claudia Cortese, "Even During a Pandemic, Fatphobia Won't Take a Day Off," *Bitch,* April 21, 2020, www.bitchmedia.org/article/fatphobia-in-coronavirus -treatment.

79. See Mary Anne Dunkin, "Lipedema," *WebMD,* Oct. 18, 2021, www.webmd .com/women/guide/lipedema-symptoms-treatment-causes.

80. Virginia Sole-Smith, "'I Sometimes Wonder What I Would Be Capable of If My Legs Didn't Hurt': Talking Lipedema and Lumpy Fat Ladies with Linda Ger- hardt," *Burnt Toast,* Substack, Oct. 6, 2022, virginiasolesmith.substack.com/p/ lumpy-fat-ladies-lipedema#details.

CHAPTER 3: VENUS IN RETROGRADE

1. Susan E. Hill, *Eating to Excess: The Meaning of Gluttony and the Fat Body in the Ancient World* (Santa Barbara, Calif.: Praeger, 2011), 4–5.

2. See, for example, Jessica Liew, "Venus Figurine," in *World History Encyclopedia,* July 10, 2017, www.worldhistory.org/Venus_Figurine/.

3. Hill, *Eating to Excess,* 5.

4. Ibid.

5. Ibid., 6.

6. Ibid., chap. 1.

7. Although Hippocrates, the ancient Greek physician, admittedly had more to say about the fat body, he was largely neutral about it, contrary to the impression one might form based on certain cherry-picked quotations from him to be found in contemporary diet books. For a fascinating discussion of the widespread miscon- strual of Hippocrates as a "spokesman against obesity, which he was not," see Helen Morales, "Fat Classics: Dieting, Health, and the Hijacking of Hippocrates," *Eidolon,* June 22, 2015, eidolon.pub/fat-classics-76db5d5578f4, as well as Hill, *Eating to Excess,* chap. 3.

8. Hill, *Eating to Excess,* 2.

9. For discussion, see ibid., 30.

10. Ibid., 2.

11. Ibid., chap. 6.

12. The conflation of "Budai" with "Buddha" may be due partly to a simple con-

fusion among cultural outsiders between their similar-sounding names. Many Chinese Buddhists do believe, however, that Budai was a reincarnation of Maitreya, who will become the *next* Buddha after Gautama Buddha (who is usually depicted with a thin body). See B. Kotaiah, "Laughing Buddha: Spreading Good Cheer, World Over," *Hindu,* June 13, 2016, www.thehindu.com/news/cities/ Hyderabad//article60438587.ece, for some basic information about this figure.

13. Note that this practice cuts across religious and cultural lines, being employed among Tunisian Jews as well as various Arab communities across Africa.

14. Soukaina Rachidi, "Ancient Leblouh Tradition Continues to Endanger the Lives of Mauritanian Women," *Inside Arabia,* March 16, 2019, insidearabia.com/ ancient-leblouh-tradition-endanger-lives-mauritanian-women/.

15. Desire Alice Naigaga et al., "Body Size Perceptions and Preferences Favor Overweight in Adult Saharawi Refugees," *Nutrition Journal* 17, art. no. 17 (2019).

16. Sabrina Strings, *Fearing the Black Body: The Racist Origins of Fat Phobia* (New York: New York University Press, 2019), chaps. 1 and 2.

17. Ibid., chap. 1.

18. Ibid., 50.

19. Ibid., 63.

20. Ibid., 60.

21. Ibid., chap. 2.

22. Ibid., 63.

23. Ibid., 100–107.

24. Ibid., 75–77.

25. Ibid., 85.

26. Ibid., 80. To be fair, Diderot here leaned on the views of his friend, the philosopher Jean-Baptiste-Pierre Le Romain, who lived in the Caribbean.

27. Ibid., 86.

28. Ibid.

29. Ibid., 209. Here, Strings draws on a Heideggerian notion.

30. Ibid., 9.

31. Ibid., 91–92.

32. Here, Strings (ibid.) is quoting Clifton C. Crais and Pamela Scully, *Sara Baartman and the Hottentot Venus: A Ghost Story and a Biography* (Princeton, N.J.: Princeton University Press, 2009), 80.

33. Strings, *Fearing the Black Body*, 92–93. Note too that one of the men who enslaved her, Georges Cuvier, wrote of Sara, "Her shape is all the more shocking because of the enormity of her hips," each one larger than eighteen inches, "and by the projection of her buttocks, which was larger than a half a foot." Indeed, he deemed her hips and buttocks veritable "deformities." Ibid., 96.

34. Ibid., 98.

35. Ibid., 187–88.

36. Ibid., 198–99.

37. In philosophy, the idea that one can't derive an "ought" claim from an "is" claim is known as the "is-ought" gap, and stems from the work of the eighteenth-century Scottish philosopher David Hume.

38. Your Fat Friend (a.k.a. Aubrey Gordon), "The Bizarre and Racist History of the BMI," Medium, Oct. 15, 2019, elemental.medium.com/the-bizarre-and-racist-history-of-the-bmi-7d8dc2aa33bb; Strings, *Fearing the Black Body*, 198–99.

39. Ancel Keys et al., "Indices of Relative Weight and Obesity," *Journal of Chronic Diseases* 25 (1972): 330.

40. Some of Keys's research was conducted on Japanese men, as well as Black Bantu men in South Africa. But, as they note in their study, the latter sample was not representative of that group, so their results failed to generalize to this population. See ibid., 333; and Your Fat Friend, "Bizarre and Racist History of the BMI."

41. Keys et al., "Indices of Relative Weight and Obesity," 339.

42. Ibid., 340.

43. See, for example, Amber Charles Alexis, "Is BMI a Fair Health Metric for Black Women?," *Healthline,* Dec. 1, 2021, www.healthline.com/nutrition/bmi-for-black-women, for a good lay overview of the recent empirical evidence. (As this article discusses, the BMI is also held by some to underestimate health risks associated with so-called obesity in certain Asian populations.) And for one important instance of the original research regarding the BMI's inaccuracy as a health measure for African American women, see Peter T. Katzmarzyk et al., "Ethnic-Specific BMI and Waist Circumference Thresholds," *Obesity* 19, no. 6 (2011): 1272–78.

44. See Gordon, *"You Just Need to Lose Weight,"* 98–108, for the definitive account of this episode, including pharmaceutical companies' stake in the decision and the influence this might have had on it. As usual, following the money tends to lead to no place auspicious.

45. Strings, *Fearing the Black Body,* 205–7.

46. Kavitha A. Davidson, "Caroline Wozniacki Mimics Serena Williams, Stuffs Her Bra and Skirt During Exhibition Match (VIDEO)," *Huffington Post,* Dec. 10, 2012, www.huffpost.com/entry/caroline-wozniacki-mimics-serena-williams-bra-skirt_n_2272271.

47. A bitter irony: when a serious health concern for Williams *did* arise, shortly after she delivered her baby daughter, the medical staff did not listen to her properly, and Williams nearly died as a result of this. See P. R. Lockhart, "What Serena Williams's Scary Childbirth Story Says About Medical Treatment of Black Women," *Vox,* Jan. 11, 2018, www.vox.com/identities/2018/1/11/16879984/serena-williams-childbirth-scare-black-women.

48. Katelyn Esmonde, "What Celeb Trainer Jillian Michaels Got Wrong About Lizzo and Body Positivity," *Vox,* Jan. 15, 2020, www.vox.com/culture/2020/1/15/21060692/lizzo-jillian-michaels-body-positivity-backlash.

49. See Centers for Disease Control and Prevention, Pregnancy Mortality Surveillance System, www.cdc.gov/reproductivehealth/maternalinfanthealth/pregnancy-mortality-surveillance-system.htm; and Linda Villarosa, "Why America's Black Mothers and Babies Are in a Life-or-Death Crisis," *New York Times,* April 11, 2018, www.nytimes.com/2018/04/11/magazine/black-mothers-babies-death-maternal-mortality.html, for discussion. Note too that this differential mortality rate cannot be explained by the comparative poverty of Black women alone; see New York City Department of Health and Mental Hygiene, Severe Maternal Morbidity in New York City, 2008–2012, New York, 2016, www1.nyc.gov/assets/doh/downloads/pdf/data/maternal-morbidity-report-08-12.pdf.

50. For reference, Monroe's measurements indicate that her BMI hovered between 19 and 20 much of the time, although she does appear to have been slightly heavier in the late 1950s. Whatever the case, she was in no way a large woman. That did not stop Elizabeth Hurley from famously commenting, in the year 2000, that "I'd kill myself if I was that fat." See "Marilyn Monroe's True Size," themarilynmonroecollection.com/marilyn-monroe-true-size/, for discussion.

51. Chioma Nnadi, "Kim Kardashian Takes Marilyn Monroe's 'Happy Birthday, Mr. President' Dress Out for a Spin," *Vogue,* May 2, 2022, www.vogue.com/article/kim-kardashian-met-gala-2022.

52. Moreover, as Telusma pointed out, this image of Kardashian was a direct re-creation of the photographer Jean-Paul Goude's 1982 portrait of a nude Black woman popping champagne in the same fashion, from a book with the appalling title *Jungle Fever.* Blue Telusma, "Kim Kardashian Doesn't Realize She's the Butt of an Old Racial Joke," *Grio,* Nov. 12, 2014, thegrio.com/2014/11/12/kim-kardashian-butt/.

53. Tressie McMillan Cottom, "Brown Body, White Wonderland," *Slate,* Aug. 29, 2013, slate.com/human-interest/2013/08/miley-cyrus-vma-performance-white-appropriation-of-black-bodies.html.

54. For some relevant original studies, see, for example, Jean-Luc Jucker et al., "Nutritional Status and the Influence of TV Consumption on Female Body Size Ideals in Populations Recently Exposed to the Media," *Scientific Reports* 7, art. no. 8438 (2017); and Anne E. Becker et al., "Eating Behaviours and Attitudes Following Prolonged Exposure to Television Among Ethnic Fijian Adolescent Girls," *British Journal of Psychiatry* 180 (2002): 509–14. And see Susie Orbach, *Bodies* (New York: Picador, 2009), 15, 168–69, for illuminating discussion.

55. Harrison, *Belly of the Beast,* chap. 4. In that chapter, they also draw on work by Nicole Gonzalez Van Cleve to theorize the horrific practice among prosecutors in Cook County, Illinois, known as "The Two-Ton Contest," or "N*****s by the Pound." The objective was to convict enough Black people, predominantly men, to reach the four-thousand-pound total weight goal. So fat Black men, in being worth more "points," were explicitly the main targets. Ibid., 61.

56. See Jamelle Bouie, "Michael Brown Wasn't a Superhuman Demon," *Slate,* Nov. 26, 2014, slate.com/news-and-politics/2014/11/darren-wilsons-racial-portrayal-of-michael-brown-as-a-superhuman-demon-the-ferguson-police-officers-account-is-a-common-projection-of-racial-fears.html.

57. Ibid.

58. Philomena R. Condoll, "Police Commander: Eric Garner Killing 'Not a Big Deal,'" *Liberation News,* June 28, 2019, www.liberationnews.org/police-commander-eric-garner-killing-not-a-big-deal/. The title of this article refers to the fact that, shockingly, when the police commander Lieutenant Christopher Bannon received a text message saying that Garner was "most likely DOA," his response was, "not a big deal." This emerged in the disciplinary hearings five years after Garner's murder, which eventually led to Pantaleo's firing. But he was never indicted, nor charged with a civil rights violation.

59. Harrison, *Belly of the Beast,* 48–49. Note that Harrison, drawing on Zakiyyah Iman Jackson and Saidiya Hartman, explicitly disavows the idea that construing Black people as "beastly" is an exercise in dehumanization. Rather, people so

derogated are constructed as a *kind* of human—an inferior, disposable kind—within a white supremacy. They write, "Black subjects are not denied humanity, or dehumanized through slavery, but rather are forced to become the Beast of humanity; the lowest on the scale of hegemonic humanity and placed among 'the animal'" (ibid., 56). I am similarly skeptical of the dehumanization hypothesis, at least in its contemporary application; and I worry, moreover, about its exonerating political upshot. (If only they knew they were dealing with a human being, then they'd be sure to treat them properly, is the naive thought sometimes betrayed by humanist discourse.) For that reason, I avoid the specific language of dehumanization in this book when it comes to fatphobia's current incarnations. See my book, *Down Girl*, chap. 5, for discussion. But other theorists may have different views about the nature and utility of the concept when it comes to fatphobia, and I won't try to litigate this delicate issue in these pages.

60. Paul Campos, *The Obesity Myth: Why America's Obsession with Weight Is Hazardous to Your Health* (New York: Gotham, 2004), 68.

61. Ibid.

62. In the course of my research for this chapter, I discovered this website still exists; no, I won't link to it.

63. Amy Erdman Farrell, *Fat Shame: Stigma and the Fat Body in American Culture* (New York: New York University Press, 2011), 17–18.

64. See also breast-feeding rather than using formula, for one other example here.

CHAPTER 4: DEMORALIZING FATNESS

1. Kate Manne, "Diet Culture Is Unhealthy. It's Also Immoral," *New York Times,* Jan. 3, 2022, www.nytimes.com/2022/01/03/opinion/diet-resolution.html.

2. Some of the insistence was, of course, rude and even abusive. C'est la vie on the internet.

3. See, for example, Ian Gillson and Amir Fouad, who write in the overview of their edited volume on this topic, "There is no global food shortage. The problem is local—or sometimes regional—and centers on moving food, often across borders, from areas of food surplus to areas of food deficit." Ian Gillson and Amir Fouad, eds., *Trade Policy and Food Security: Improving Access to Food in Developing Countries in the Wake of High World Prices* (Washington, D.C.: World Bank, 2015), 6. Similarly, they write, "Food security today is less a question of whether the Earth is capable of producing enough food for such a large and growing population; indeed, food shortage at the global level has yet to pose a legitimate threat. Rather, the role that political factors, ownership, institutions, and inequal-

ity play in the distribution of food remains pivotal" (ibid., 1–2). They draw here on Amartya Sen's seminal work, *Poverty and Famines: An Essay on Entitlement and Deprivation* (Oxford: Clarendon Press, 1981).

4. The metaphors of "eating crow" and "humble pie" both refer to getting one's comeuppance and tasting the ignominy of submission, apology, or retraction. The former reportedly comes from an American story published around 1850 in which a stingy farmer is tricked by his boarders into eating a crow stuffed with snuff. But the thought was that a crow, a carrion eater, would not make for a tasty meal anyway. Compare also the expressions "eating one's shoe," "eating one's hat," "eating dirt," and "eating one's words."

5. For an illuminating general discussion of moral panics in relation to fatness, see Kathleen LeBesco, "Fat Panic and the New Morality," in Metzl and Kirkland, *Against Health,* 72–82.

6. The disciplinary scenario involved a salesperson giving NFL tickets as a gift to customers, in violation of company policy. See Joseph A. Bellizzi and Ronald W. Hasty, "Territory Assignment Decisions and Supervising Unethical Selling Behavior: The Effects of Obesity and Gender as Moderated by Job-Related Factors," *Journal of Personal Selling and Sales Management* 18, no. 2 (1998): 35–49.

7. Natasha A. Schvey et al., "The Influence of a Defendant's Body Weight on Perceptions of Guilt," *International Journal of Obesity* 37, no. 9 (2013): 1275–81.

8. Sole-Smith, "'I Sometimes Wonder What I Would Be Capable of If My Legs Didn't Hurt.'"

9. This trope was first named and theorized by Dr. Charlotte Cooper, "Headless Fatties," blog post, 2007, charlottecooper.net/fat/fat-writing/headless-fatties -01-07/.

10. Cathy E. Elks et al., "Variability in the Heritability of Body Mass Index: A Systematic Review and Meta-regression," *Frontiers in Endocrinology* 3, art. no. 29 (2012): 5, in which the researchers found similar overall heritability estimates for men (0.73; 95 percent CI: 0.71–0.76) and women (0.75; 95 percent CI: 0.73–0.77), based on estimates from twin studies. Estimates of heritability from family studies are often lower, but have also been argued to be underestimates (ibid., 10).

11. Linda Geddes, "Genetic Study Homes in on Height's Heritability Mystery," *Nature,* April 23, 2019, www.nature.com/articles/d41586-019-01157-y.

12. Albert J. Stunkard et al., "An Adoption Study of Human Obesity," *New England Journal of Medicine* 314 (1986): 193–98.

13. Gina Kolata, "One Weight Loss Approach Fits All? No, Not Even Close," *New York Times*, Dec. 12, 2016, www.nytimes.com/2016/12/12/health/weight-loss-obesity.html.

14. Giovanni Luca Palmisano et al., "Life Adverse Experiences in Relation with Obesity and Binge Eating Disorder: A Systematic Review," *Journal of Behavioral Addiction* 5, no. 1 (2016): 11–31. And see Gordon, *"You Just Need to Lose Weight,"* 73–80, for some wise words of caution about this kind of research and the danger of inferring far too much from it.

15. Gay, *Hunger*, 16.

16. Ibid., 43.

17. Ibid., 17.

18. Ibid., 23.

19. Ibid., 38.

20. See, for example, "Why People Become Overweight," Harvard Health Publishing, June 24, 2019, www.health.harvard.edu/staying-healthy/why-people-become-overweight; "When Your Weight Gain Is Caused by Medicine," in *University of Rochester Medical Center Health Encyclopedia*, www.urmc.rochester.edu/encyclopedia/content.aspx?contenttypeid=56&contentid=DM300; and Elizabeth Scott, "How Stress Can Cause Weight Gain: The Role of Cortisol in the Body," *Very Well Mind*, Jan. 5, 2021, www.verywellmind.com/how-stress-can-cause-weight-gain-3145088, for some decent lay overviews of the relevant health research (with, unfortunately, the inevitable side of fatphobia).

21. Robin Marantz Henig, "Fat Factors," *New York Times Magazine*, Aug. 13, 2006, www.nytimes.com/2006/08/13/magazine/13obesity.html.

22. Obviously, I'm not denying the strong desire to *try* a wholly unfamiliar food; this is not plausibly a craving, though, but rather the mark of culinary curiosity or an adventurous appetite. And so sometimes we discover, upon tasting it, that we didn't *really* want the food, though we did want to try it.

23. Marquisele Mercedes, "Public Health's Power-Neutral, Fatphobic Obsession with 'Food Deserts,'" Medium, Nov. 13, 2020, marquisele.medium.com/public-healths-power-neutral-fatphobic-obsession-with-food-deserts-a8d740dea81. As Mercedes notes, the preferred term in many activist spaces is hence now "food apartheid," coined by Karen Washington.

24. Ibid.

25. It's worth noting, however, that the relationship between so-called obesity and socioeconomic status is actually complex, and appears to vary with race and

gender. One important study endorsed by the CDC found that, for women, "obesity" prevalence decreased with increasing income, but the same patterns did not hold for men. Similarly, lower "obesity" prevalence was found for college graduates compared with people with less education among whites and Black and Hispanic women, but not for Asians or Black and Hispanic men. The authors concluded that "the association between obesity and income or educational level is complex and differs by sex and race." Cynthia L. Ogden et al., "Prevalence of Obesity Among Adults, by Household Income and Education—United States, 2011–2014," *MMWR Morbidity Mortality Weekly Report* 66, no. 50 (2017): 1369–73.

26. For example, SNAP benefits typically can't be used to purchase hot food (including rotisserie chickens) from a grocery store, even though this may provide exactly the sort of quick, filling meal that people working long hours need to feed themselves and their families. Thanks to Joel Sati for discussion on this point.

27. Pieter H. M. van Baal et al., "Lifetime Medical Costs of Obesity: Prevention No Cure for Increasing Health Expenditure," *PLOS Medicine* 5, no. 2 (2008): e29.

28. I use these particular examples because of the high degree of risk associated with each of these activities, with the chance of dying roughly calculated to be 1 in 60 for every instance of BASE jumping, 1 in 167 annually for mountain climbing in Nepal, and 1 in 100 for Grand Prix racers. See the relevant sources and infographic in Patrick McCarthy, "Infographic: Your Chances of Dying from Common Activities," *OffGrid*, Nov. 10, 2018, www.offgridweb.com/survival/infographic-your-chances-of-dying-from-common-activities/.

29. A. W. Eaton, "Taste in Bodies and Fat Oppression," in *Body Aesthetics*, ed. Sherri Irvin (Oxford: Oxford University Press, 2016), 46. Note that Eaton offers this example in the course of giving a distinct, but complementary, argument, to the conclusion that unhealthy choices other than fatness are sometimes *aesthetically* venerated (rather than morally tolerated, as I am arguing). She writes, "The known unhealthiness of a particular bodily state [like tanning, particularly as a light-skinned person] does little or nothing to undermine that state's attractiveness and desirability. This strongly suggests that our collective revulsion to fat bodies is not ultimately a response to the (mistaken) belief that fat is unhealthy." Ibid.

30. Compare the important fat activists Kate Harding and Marianne Kirby, who write, bracingly, in their co-authored book, "Health is not a moral imperative. You are not a bad person if you just don't like working out or eating vegetables, if you have priorities other than trying to live to be one hundred, or if you have a disability that keeps you from ever truly feeling 'healthy.'" Kate Harding and Mari-

anne Kirby, *Lessons from the Fat-o-Sphere: Quit Dieting and Declare a Truce with Your Body* (Toronto: Penguin, 2009), 15.

31. Typically, a libertarian position would be that there should be no *laws* mandating seatbelts and motorcycle helmets, given that these are purely individual choices. But this frequently goes hand in hand with a sense that individuals are not *morally* obligated to exercise these precautions either. To which it is natural and, in my view, fair to point out that we live in a society, and that our close dependence on others makes it reasonable to expect people to take minimal, non-burdensome precautions against health risks that could indeed make them very costly to their relatives, among others.

32. Admittedly, masking is and has always been controversial in the United States. But it shouldn't be. Anyone without a serious respiratory issue who has worn a mask for any length of time, is adequately community-minded (particularly bearing in mind disabled, immunocompromised, and immunosuppressed people), and admits to the true risks of COVID, can testify that it's really not a big deal to wear one in high-transmission settings. Medical professionals also manage to wear masks for extremely long shifts while doing extremely hard jobs, which adds to the point that those who refuse to wear one are being selfish and, often, whiny.

33. See, for example, Nicholas A. Christakis and James H. Fowler, "The Spread of Obesity in a Large Social Network over 32 Years," *New England Journal of Medicine* 357, no. 4 (2007): 370–79. The study—which uses the language of the "obesity epidemic" uncritically and tries to account for the "spread" of what is framed as an obviously undesirable and dangerous way of being in the world, much like a painful disease or illness—attracted significant criticism at the time. This led one of its authors, Christakis, to helpfully clarify: "We're not suggesting that people should sever their ties with overweight friends. Having friends is healthy for you." Also, they are your friends, so. See Roxanne Khamsi, "Is Obesity Contagious?," *New Scientist,* July 25, 2007, www.newscientist.com/article/dn12343-is-obesity-contagious/#ixzz7VwC4oyC5.

34. See Gordon, *"You Just Need to Lose Weight,"* 7–8, on "gainers," who simply want to live their lives in larger bodies—much as some people want to be tattooed, or muscular, or have piercings. Again, such desires strike me as precisely none of our business.

35. Eaton, "Taste in Bodies and Fat Oppression," 46.

36. For the original discussion of healthism, see R. Crawford, "Healthism and the Medicalization of Everyday Life," *International Journal of Health Services* 10, no. 3 (1980): 365–88.

37. See, for example, "People with Low Socioeconomic Status and Commercial Tobacco: Health Disparities and Ways to Advance Health Equity," Centers for Disease Control and Prevention, www.cdc.gov/tobacco/health-equity/low-ses/index.htm, on the disproportionate poverty of smokers. And, in this vein, see Barbara Ehrenreich, *Nickel and Dimed: On (Not) Getting By in America* (New York: Henry Holt, 2001), 31, on the small pleasures of smoking as something "you do for yourself" when life is otherwise arduous.

38. Thalia Wheatley and Jonathan Haidt, "Hypnotic Disgust Makes Moral Judgments More Severe," *Psychological Science* 16, no. 10 (2005): 780–84. See also note 41, below, for some important replications.

39. Ibid., 781.

40. I draw intermittently throughout this section on discussion in *Down Girl,* 256–59.

41. Wheatley and Haidt, "Hypnotic Disgust Makes Moral Judgments More Severe," 783.

42. See Simone Schnall et al., "Disgust as Embodied Moral Judgment," *Personality and Social Psychology Bulletin* 34, no. 8 (2008): 1096–1109.

43. L. R. Vartanian, "Disgust and Perceived Control in Attitudes Toward Obese People," *International Journal of Obesity* 34 (2010): 1302–7. Moreover, disgust fully mediated the association between perceived control over one's weight and such fatphobic judgments (whereas perceived control over one's weight did not mediate the link between these disgust reactions and these fatphobic judgments). What this means is that someone's perception that people are in control of their weight predicts how much disgust she likely feels toward fat bodies, which in turn predicts the extent to which she will harbor fatphobic judgments. So this study underscores the important role of disgust in the etiology of fatphobia twice over. Note that these results held even controlling for an individual's degree of disgust sensitivity (ibid., 1306). Thanks to Eleni Man and Shaun Nichols for their valuable help in understanding these findings. Of course, any errors or omissions are my sole responsibility.

44. See Eaton, "Taste in Bodies and Fat Oppression," 43–44, for related discussion.

45. Daniel Kelly, *Yuck: The Nature and Moral Significance of Disgust* (Cambridge, Mass.: MIT Press, 2011), 46–47.

46. Yoel Inbar and David A. Pizarro, "Pathogens and Politics: Current Research and New Questions," *Social and Personality Psychology Compass* 10, no. 6 (2014): 365–74.

47. For a state-of-the-art discussion, see Jakob Fink-Lamotte et al., "Are You Looking or Looking Away? Visual Exploration and Avoidance of Disgust- and Fear-Stimuli: An Eye-Tracking Study," *Emotion* 22, no. 8 (2022): 1909–18.

48. See Orlando Patterson, *Slavery and Social Death: A Comparative Study* (Cambridge, Mass.: Harvard University Press, 1982), especially chap. 11.

CHAPTER 5: SOMETHING TO BE DESIRED

1. Note that names have been changed throughout this chapter.

2. See *Down Girl*, 59.

3. Ogi Ogas and Sai Gaddam, *A Billion Wicked Thoughts: What the Internet Tells Us About Sexual Relationships* (New York: Penguin, 2011), 52–53, which revealed that porn website searches for a "fat" girl are almost three times more common than searches for a "skinny" one. Moreover, they found that, on the Alexa Adult list, there were more than 504 sites devoted to fat women and only 182 explicitly devoted to thin ones at the time of their book's publication. Of course, this doesn't necessarily mean that fat female bodies are *more* popular than thin ones, since, as the authors go on to note, mainstream pornography tends to feature thin women, who therefore don't need to be found using special search terms. But it does suffice to show that fatness is hardly a rare sexual interest.

4. See Strings, *Fearing the Black Body*, a work that crucially informed chapter 3 throughout.

5. I discuss the misogyny directed against Gillard at length in *Down Girl*, chap. 8. For Greer's defense of her comment—"women are fat-arsed creatures"—see "Greer Defends 'Fat Arse' PM Comment," *Sydney Morning Herald*, Aug. 28, 2012, www.smh.com.au/politics/federal/greer-defends-fat-arse-pm-comment -20120828-24x5i.html.

6. See, for example, "Germaine Greer: Transgender Women Are 'Not Women,'" BBC News, Oct. 24, 2015, https://www.bbc.com/news/av/uk-34625512.

7. Aubrey Gordon, *What We Don't Talk About When We Talk About Fat* (Boston: Beacon Press, 2020), 90–91.

8. Lindy West, *Shrill: Notes from a Loud Woman* (New York: Hachette, 2016), 76.

9. Gordon, *What We Don't Talk About When We Talk About Fat*, 91–92.

10. See my book *Entitled*, chap. 4, for more about such cases of consensual but unwanted sex and their harmfulness.

11. Ashifa Kassam, "Canada Judge Says Sexual Assault Victim May Have Been

'Flattered' by the Incident," *Guardian*, Oct. 27, 2017, www.theguardian.com/world/2017/oct/27/canada-judge-says-sexual-assault-victim-may-have-been-flattered-by-the-incident.

12. Alexandra M. Zidenberg et al., "Tipping the Scales: Effects of Gender, Rape Myth Acceptance, and Anti-fat Attitudes on Judgments of Sexual Coercion Scenarios," *Journal of Interpersonal Violence* 36, no. 19–20 (2021): NP10178–NP10204.

13. Margaret Tilley, "The Role of Lifestyles and Routine Activities on Youth Sexual Assault and Intimate Partner Victimization" (PhD diss., Kennesaw State University, 2015).

14. Thanks to my agent, Lucy V. Cleland, for this pithy formulation.

15. See Quill Kukla (writing as Rebecca Kukla), "Sex Talks," *Aeon*, Feb. 4, 2019, aeon.co/essays/consent-and-refusal-are-not-the-only-talking-points-in-sex. Note that Kukla's category of "sexual gifts" complicates their views on the popular idea I subscribe to here, that consent should be enthusiastic. For further discussion, see their paper, "That's What She Said: The Language of Sexual Negotiation," *Ethics* 129 (Oct. 2018): 70–97.

16. For a notable and salutary exception, see Louise Richardson-Self on what she calls "unfuckable objectification," wherein some women are depicted as "sexually undesirable to all men, the implication of which is that these women have no value whatsoever. They have failed in one of their most fundamental service work roles: being attractive for Men; thus, they are not wanted by Men. Once more, Men are figured as the only real (sexual) agents, since all Men can, but never would choose to fuck that 'lot' of (Bad) Women." See Louise Richardson-Self, *Hate Speech Against Women Online: Concepts and Countermeasures* (Lanham, Md.: Rowman & Littlefield, 2021), 86–87. Though I am in sympathy with Richardson-Self's account, I prefer to theorize this possibility not as a separate type of objectification per se but rather as a natural outgrowth of objectification's common fixation on hierarchy.

17. This list is reordered and slightly simplified from Martha C. Nussbaum, "Objectification," *Philosophy and Public Affairs* 24, no. 4 (1995): 257. Note that Nussbaum theorizes objectification as a fairly loose cluster concept, with instances involving at least one, and typically more than one, of the above features.

18. Nussbaum touches on the idea of sexual hierarchies only once, at the very end of her extensive discussion, and doesn't use it to amend or complicate her list of the seven features of objectifying treatment. Rather, it crops up in passing in her criticism of Richard D. Mohr's idea that treating people as fungible can actually be a boon to treating them properly, since he believed it makes for a kind of sexual

democracy evident among gay men in the sexual bathhouse culture he celebrated. Ibid., 287–88.

19. Rae Langton, *Sexual Solipsism: Philosophical Essays on Pornography and Objectification* (Oxford: Oxford University Press, 2009), 228–29.

20. Zadie Smith, *On Beauty: A Novel* (New York: Penguin, 2005), 205–6. Thanks to my editor, Amanda Cook, for suggesting this example.

21. Ibid., 207.

22. For an excellent recent philosophical treatment of wellness culture in relation to fatphobia, see Emma Atherton, "Moralizing Hunger: Cultural Fatphobia and the Moral Language of Contemporary Diet Culture," in "Feminism and Food," special issue, *Feminist Philosophy Quarterly* 7, no. 3 (2021).

23. Harrison, *Belly of the Beast.*

24. Javier C. Hernández, "He Quit Singing Because of Body Shaming. Now He's Making a Comeback," *New York Times,* Jan. 23, 2023, www.nytimes.com/2023/01/23/arts/music/limmie-pulliam-opera-body-shaming.html.

25. Seth Stephens-Davidowitz, "Google, Tell Me. Is My Son a Genius?," *New York Times,* Jan. 18, 2014, www.nytimes.com/2014/01/19/opinion/sunday/google-tell-me-is-my-son-a-genius.html. Additionally, parents were around twice as likely to ask how to get their daughters to lose weight, and one and a half times more likely to wonder if their daughters were beautiful, as compared with their sons. They were two and a half times more likely to wonder if their son was "gifted," and showed a similar bias in the use of the word "genius." This, even though girls are more likely to display advanced vocabulary at a young age and be placed into gifted programs in school. As Stephens-Davidowitz writes, "The disturbing results outlined here leave us with many open questions, but the most poignant may be this one: How would American girls' lives be different if parents were half as concerned with their bodies and twice as intrigued by their minds?"

26. Erin M. Lenz, "Influence of Experienced and Internalized Weight Stigma and Coping on Weight Loss Outcomes Among Adults" (PhD diss., University of Connecticut, 2017).

27. Molly Olmstead, "Cornell Frat Suspended for Game in Which Men Compete to Have Sex with Overweight Women," *Slate,* Feb. 7, 2018, slate.com/news-and-politics/2018/02/cornell-fraternity-zeta-beta-tau-suspended-for-offensive-pig-roast-game.html. And for an important academic treatment of this practice, see Ariane Prohaska and Jeannine Gailey, "Fat Women as 'Easy Targets': Achieving Masculinity Through Hogging," in *The Fat Studies Reader,* ed. Esther Rothblum and Sondra Solovay (New York: New York University Press, 2009), 158–66.

28. Hanne Blank, *Fat* (New York: Bloomsbury, 2020), 93.

29. It is striking that despite the ways men regularly derogate women's appearances, by invoking the standards of beauty enshrined by a white supremacist, heteronormative, and fatphobic patriarchy, it remains vanishingly rare for women to lash out against men on this basis. And this is one reason among many why I remain unflinchingly unsympathetic to the heterosexual men known as incels. They might have been rejected or made to feel undesirable by the people they desire, and this can be disappointing. (Although some incels, to be clear, are young men who never reached out to the "hot" women they wanted to date in the first place, and more or less expected these women to turn up at their doorstep ready and eager to date them.) But when it comes to those of us made to feel unworthy of sex, love, and aesthetic veneration, it is women and other marginalized genders who primarily suffer. And yet, somehow, we manage not to commit murders for this reason. See my book, *Entitled,* chap. 2, for further discussion.

30. See Hebl and Mannix, "The Weight of Obesity in Evaluating Others," a study discussed in chap. 1 here.

31. Elena Ferrante, *The Story of the Lost Child* (New York: Europa, 2015), 237.

32. Ibid., 238.

33. Ibid., 239.

34. Ibid., 240.

35. Ibid., 243.

36. Ibid., 242.

37. For a fuller account of this episode, see my piece "Good Girls: How Powerful Men Get Away with Sexual Predation," *Huffington Post,* March 24, 2017 (updated March 28, 2017), www.huffpost.com/entry/good-girls-or-why-powerful-men-get-to-keep-on-behaving_b_58d5b420e4b0f633072b37c3.

CHAPTER 6: SMALL WONDER

1. Plato, *Theaetetus,* trans. Benjamin Jowett (Indianapolis: Hackett, 2014), 155d.

2. To understand these social realities and general atmosphere in philosophy, Kristie Dotson's famous paper, "How Is This Paper Philosophy?," *Comparative Philosophy* 3, no. 1 (2012): 3–29, is essential reading.

3. Katherine Mangan, "In the Humanities, Men Dominate the Fields of Philosophy and History," *Chronicle of Higher Education,* Oct. 12, 2012, www.chronicle.com/article/in-the-humanities-men-dominate-the-fields-of-philosophy-and-history/.

4. See, for example, Rebecca Ratcliffe and Claire Shaw, " 'Philosophy Is for Posh, White Boys with Trust Funds'—Why Are There So Few Women?," *Guardian,* Jan. 5, 2015, www.theguardian.com/higher-education-network/2015/jan/05/philosophy-is-for-posh-white-boys-with-trust-funds-why-are-there-so-few-women, featuring perspectives by Jennifer Saul and many others. For a now-classic discussion of these issues, see Sally Haslanger, "Changing the Ideology and Culture of Philosophy: Not by Reason (Alone)," *Hypatia* 23, no. 2 (2008): 210–23. For a recent fascinating diagnosis, see Christia Mercer's article "The Philosophical Origins of Patriarchy," *Nation,* July 1, 2019, www.thenation.com/article/archive/patriarchy-sexism-philosophy-reproductive-rights/, and her paper "The Philosophical Roots of Western Misogyny," *Philosophical Topics* 46, no. 2 (2018): 183–208.

5. Ratcliffe and Shaw, " 'Philosophy Is for Posh, White Boys with Trust Funds.' "

6. For some representative pieces about sexual harassment in philosophy, see, for example, Jennifer Schuessler, "A Star Philosopher Falls, and a Debate over Sexism Is Set Off," *New York Times,* Aug. 2, 2013, www.nytimes.com/2013/08/03/arts/colin-mcginn-philosopher-to-leave-his-post.html; Colleen Flaherty, "Another Harasser Resigns," *Inside Higher Ed,* Nov. 4, 2015, www.insidehighered.com/news/2015/11/04/northwestern-philosophy-professor-resigns-during-termination-hearing-over-sexual; Katie J. M. Baker, "The Famous Ethics Professor and the Women Who Accused Him," *BuzzFeed News,* May 20, 2016, www.buzzfeednews.com/article/katiejmbaker/yale-ethics-professor; and Katie J. M. Baker, "UC Berkeley Was Warned About Its Star Professor Years Before Sexual Harassment Lawsuit," *BuzzFeed News,* April 7, 2017, www.buzzfeednews.com/amphtml/katiejmbaker/john-searle-complaints-uc-berkeley. For general discussion, see Janice Dowell and David Sobel, "Sexual Harassment in Philosophy," *Daily Nous,* Aug. 29, 2019, dailynous.com/2019/08/29/sexual-harassment-philosophy-guest-post-janice-dowell-david-sobel/. For some brief (and necessarily partial) indication of philosophy's racism problem, see, for example, David Rutledge, "Racist Attitudes 'Whitewashed' Modern Philosophy. What Can Be Done to Change It?," ABC News, *The Philosopher's Zone* podcast, Nov. 9, 2019, www.abc.net.au/news/2019-11-10/modern-philosophical-canon-has-always-been-pretty-whitewashed/11678314, featuring the perspective of Bryan van Norden about the existing canon.

7. For some recent pieces on the transphobia of philosophy, see, for example, Talia Mae Bettcher, "When Tables Speak: On the Existence of Trans Philosophy," *Daily Nous,* May 30, 2018, dailynous.com/2018/05/30/tables-speak-existence-trans-philosophy-guest-talia-mae-bettcher/; t philosopher, "I Am Leaving Academic Philosophy Because of Its Transphobia Problem," Medium, May 20, 2019, medium.com/@transphilosopher33/i-am-leaving-academic-philosophy-because

-of-its-transphobia-problem-bc618aa55712; and Robin Dembroff, "Cisgender Commonsense and Philosophy's Transgender Trouble," *Transgender Studies Quarterly* 7, no. 3 (2020): 399–406. For a sense of philosophy's classism, see John Proios, "Ethical Narratives and Oppositional Consciousness," *APA Newsletter on Feminism and Philosophy* 20, no. 3 (2021): 11–15. For some discussions of ableism in philosophy, see Shelley Tremain's "Dialogues on Disability" series on the blog *Biopolitical Philosophy,* biopoliticalphilosophy.com/.

8. See, for example, Rachel Moss, "For Tolerance of Body Diversity, Academia Gets a Big, Fat Zero," *Times Higher Education,* Sept. 29, 2021, www.timeshigher education.com/opinion/tolerance-body-diversity-academia-gets-big-fat-zero.

9. True, arguments are sometimes criticized as lightweight or insubstantial. But the imagined contrast here is generally with a robust and muscular, masculine body, not a fat one—so metaphors of this kind are not anti-fatphobic so much as antifeminist.

10. Willard V. Quine, "On What There Is," *Review of Metaphysics* 2, no. 5 (1948): 23.

11. I draw intermittently in this section on my piece "Diet Culture Is Unhealthy."

12. Quine, "On What There Is," 23.

13. I don't mean to suggest, of course, that Quine set out to invoke these tropes as such, that is, *as* instantiations of classism and fatphobia. (Even setting aside the obvious anachronism, does anyone?) My point is just that he deployed these tropes not merely by accident, oblivious to their cultural meaning, but in an effort to be witty and pointed in his choice of metaphors, in a way that turns crucially on their having these very meanings.

14. Quine, "On What There Is," 23–24.

15. Here, I invert the famous idea of the "mind-body" problem, usually credited to Descartes, which is (very roughly) the problem of understanding the relationship between the mind and the body—or, more specifically, how, if at all, our minds can be instantiated by our brains and their associated neurophysiology. The "body-mind" problem I point to here is obviously a considerably more prosaic one.

16. Robert Paul Wolff, *About Philosophy,* 11th ed. (Boston: Pearson, 2012), 21.

17. See Talia Mae Bettcher, who writes poignantly about what it's like to be a trans woman in philosophy when other philosophers evince blithe ignorance as well as bigotry toward people like her: "It's one thing to spout views about [abstract metaphysical problems] with both arrogance and ignorance. It happens. It's annoying. But it's quite another thing to do this when we're talking about *people*—

people who are in the room, people trying (and succeeding) to philosophize themselves." See her "When Tables Speak."

18. Philippa Foot, "The Problem of Abortion and the Doctrine of Double Effect," *Oxford Review* 5 (1967): 5–15.

19. Judith Jarvis Thomson, "The Trolley Problem," *Yale Law Journal* 94, no. 6 (1985): 1395–415.

20. David Edmonds, *Would You Kill the Fat Man? The Trolley Problem and What Your Answer Tells Us About Right and Wrong* (Princeton, N.J.: Princeton University Press, 2014).

21. In an online survey of answers to the trolley problem and the "fat man" variant, 84 percent of the nearly 140,000 respondents say the trolley should be diverted, but only 41 percent say the fat man should be thrown from the bridge; see https://www.philosophyexperiments.com/fatman/Default.aspx. The creators actually admit that the man's fatness may be a source of bigotry, but argue (among other things) that if it was, then we'd expect a larger number of people to say we should *not* turn the trolley but *should* sacrifice the fat man. It would be a pretty extreme form of fatphobia that would generate such a pattern, though. Moreover, as I argue below, distorting the results is hardly the only problem with setting up the case in this manner.

22. This case is also discussed by Foot (who writes that it is already "well known to philosophers") in "The Problem of Abortion and the Doctrine of Double Effect," 5–6. "Obviously the right thing to do is to sit down and wait until the fat man grows thin," she quips initially. The concluding line of her paper, though: "The levity of the examples is not meant to offend," 15.

23. Plato, *Timaeus,* trans. Donald J. Zeyl (Indianapolis: Hackett, 2000), 62d.

24. Hill, *Eating to Excess,* 47.

25. Plato, *Timaeus,* 63b.

26. Ibid. The fact that the mouth both speaks and takes in food is a potentially awkward fact that Plato considers when he writes, again in the voice of Timaeus, "Our makers fitted the mouth out with teeth, a tongue, and lips in their current arrangement, to accommodate both what is necessary and what is best: they designed the mouth as the entry passage for what is necessary and as the exit for what is best: for all that comes in and provides nourishment for the body is necessary, while that stream of speech that flows out through the mouth, that instrument of intelligence, is the fairest and best of all streams." Ibid., 69e.

27. Ibid., 64e.

28. Ibid., 66e.

29. Hill, *Eating to Excess*, 50.

30. Strings, *Fearing the Black Body*, chap. 4.

31. Plato, *Timaeus*, 86.

32. Hill, *Eating to Excess*, 54. And compare *The Republic*, for Plato's somewhat more egalitarian picture of the nature and role of women—in particular, his inclusion of female guardians in an ideal city.

33. Hill, *Eating to Excess*, 52.

34. Aristotle notes in the very beginning of this discussion, "Similarly health is ruined by eating and drinking either too much or too little, while it is produced, increased, and preserved by taking the right quantity of drink and victuals." However, as we'll see, he held that eating too little is not a common human temptation. *Nicomachean Ethics*, bk. 2, chap. 2, in *The Ethics of Aristotle*, trans. J. A. K. Thomson (London: Routledge, 1953).

35. Ibid.

36. Aristotle famously used the example of food to establish that finding a mean between extremes is neither straightforward nor a mathematically precise, rote matter. "Let ten pounds of food be a large, and two pounds a small, allowance for an athlete. It does not follow that the trainer will prescribe six pounds. That might be a large or it might be a small allowance for the particular athlete who is to get it. It would be little for Milo but a lot for a man who has just begun his training." Ibid., bk. 2, chap. 4.

37. Aristotle points out that we do not call people intemperate for being too apt to indulge in the pleasures of, for example, ambition, learning, or storytelling. Rather, he argues, temperance is concerned "with those pleasures which man shares with the lower animals, and which consequently appear slavish and bestial"—most notably sex and the consumption of food and drink. Ibid., bk. 3, chap. 10.

38. Aristotle also drew an important distinction between self-indulgent "belly-gorgers," who eat too much, and the morally weak who gain excessive pleasure from indulging particular appetites. Ibid., bk. 3, chap. 11.

39. Ibid., bk. 2, chap. 7.

40. Interestingly, Aristotle does not seem to consider people who deprive themselves of food not because of an inability to take pleasure from it but because they deny themselves this pleasure. This, even though Aristotle surely knew of ascetics,

people who thought that every pleasure is bad. It's worth noting here, however, that there's no clear evidence of disordered eating in the ancient world, which may point both to its socially constructed nature and to its tendency to afflict people in particularly calorie-abundant social environments. On the other hand, anorexia appears to have been not uncommon in women—mostly nuns—during the Middle Ages. For interesting discussion of so-called anorexia mirabilis, see Whitney May, "Holy Anorexia: How Medieval Women Coped with What Was Eating at Them," *A Medieval Woman's Companion,* amedievalwomanscompanion.com/holy-anorexia-how-medieval-women-coped-with-what-was-eating-at-them/, as well as Caroline Bynum's book *Holy Feast and Holy Fast* (Berkeley: University of California Press, 1987), chap. 6. Thanks to Rachana Kamtekar and many other historically minded colleagues for valuable discussion on this point and others in this section and the preceding one. Of course, any mistakes and omissions are my sole responsibility.

41. C. D. C. Reeve, introduction to *Politics,* by Aristotle, trans. C. D. C. Reeve (New York: Hackett, 1998), xxxv.

42. Ibid., xxxvi.

43. Ibid.

44. This study was conducted by none other than Ancel Keys—whose fatphobia we encountered in chapter 3—along with the psychologist Josef Brozek. See David Baker and Natacha Keramidas, "The Psychology of Hunger," *Monitor on Psychology* 44, no. 9 (2013): 66, for a good overview of this research and its legacy.

45. The researchers showed this, specifically, by "preloading" participants with a milkshake before they tasted various ice creams, to which they had unrestricted access. Instead of eating less, because they were already fuller, ordinarily "restrained eaters" ate more than they did without this "preload"—seemingly because, having already had a milkshake, they now had a kind of "fuck it" mindset. See C. P. Herman and D. Mack, "Restrained and Unrestrained Eating," *Journal of Personality* 43, no. 4 (1975): 647–60, for the original, famous study. It has been widely replicated, discussed, and subject to numerous variations in the subsequent literature on "restrained eating."

46. Clara M. Davis, "Results of the Self-Selection of Diets by Young Children," *Canadian Medical Association Journal* 41, no. 3 (1939): 257–61.

47. Amy T. Galloway et al., "'Finish Your Soup': Counterproductive Effects of Pressuring Children to Eat on Intake and Affect," *Appetite* 46, no. 3 (2006): 318–23. Currently, many feeding specialists and dietitians trained in a new paradigm devised by Ellyn Satter, known as "division of responsibility," hence recommend

routinely serving a small portion of dessert alongside dinner, not distinguishing between "good foods" and "bad foods," and allowing some windows of unfettered access to "unhealthy" foods to partly temper the allure they might take on otherwise. (At most times, parents are responsible for deciding what, when, and where children eat; children are responsible for deciding how much to eat of the foods offered—hence the name of the paradigm.) Those of us who've tried this with our kids, often with trepidation, tend to find that they're surprisingly willing to eat a wide range of foods and don't become obsessive over "treat" foods when they don't fear losing access to them. More important, they learn to trust themselves, their bodies, and their appetites. See Ellyn Satter, *Secrets of Feeding a Healthy Family: How to Eat, How to Raise Good Eaters, How to Cook* (New York: Kelcy Press, 2008). For another excellent source of insights on this way of approaching the family dinner table, see Virginia Sole-Smith and Amy Palanjian, *Comfort Food,* podcast, comfortfoodpodcast.libsyn.com/, and Sole-Smith's book *Fat Talk.*

48. For a more recent study that suggested adults may also possess such "nutritional wisdom," see Jeffrey M. Brunstrom and Mark Schatzker, "Micronutrients and Food Choice: A Case of 'Nutritional Wisdom' in Humans?," *Appetite* 174 (2022): 106055.

49. Thomas Nagel, "Free Will," in *What Does It All Mean? A Very Short Introduction to Philosophy* (New York: Oxford University Press, 1987), 47.

50. For a more recent example along these lines, this time involving weakness of the will and having a cookie, thus breaking your diet, see Agnes Callard, *Aspiration: The Agency of Becoming* (New York: Oxford University Press, 2018), chap. 4.

51. Steven Pinker, *Rationality: What It Is, Why It Seems Scarce, Why It Matters* (New York: Viking, 2021), 36.

52. Ibid., 51.

53. Tyler Kingkade, "Geoffrey Miller Censured by University of New Mexico for Lying About Fat-Shaming Tweet," *Huffington Post,* Aug. 7, 2013, https://www.huffpost.com/entry/geoffrey-miller-censured-unm_n_3716605. As this article explains, technically, Miller was reprimanded for lying about his motives for tweeting this out—he claimed it was part of his research, a claim which UNM rejected.

54. Jacob M. Burmeister et al., "Weight Bias in Graduate School Admissions," *Obesity* 21, no. 5 (2013): 918–20. Another study by Viren Swami and Rachael Monk found that women whose BMI put them in the obese category (or the "emaciated" one) were less likely to be offered a place in university in a hypothetical scenario. "Weight Bias Against Women in a University Acceptance Scenario," *Journal of General Psychology* 140, no. 1 (2013): 45–56.

55. See also Kristin Rodier and Samantha Brennan, "Teaching (and) Fat Stigma in Philosophy," *Teaching Philosophy* (forthcoming), for illuminating reflections on teaching students *about* fat stigma as self-identified fat women in philosophy.

56. "Because If You Had Been, It Would All Have Been OK?," *What Is It Like to Be a Woman in Philosophy?*, Oct. 21, 2010, beingawomaninphilosophy.wordpress .com/2010/10/21/because-if-you-had-been-it-would-all-have-been-ok/. This blog is an invaluable source of information about philosophy's sexism and misogyny (among other things) in general.

57. In some media, fat characters even get smarter when they lose weight: "Fat Monica" on *Friends* is one such. She is a noticeably different character in her thin and sleek contemporary incarnation than in the flashbacks that depict her as a fat, naive, food-obsessed buffoon, courtesy of Courteney Cox in a fat suit. Whereas in the show's present day, after her transformational glow-up, she was supposed to be one of the smartest central characters. Thanks to Esa Díaz León for suggesting this example.

58. *The Simpsons*, season 4, episode 6, "Itchy and Scratchy: The Movie," aired Nov. 3, 1992, www.youtube.com/watch?v=NfBVRqZPb2w&ab_channel=Anand Venkatachalam.

59. The film's main message is that it's not fatphobia that's standing between a (supposedly somewhat) fat woman and her success in the world: rather, it's her lack of self-confidence. Blech.

60. Owen Gleiberman, "'The Whale' Review: Brendan Fraser Is Sly and Moving as a Morbidly Obese Man, but Darren Aronofsky's Film Is Hampered by Its Contrivances," *Variety*, Sept. 4, 2022, variety.com/2022/film/reviews/the-whale -review-brendan-fraser-darren-aronofsky-1235359338/.

61. Carmen Maria Machado, "The Trash Heap Has Spoken," *Guernica*, Feb. 13, 2017, www.guernicamag.com/the-trash-heap-has-spoken/.

62. On the other hand, Ursula *is* a villain. See Sophie Carter-Kahn and April Quioh, "Boo! Fear the Fat," Oct. 26, 2017, in *She's All Fat*, podcast, shesallfat pod.com/pod/s1e8, for an interesting take on the subsequent ambiguity in terms of fat representation.

63. Sonya Renee Taylor, *The Body Is Not an Apology: The Power of Radical Self-Love* (Oakland: Berrett-Koehler, 2018).

64. In fairness, Samuel Hunter responded to such criticism by discussing his rapid weight gain in his early twenties, before he lost the weight over the decade prior to the play's initial production in 2012. But this, to my mind, is pretty cold comfort: As many fat activists have pointed out, some formerly fat people are among

the most horrified by the bodies they imagine they were heading toward having. They can hence perpetuate particularly noxious forms of fatphobia in venting their unprocessed emotions about fatness. As Michael Schulman put it in *The New Yorker:* "Charlie's obesity grew out of Hunter's lived experience, but also out of worst-case speculation. 'What would happen to me if I hadn't turned that corner? . . . I was looking at the way I was gaining weight back then and how rapidly it was happening—I was, like, "This could have been me."'" But it wasn't, and that matters. Michael Schulman, "About Brendan Fraser's Fat Suit in *The Whale,*" *New Yorker,* Dec. 7, 2022, www.newyorker.com/culture/notes-on-hollywood/the-whale-and-the-fat-suit-brendan-fraser-darren-aronofsky.

65. Annette Richmond, "Ash of *The Fat Lip* Podcast Wants You to Know That Sizes Above 32 Exist," *Ravishly,* Feb. 26, 2018, www.ravishly.com/ash-fat-lip-podcast. For just a few other excellent sources of fat creators' stories and testimony, see the podcast *Unsolicited: Fatties Talk Back,* by Marquisele Mercedes, Da'Shaun L. Harrison, Caleb Luna, Bryan Guffey, and Jordan Underwood; the podcast *She's All Fat,* by April Quioh and Sophie Carter-Kahn; and the *Comfy Fat* blog, published by J Aprileo.

66. See Miranda Fricker, *Epistemic Injustice: Power and the Ethics of Knowing* (Oxford: Oxford University Press, 2007), chaps. 1–2.

67. See Kristie Dotson, "Tracking Epistemic Violence, Tracking Practices of Silencing," *Hypatia* 26, no. 2 (2011): 242. For an illuminating discussion of this problem for fat theorists in philosophy in particular and academia in general, see Alison Reiheld's interview with Shelley Tremain, in which she says, "Just as women doing feminist philosophy and people of color doing race theory are often derided as doing 'me studies' and ironically granted less epistemic authority than men talking about gender or white folks talking about race, fat folks theorizing fatness often get discounted. This general attitude within academia and within philosophy is simply poor knowledge-seeking. It also contributes to derision for these people as philosophers, and as academics. We cannot pursue knowledge if we so arrogantly restrict both who gets to be knowers and what is worth knowing." Shelley Tremain, "Dialogues on Disability: Shelley Tremain Interviews Alison Reiheld," *Biopolitical Philosophy,* Sept. 18, 2019, biopoliticalphilosophy.com/2019/09/18/dialogues-on-disability-shelley-tremain-interviews-alison-reiheld/.

68. Richmond, "Ash of *The Fat Lip* Podcast Wants You to Know That Sizes Above 32 Exist."

69. See the user @ash.fatlip's Instagram post, Nov. 3, 2022, www.instagram.com/p/CkgNl4yu1kI/?igshid=MDJmNzVkMjY%3D.

70. Ash, "You Can Still Fly with Limited Mobility," *The Fat Lip* (blog), July 8, 2019, thefatlip.com/2019/07/08/you-can-still-fly-with-limited-mobility/.

71. Ash, "Make Your Home Work for You," *The Fat Lip* (blog), Aug. 1, 2019, thefatlip.com/2019/08/01/home-accomodations/.

72. Ash, "UPDATED 2022: 27 Sturdy Chairs for Fat People (up to and Beyond 500lbs!)," *The Fat Lip* (blog), Nov. 9, 2019, thefatlip.com/2019/11/09/27-sturdy-chairs-for-fat-people/.

73. Ash, "Our 600 Pound Lives," *The Fat Lip* (blog), March 21, 2020, thefatlip.com/2020/03/21/our-600-pound-lives/.

74. Nor should we assume, for that matter, that people who *do* have cognitive disabilities, including what are often termed "severe" ones, should be construed as mentally "lacking" either. Although this issue is well beyond the scope of this book to wrestle with, the ableism of philosophy in this connection has been brilliantly called out by the philosopher Eva Kittay. She has shown that cognitively disabled people are not only equally valuable and deserving of humane, dignified treatment, but that they may also teach non-disabled people many valuable and subtle lessons. See her *Learning from My Daughter: The Value and Care of Disabled Minds* (New York: Oxford University Press, 2019).

75. See my book *Entitled*, chap. 8, for a discussion of the notion of epistemic entitlement in connection with Solnit's groundbreaking work on this topic—though the coinage "mansplaining" is not due to her and she reports somewhat mixed feelings about it. For Solnit's classic original discussion of this phenomenon, see "Men Explain Things to Me," reprinted in *Guernica*, Aug. 20, 2012, www.guernicamag.com/rebecca-solnit-men-explain-things-to-me/.

76. Peter Singer, "Weigh More, Pay More," *Straits Times*, March 16, 2012, www.straitstimes.com/world/peter-singer-weigh-more-pay-more.

77. Chris Uhlik, "What Is the Cost of Fuel Burned for 1 Kg in 1 Hour for an A320 Aircraft?," Quora, www.quora.com/What-is-the-cost-of-fuel-burned-for-1-kg-in-1-hour-for-an-A320-aircraft/answer/Chris-Uhlik. Note that even if Uhlik's estimate of these costs is off, it would have to be off by hundreds of orders of magnitude to justify Singer's point about the great expense of transporting fat bodies.

78. Singer is most controversial with respect to another issue of basic humanity: the value of the lives of even "severely" disabled people, which he implicitly denies in arguing that if a parent has the legal option to euthanize an infant who will be seriously disabled, they should take it. To which the late disability rights activist and lawyer Harriet McBryde Johnson forcefully replied, "I enjoy my life. . . .

[T]he presence or absence of a disability doesn't predict quality of life." See her classic piece, "Unspeakable Conversations," *New York Times Magazine,* Feb. 16, 2003, www.nytimes.com/2003/02/16/magazine/unspeakable-conversations .html. And in fact disabled and nondisabled people report a similar level of life satisfaction when surveyed. For three excellent recent philosophical treatments of this issue, see Elizabeth Barnes, *The Minority Body: A Theory of Disability* (Oxford: Oxford University Press, 2016); Joseph A. Stramondo, "Bioethics, Adaptive Preferences, and Judging the Quality of a Life with Disability," *Social Theory and Practice* 47, no. 1 (2021): 199–220; and Joel Michael Reynolds, *The Life Worth Living: Disability, Pain, and Morality* (Minneapolis: University of Minnesota Press, 2022).

79. Daniel Callahan, "Obesity: Chasing an Elusive Epidemic," *Hastings Center Report* 43, no. 1 (2013): 37.

80. Ibid., 40.

81. Ibid., 37–38.

82. Ibid., 35.

83. These complaints are also, of course, ableist. Such technologies are enormously beneficial for many disabled people, including people living with arthritis, multiple sclerosis, Parkinson's, limb differences, and so on.

84. Ibid., 39.

CHAPTER 7: DINNER BY GASLIGHT

1. See chapter 2, "Shrinking Costs," for discussion.

2. See Anna Guerdjikova and Harold C. Schott, "Why Dieting Can Be Harmful," Lindner Center blog, Feb. 8, 2021, lindnercenterofhope.org/blog/why-dieting -can-be-harmful/.

3. See "Overview of the $58 Billion U.S. Weight Loss Market 2022," *Globe News Wire,* March 23, 2022, https://www.globenewswire.com/en/news-release/2022/ 03/23/2408315/28124/en/Overview-of-the-58-Billion-U-S-Weight-Loss -Market-2022.html.

4. See *Saturday Night Live,* "Cinema Classics: Gaslight," aired Jan. 22, 2022, www.youtube.com/watch?v=xZU9D_DcbMs&ab_channel=SaturdayNightLive.

5. Patrick Hamilton, *Angel Street: A Victorian Thriller in Three Acts* (copyrighted under the title *Gas Light*) (New York: Samuel French, 1939), 18.

6. Ibid., 34–35.

7. Manne, *Entitled,* 148.

8. It's not clear whether this injury was an accident, and then blamed on Bella, or whether Mr. Manningham deliberately inflicted it as part of his diabolical campaign against her. It's also not clear what the point of his campaign is: perhaps to send her to the madhouse, having gotten what he wanted from her, in the form of her money to buy the Barlow house. Or perhaps "the cruelty is the point," to borrow a line from Adam Serwer in his recent book of the same title.

9. I use quotation marks here given the ableism of the term "crazy," which is nevertheless hard to avoid in doing justice to the characteristic aims and perspective of a prototypical gaslighter, such as Mr. Manningham.

10. For my full definition of gaslighting, see my paper "Moral Gaslighting," *Aristotelian Society Supplementary Volume* 97, no. 1 (2023). I draw in this work on existing philosophical work on gaslighting, including by Kate Abramson, "Turning Up the Lights on Gaslighting," *Philosophical Perspectives* 28, no. 1 (2014): 1–30; Veronica Ivy (writing as Rachel V. McKinnon), "Allies Behaving Badly: Gaslighting as Epistemic Injustice," in *The Routledge Handbook of Epistemic Injustice,* ed. Gaile Pohlhaus, Jr., Ian James Kidd, and José Medina (New York: Routledge, 2017), 167–75; and Elena Ruíz, "Cultural Gaslighting," *Hypatia* 35, no. 4 (2020): 687–713.

11. Note that even when there is an individual perpetrator, gaslighting need not be intentional: Imagine a formerly alcoholic agent who makes you feel guilty for questioning his obvious relapse by saying things like "Don't you trust me?" and "If you keep questioning me, I *will* relapse." This would still count as gaslighting, in my view, even though he is not *intending* to mentally deter you from believing the truth; rather, he is trying to conceal something he is deeply ashamed of.

12. See, in particular, Ruíz, "Cultural Gaslighting"; and Angelique M. Davis and Rose Ernst, "Racial Gaslighting," *Politics, Groups, and Identities* 7, no. 4 (2019): 761–74.

13. Physically wiring people's jaws shut to "help" them lose weight was popular as late as the 1980s. Safety concerns about such measures abound, including that someone who cannot open their mouth could easily choke on their own vomit. See Daniel Davies, "Researchers Develop Weight-Loss Tool That Uses Magnets to Lock Your Mouth Shut," *Men's Health,* July 14, 2021, www.menshealth.com/uk/health/a37020381/dental-slim-diet-control-magnet-device/.

14. See Virginia Sole-Smith, "A Weight Watchers App for Kids Raises Concerns," *New York Times,* April 17, 2020, www.nytimes.com/2020/04/17/parenting/big-kid/weight-watchers-kids.html. Admittedly, this app is free for the basic version, with a paid subscription option for additional "health coaching." But the

point is surely to hook children and their parents on this approach to food and bodies, making them ready consumers for Weight Watchers (now rebranded "WW —WIth the updated tagline "Wellness that works") products in the future.

15. Virginia Sole-Smith and Amy Palanjian, "Can You Be Addicted to Sugar? (with Lisa Du Breuil)," Jan. 17, 2019, in *Comfort Food,* podcast, comfortfood podcast.libsyn.com/episode-24-can-you-be-addicted-to-sugar-with-lisa -dubreuil. The answer to the episode's titular question is no, incidentally: sugar is not well understood as any kind of addictive substance.

16. Amanda Milkovits, "'I Don't Buy for a Second the Coaches Didn't Know': Former Students Wonder Why No One Stopped Coach Aaron Thomas and 'Fat Tests,'" *Boston Globe,* Jan. 24, 2022, www.bostonglobe.com/2022/01/24/ metro/i-dont-buy-second-coaches-didnt-know-former-students-wonder-why-no -one-stopped-coach-aaron-thomas-fat-tests/.

17. "Teen's Death at Camp Fuels Debate, Inquiry," *Los Angeles Times,* Dec. 5, 1999, www.latimes.com/archives/la-xpm-1999-dec-05-mn-40755-story.html.

18. Harrison, *Belly of the Beast,* 38.

19. Marquisele Mercedes, Da'Shaun L. Harrison, Caleb Luna, Bryan Guffey, and Jordan Underwood, "Solicited: I'm Just Asking Questions," March 27, 2022, in *Unsolicited: Fatties Talk Back,* podcast, unsolicitedftb.libsyn.com/im-just-asking -questions.

20. And given the ubiquity of diet culture, there's a general problem of the gaslit unwittingly gaslighting others and convincing vulnerable people of the impor- tance of shrinking their bodies.

21. The invidious comparison between the adult's and the child's body also hints at the fact that, for girls, policing the body is connected with policing sexuality and preventing the body from looking "mature" before it is deemed proper.

22. Hamilton, *Angel Street,* 10.

23. Ibid., 11.

24. Ibid., 12.

25. Ibid., 16.

26. Ibid., 26.

27. To be fair, though, it is a man, Anthony Marentino—one of the series's and franchise's appointed and much-stereotyped "gay best friends"—who initially draws attention to Samantha's extra few pounds of flesh. "Mother of God! What's with the gut?!"

28. For a good lay overview of the risks here, with excerpts from interviews with nutritionists and other experts, see Jenny Sugar, "If Dieting Makes You Feel Anxious, Distracted, Stressed, or Depressed, Experts Explain Why," *Pop Sugar,* April 13, 2020, www.popsugar.com/fitness/photo-gallery/47337017/image/47369438/Dieting-Affects-Sleep.

29. Harriet Brown, "The Weight of the Evidence," *Slate,* March 24, 2015, slate.com/technology/2015/03/diets-do-not-work-the-thin-evidence-that-losing-weight-makes-you-healthier.html. See also her book *Body of Truth: How Science, History, and Culture Drive Our Obsession with Weight—and What We Can Do About It* (Boston: Da Capo Press, 2015) for further valuable reflections on the topic.

30. Kolata, "One Weight Loss Approach Fits All?" This man had maintained his weight loss of forty-two pounds for two and a half years at the time—well short of the five years that represents the gold standard in the business.

31. Ibid.

32. Ibid.

33. Lucy Wallis, "Do Slimming Clubs Work?," BBC News, Aug. 8, 2013, www.bbc.com/news/magazine-23463006.

34. Ibid.

35. Ibid.

36. Hamilton, *Angel Street,* 92.

CHAPTER 8: THE AUTHORITY OF HUNGER

1. I draw here on my "Diet Culture Is Unhealthy," though my argument in what follows has evolved considerably.

2. *Fantasy Island,* season 1, episode 1, "Hungry Christine/Mel Loves Ruby," Aug. 10, 2021. The showrunners, Liz Craft and Sarah Fain, made it clear on their podcast, *Happier in Hollywood,* that they admire and applaud Christine's abstemious lifestyle, having based the character loosely on Craft's sister-in-law, also a morning news anchor, who has to stay in what they described as "incredible shape" for her job too. (The episode even portrays Christine as the victim of an "evil donut-bringer," a regular trope on the podcast, as they bemoan people who bring in "fattening" food to share at the office and tempt them to break their own diets.)

3. If you're in the minority of people who are okay with throwing the fat man off the bridge, consider an even more obviously vicious act: cutting up one healthy person—thereby killing them—to harvest their organs in order to save five ailing

people (who would die without this intervention). Utilitarianism seems to prescribe this horrific action, in the hypothetical "surgeon case" (also offered, in its original form, in Philippa Foot's "The Problem of Abortion and the Doctrine of Double Effect," 9). Relatively few people think utilitarianism survives these sorts of counterexamples, at least without major modifications, which arguably then make the theory much less simple and attractive.

4. Peter Singer, "Famine, Affluence, and Morality," *Philosophy and Public Affairs* 1, no. 3 (1972): 229–43. Singer also defends a stronger (that is, more committal) principle, according to which, "if it is in my power to prevent something bad from happening, without thereby sacrificing anything of *comparable* moral importance, we ought, morally, to do it" (ibid., 231, my italics). The weaker principle will suffice for present purposes. I discuss Singer's conclusions and some of my qualms about them, including their impugning of small indulgences, in a Substack post: "Against Swooping In," *More to Hate,* June 30, 2022, katemanne.substack.com/p/against-swooping-in.

5. See, for example, Singer's "Animal Liberation," in *Animal Rights,* ed. Robert Garner (London: Palgrave Macmillan, 1973), 7–18.

6. As the economist Emily Oster put it, in rather less pointed (and critical) terms, "The simplest diet, then, is just . . . eat less. This is best epitomized by a good book I once read called *The Economists' Diet.* The primary message was that to lose weight you need to weigh yourself every day and eat less. And, also, that you'll be hungry a lot of the time. It was sort of beautiful in its simplicity, but I can see why this hasn't caught on." Emily Oster, "Diets and Data," *ParentData,* Substack, Jan. 6, 2022, emilyoster.substack.com/p/diets-and-data.

7. See Colin Klein, "An Imperative Theory of Pain," *Journal of Philosophy* 104, no. 10 (2007): 517–32; and Colin Klein, *What the Body Commands: The Imperative Theory of Pain* (Cambridge, Mass.: MIT Press, 2015).

8. I draw here on my paper "Locating Morality: Moral Imperatives as Bodily Imperatives," in *Oxford Studies in Metaethics 12,* ed. Russ Shafer-Landau (Oxford: Oxford University Press, 2017), 1–26. Note that while utilitarianism and the like offer an *ethical* theory—predictions about what is right and wrong and why—the idea of bodily imperatives is offered in service of the complementary but more fundamental level of analysis that philosophers call "metaethical," which gives answers to questions about morality's *source* or *nature* (among other things). Note too that my metaethical view is not committal with respect to a specific ethical theory: it certainly does not entail or require a commitment to utilitarianism (or indeed any theory in the broader family of theories utilitarianism belongs to, which are called consequentialist, and hold that the morality of an action depends only on its consequences).

9. One of the relatively few things that can interfere with the bodily imperative to eat—or "the eating instinct," as Virginia Sole-Smith calls it—is having to prioritize the bodily imperative to *breathe*. This happened to Sole-Smith's baby daughter Violet, due to a congenital condition that caused heart failure, leaving her tiny body prioritizing getting enough oxygen over ingesting enough milk. This adaptive, hardwired instinct, together with medical trauma, led to a subsequent oral aversion that lasted far longer than doctors anticipated. Violet hence became dependent on a feeding tube. For a moving account of gradually teaching Violet to eat again, over the two years that followed, and the way this helped Sole-Smith reckon with her own sense of discomfort around food, see her book *The Eating Instinct: Food Culture, Body Image, and Guilt in America* (New York: Henry Holt, 2018), chap. 1.

10. In my work in metaethics, I take the kinds of measures that can be used to torture people as an epistemic criterion for a bodily imperative. And this delivers a decisive answer to a question I am often asked: Are sexual urges bodily imperatives? No, they are merely desires. For, while raping or otherwise sexually violating someone is a well-established torture method—would that it were otherwise—nobody (as far as I know) has actually been tortured merely by withholding sex from them, contra incel logic.

11. This framework also helps to explain why there are such strong reasons not to develop an addiction, which will then create newfound bodily imperatives to satisfy the addiction that both are difficult to satisfy and will frequently lead to serious further issues, including health problems (and unmet bodily imperatives) down the line. However, I do believe that we have a moral duty to minister humanely to people who have already developed an addiction—by offering methadone treatment rather than expecting people to quit heroin "cold turkey," for example. And this is for intrinsic moral reasons, to do with minimizing the suffering constituted by unmet bodily imperatives, as well as the instrumental reason that such treatments are generally more effective.

12. Note that, like most contemporary moral philosophers, I use the terms "ethical" and "moral" interchangeably.

13. See the introduction to my book *Down Girl* for an extended discussion of the (typically gendered) crime of strangulation.

14. For a vivid account of such suffering, as in acute respiratory distress syndrome, see Cheryl Misak, "ICU Psychosis and Patient Autonomy: Some Thoughts from the Inside," *Journal of Medicine and Philosophy* 30, no. 4 (2005): 411–30.

15. An even more extreme practice is the "Uberman" method, which tells you to sleep twenty minutes out of every four hours (a form of "polyphasic sleep," with

a large dose of sleep deprivation added for good measure). For a recent account of what this can do to a person, complete with hallucinations, depression, and a fugue-like state of which he has no recollection, see Mark Serrels, "I Tried Poly-phasic Sleep and Almost Lost My Mind," CNET, July 12, 2022, www.cnet.com/culture/features/i-tried-polyphasic-sleep-and-almost-lost-my-mind/. He writes, "Looking back, the whole thing seems ridiculous. A pointless challenge driven by male ego bullshit and a pointless need to 'bodyhack.' Weaponized toxic masculin-ity in its purest form." He adds, "It made for a good story, though."

16. See "The Nap Ministry," thenapministry.wordpress.com/.

17. Moreover, a progression to full-syndrome EDs was reported in 14 percent, 33 percent, 37.5 percent, and 46 percent of those who had originally been classi-fied as having partial-syndrome EDs in four other studies. See Catherine M. Shisslak et al., "The Spectrum of Eating Disturbances," *International Journal of Eating Disorders* 18, no. 3 (1995): 213–14.

18. See, for example, "Eating Disorder Statistics," South Carolina Department of Mental Health, www.state.sc.us/dmh/anorexia/statistics.htm.

19. Specifically, the researchers found, in a community sample of nearly five hun-dred adolescent females followed over eight years, that "lifetime prevalence [of an eating disorder] by age 20 was 0.8% for anorexia nervosa (AN), 2.6% for bulimia nervosa (BN), 3.0% for binge eating disorder (BED), 2.8% for atypical AN, 4.4% for subthreshold BN, 3.6% for subthreshold BED, 3.4% for purging disorder (PD); with a combined prevalence of 13.1% (5.2% had AN, BN, or BED; 11.5% had a Feeding and Eating Disorders Not Elsewhere Classified; FED-NEC)." Eric Stice et al., "Prevalence, Incidence, Impairment, and Course of the Proposed DSM-5 Eating Disorder Diagnoses in an 8-Year Prospective Community Study of Young Women," *Journal of Abnormal Psychology* 122, no. 2 (2013): 445–57. Re-cent evidence has also suggested that the prevalence of atypical anorexia may be even higher for nonbinary and gender nonconforming people; see Erin N. Harrop et al., "Restrictive Eating Disorders in Higher Weight Persons: A Systematic Re-view of Atypical Anorexia Nervosa Prevalence and Consecutive Admission Litera-ture," *International Journal of Eating Disorders* 54, no. 8 (2021): 1328–57.

20. For an edifying if harrowing discussion of these symptoms, among others, see Aubrey Gordon and Michael Hobbes's interview with Erin Harrop, "Eating Dis-orders," March 30, 2021, in *Maintenance Phase,* podcast, player.fm/series/maintenance-phase/eating-disorders.

21. See, for example, Margot Rittenhouse, "What Is Atypical Anorexia Nervosa: Symptoms, Causes, and Treatment," Eating Disorder Hope, updated Aug. 30, 2021, www.eatingdisorderhope.com/information/atypical-anorexia.

22. Michael Hobbes, "Everything You Know About Obesity Is Wrong," *Huffington Post,* Sept. 19, 2018, highline.huffingtonpost.com/articles/en/everything-you-know-about-obesity-is-wrong/, in which he summarizes some of Harrop's dissertation research (see also note 20). In contrast, anorexia nervosa will be diagnosed two and a half years after onset, on average; see Kate Shiber, "You Don't Look Anorexic," *New York Times Magazine,* Oct. 18, 2022, www.nytimes.com/2022/10/18/magazine/anorexia-obesity-eating-disorder.html, which also draws on work by Harrop.

23. See Christina van Dyke, "Manly Meat and Gendered Eating: Correcting Imbalance and Seeking Virtue," in *Philosophy Comes to Dinner: Arguments on the Ethics of Eating,* ed. Andrew Chignell, Terence Cuneo, and Matthew C. Halteman (New York: Routledge, 2016), 39–55; and Megan A. Dean, "Eating as a Self-Shaping Activity: The Case of Young Women's Vegetarianism and Eating Disorders," *Feminist Philosophy Quarterly* 7, no. 3 (2021), for two nuanced feminist discussions of considerations of this nature.

24. Many other books, written by qualified experts like nutritionists and dietitians and psychologists, get into the details of this practice and offer advice well above my pay grade to give as a philosopher about how to implement it. See, for example, Evelyn Tribole and Elyse Resch, *Intuitive Eating: A Revolutionary Anti-diet Approach,* 4th ed. (New York: St. Martin's Press, 2020); Harrison, *Anti-diet;* and Conason, *Diet-Free Revolution,* for some excellent starting points. And many certified intuitive eating counselors offer the personal support and individualized guidance that many people will need or at least benefit from in order to implement the principles of this approach to eating without falling back into a diet mentality. Suffice it to say here that the general paradigm of intuitive eating dovetails nicely with my philosophical ideas about the authority of hunger, the importance of listening to your body, and pushing back against gaslighting by trusting your own instincts. And, although intuitive eating is not without its critics and detractors, for me personally, it's been vital.

25. Pinker, *Rationality,* 52.

26. For an illuminating philosophical meditation on bodily alienation in relation to the cultivation of a "thigh gap," which requires extreme thinness for most body types, see Céline Leboeuf, "Anatomy of the Thigh Gap," *Feminist Philosophy Quarterly* 5, no. 1 (2019). And thanks to Fabio Cabrera for wonderful discussions of this paper.

27. Sharon Hayes and Stacey Tantleff-Dunn, "Am I Too Fat to Be a Princess? Examining the Effects of Popular Children's Media on Young Girls' Body Image," *British Journal of Developmental Psychology* 28, no. 2 (2010): 413–26.

28. Christine Roberts, "Most 10 Year-Olds Have Been on a Diet: Study; 53 Percent of 13-Year-Old Girls Have Issues with How Their Bodies Look," *New York Daily News*, July 2, 2012, www.nydailynews.com/news/national/diets-obsess -tweens-study-article-1.1106653.

29. José Francisco López-Gil et al., "Global Proportion of Disordered Eating in Children and Adolescents: A Systematic Review and Meta-analysis," *JAMA Pediatrics* 177, no. 4 (2023): 363–372.

30. Jacinta Lowes and Marika Tiggemann, "Body Dissatisfaction, Dieting Awareness, and the Impact of Parental Influence in Young Children," *British Journal of Health Psychology* 8 (2003): 135–47.

31. W. Stewart Agras et al., "Childhood Risk Factors for Thin Body Preoccupation and Social Pressure to Be Thin," *Journal of the American Academy of Child and Adolescent Psychiatry* 46, no. 2 (2007): 171–78.

32. Such overeating is a complex phenomenon that can be caused by taking common medications, such as corticosteroids, which make some people desperately want to eat even long after they are full, due to a kind of disconnection between their satiety cues and their appetites. Similar remarks apply to some people with rare genetic disorders, such as Prader-Willi syndrome.

33. Lauren Del Turco, "6 Weight Loss Surgery Myths, and the Honest Truth from Experts," *Prevention,* Jan. 6, 2020, www.prevention.com/weight-loss/ a30393486/weight-loss-surgery-myths/.

34. Among the various types of weight-loss surgery commonly performed are a sleeve gastrectomy, which reduces the stomach to around the size of a banana; a duodenal switch, a sleeve gastrectomy plus a bypassing of a large proportion of the small intestine; and a gastric bypass, the most extreme option, which connects a tiny section of the stomach to a lower part of the small intestine. Gastric band, or "lap band," surgery—which involves an adjustable band to squeeze and thus section off a portion of the stomach—is now performed less frequently, since it is considered a less powerful intervention. For a good lay overview of these differences, see ibid.

35. See "Estimate of Bariatric Surgery Numbers, 2011–2020," American Society for Metabolic and Bariatric Surgery, June 2022, asmbs.org/resources/estimate -of-bariatric-surgery-numbers.

36. John Pavlus, "What No One Tells You About Weight Loss Surgery," *Glamour,* July 30, 2007, www.glamour.com/story/weight-loss-surgery.

37. "Weight-Loss Surgery Side Effects: What Are the Side Effects of Bariatric Surgery?," National Institute of Diabetes and Digestive and Kidney Diseases,

www.niddk.nih.gov/health-information/weight-management/bariatric-surgery/side-effects.

38. Del Turco, "6 Weight Loss Surgery Myths."

39. Derek Bagley, "Unforeseen Consequences: Bariatric Surgery Side Effects," *Endocrine News*, Nov. 2018, endocrinenews.endocrine.org/unforeseen-consequences-bariatric-surgery-side-effects/.

40. "Weight-Loss Surgery Side Effects."

41. Pavlus, "What No One Tells You About Weight Loss Surgery."

42. Benjamin Clapp, "Small Bowel Obstruction After Laparoscopic Gastric Bypass with Nonclosure of Mesenteric Defects," *Journal of the Society of Laparoscopic and Robotic Surgeons* 19, no. 1 (2015): e2014.00257.

43. Lara Pizzorno, "Bariatric Surgery: Bad to the Bone, Part 1," *Integrative Medicine* 15, no. 1 (2016): 48–54.

44. Del Turco, "6 Weight Loss Surgery Myths."

45. Pavlus, "What No One Tells You About Weight Loss Surgery."

46. "Weight-Loss Surgery Side Effects."

47. Bagley, "Unforeseen Consequences." For one prominent piece of original research on this topic, see O. Backman et al., "Alcohol and Substance Abuse, Depression, and Suicide Attempts After Roux-en-Y Gastric Bypass Surgery," *British Journal of Surgery* 103, no. 10 (2016): 1336–42. This research examined suicide attempts in patients who had undergone this type of (RYGB) surgery between 2001 and 2010 in Sweden, and found that these patients were nearly three times more likely to be hospitalized following attempted suicide than members of the general population. Other studies have compared patients following bariatric surgery with "obese" or "severely obese" people, and similarly showed a substantially elevated suicide and self-harm risk (nearly double the risk in one study, and more than three times the risk for patients who underwent RYGB surgery; some studies produced even more alarming findings). See also Alexis Conason and Lisa Du Breuil, "'But Everything Is Supposed to Get Better After Bariatric Surgery!': Understanding Postoperative Suicide and Self-Injury," *Bariatric Times*, Oct. 1, 2019, bariatrictimes.com/understanding-postoperative-suicide-self-injury/; and Sara G. Miller, "Risk of Self-Harm May Rise Following Bariatric Surgery," *Scientific American*, Oct. 8, 2015, www.scientificamerican.com/article/risk-of-self-harm-may-rise-following-bariatric-surgery/.

48. Bagley, "Unforeseen Consequences."

49. Ragen Chastain, "The Inconvenient Truth About Weight Loss Surgery,"

Ravishly, March 14, 2017, www.ravishly.com/2017/03/14/inconvenient-truth
-about-weight-loss-surgery.

50. Miranda Hitti, "Lasting Damage from Fen-Phen Drug?," *WebMD,* Nov. 5,
2008, https://tlfllc.com/blog/lasting-damage-from-fen-phen-drug.

51. Gordon, *What We Don't Talk About When We Talk About Fat,* 59.

52. Alicia Mundy, *Dispensing with the Truth: The Victims, the Drug Companies,
and the Dramatic Story Behind the Battle over Fen-Phen* (New York: St. Martin's
Press, 2010), 4. In Aubrey Gordon and Michael Hobbes's "Fen Phen & Redux"
episode of their podcast *Maintenance Phase,* player.fm/series/maintenance-phase/
fen-phen-redux, they draw on Mundy's research. The drugs were taken off the
market in 1997.

53. See, for example, University of Illinois, "Phentermine, Oral Capsule," *Healthline,* Aug. 2, 2021, https://www.healthline.com/health/drugs/phentermine-oral
-capsule.

54. Amy J. Jeffers and Eric G. Benotsch, "Non-medical Use of Prescription Stimulants for Weight Loss, Disordered Eating, and Body Image," *Eating Behaviors* 15
(2014): 414–18.

55. Amanda B. Bruening et al., "Exploring Weight Control as Motivation for Illicit Stimulant Use," *Eating Behaviors* 30 (2018): 72–75.

56. See, for example, Jacquelyn Cafasso, "Can You Overdose on Adderall?"
Healthline, Jan. 24, 2023, www.healthline.com/health/can-you-overdose-on
-adderall#drug-interactions.

57. A closely related drug prescribed for type 2 diabetes—Victoza, a liraglutide—
was also recently the subject of a lawsuit due to claims it causes pancreatic cancer
in humans. The drug's manufacturer, Novo Nordisk, won the appeal from plain-
tiffs to reopen the case, however. See Brendan Pierson, "Novo Nordisk Wins Appeal over Claims That Diabetes Drug Causes Cancer," Reuters, March 29, 2022,
www.reuters.com/legal/litigation/novo-nordisk-wins-appeal-over-claims-that
-diabetes-drug-causes-cancer-2022-03-29/.

58. Even so, the off-label use of Ozempic (a lower-dose version intended for
people with type 2 diabetes) for weight loss had become so popular that it was in
scarce supply for the patients who actually need it, when this book was in press.
See Arianna Johnson, "What to Know About Ozempic: The Diabetes Drug Becomes a Viral Weight Loss Hit (Elon Musk Boasts Using It) Creating a Shortage,"
Forbes, Dec. 26, 2022, www.forbes.com/sites/ariannajohnson/2022/12/26/
what-to-know-about-ozempic/.

59. This "flattening" complaint would also apply to the idea of making disabled

people nondisabled. For an argument that aims to establish the value of disability as a form of diversity that it makes sense to take pride in and celebrate, see Barnes, *The Minority Body*.

60. Note that I'm not by any means making a blanket argument against changing one's body. My objection is to practices that help one's body conform more closely to harmful standards and values, making—for one salient example—many trans people's practices of self-expression completely disanalogous from those I flag above as problematically flattening difference. Trans people *embody* an important form of diversity and do us all the service of subverting patriarchal gender norms and strictures. More on trans as well as disability pride will follow in the conclusion.

61. Gay, *Hunger*, 15.

62. Thanks to Bianca Waked for illuminating discussion here.

63. isozyme (@isocrime), Twitter, March 16, 2021, 8:28 P.M., twitter.com/isocrime/status/1371981683822628872. Thanks to Urna Chakrabarty for bringing this tweet to my attention and for valuable discussion on this point in general.

64. West, *Shrill*, 79. The placement of the adjective in this quotation is important here; neither West nor I am saying that *only* fat women's bodies are somehow "real," as in the misguided sentiment that "*real* women have curves," and similar. The thought is that *some* real women's bodies are fat, and certain small-minded men recoil from them in cowardice; so much the worse for them, and more for the rest of us.

65. isozyme (@isocrime), Twitter, Dec. 3, 2020, 12:24 p.m., twitter.com/isocrime/status/1334548965870751744. Thanks again to Urna Chakrabarty for pointing me to this author.

66. In philosophers' terms, such a refusal would thus be "supererogatory"—good, but above and beyond the call of duty proper—to use our rather awkward label.

67. As the beauty culture critic Jessica DeFino writes, "Sure, maybe that anti-aging product *does* take the burden off of the individual buying it. Maybe it makes that *one individual* feel better about how they look. But it only compounds the original problem for the collective." See her piece "Erasing Your Wrinkles Is Not Empowerment," Medium, Jan. 12, 2021, jessica-defino.medium.com/erasing-your-wrinkles-isnt-empowerment-514c5b5c2d2e. And it's worth noting the painful irony that, now, many people are seeking cosmetic procedures such as filler to offset what has become known as "Ozempic face"—the gaunt features people

develop after rapidly losing weight via semaglutide. What a banner day for capitalism. See Amy Synnott, "Those Weight Loss Drugs May Do a Number on Your
Face," *New York Times,* Jan. 24, 2023, www.nytimes.com/2023/01/24/style/
ozempic-weight-loss-drugs-aging.html.

CONCLUSION: NOT SORRY

1. Dr. Jordan B. Peterson (@jordanbpeterson), Twitter, May 16, 2022, 3:11 p.m.,
twitter.com/jordanbpeterson/status/1526279181545390083?s=20&t=kqOL9
Yy4HUFn9zBVwZvOvw. The tweet had received 5,210 retweets, 10,900 quote
tweets, and 64,700 likes at the time of writing, June 23, 2022.

2. Dr. Jordan B. Peterson (@jordanbpeterson), Twitter, June 16, 2022, 5:51 p.m.,
twitter.com/jordanbpeterson/status/1537553423016632322?s=20&t=kqOL9
Yy4HUFn9zBVwZvOvw. The tweet had received 844 retweets, 833 quote
tweets, and 22,300 likes at the time of writing, June 23, 2022.

3. Brad Hunter, "Paige Spiranac Fat-Shamed by Male Social Media Trolls,"
Toronto Sun, Sept. 16, 2022, torontosun.com/sports/golf/paige-spiranac-fat
-shamed-by-male-social-media-trolls. Spiranac responded by talking about how
hard it is to "maintain my ideal weight all the time for year after year." "It doesn't
come naturally to me," she added.

4. For one related but distinct idea, see Lindsay Kite and Lexie Kite, *More Than a
Body: Your Body Is an Instrument, Not an Ornament* (New York: HarperCollins,
2021). I worry, however, that the notion of what our bodies are *good for,* as opposed to *whom* they are for, has an unintentionally ableist upshot. For another—
again, related, but distinct—idea in this vicinity, see the notion of "body
sovereignty" (not to be confused with the noxious sovereign citizens movement).
This important notion, developed by Indigenous authors, draws inspiration from
the idea of land sovereignty to "seek equitable rights of access for all bodies,
particularly marginalized bodies." See A. Gillon (Ngāti Awa), "Fat Indigenous
Bodies and Body Sovereignty: An Exploration of Re-presentations," *Journal of
Sociology* 56, no. 2 (2020): 213–28. However, one can be regarded as sovereign
over a body or territory while viewing oneself as its *custodian* rather than beneficiary; conversely, the beneficiary of a body or territory may *not* be sovereign over
it, as in the case of young children, for instance. So body sovereignty and reflexivity, as I intend the notion to be understood, can come apart in both directions.

5. "Body acceptance" is a mushier term, with some authors treating it as an um-
brella term for *both* the body positivity and the body neutrality movements. Others
treat it as an outgrowth of the "fat acceptance" movement, which is a term
adopted by some authors for the general political project of anti-fatphobia that this

book has its roots in. Still others think of body acceptance as a variant of body neutrality. See Equip's "How to Reframe the Way You Think About Your Body," Katie Couric Media, June 13, 2022, katiecouric.com/health/what-is-difference -between-body-neutrality-and-positivity/, for a recent illustration of this prevalent confusion. The article reads, "In some ways, body acceptance is more closely tied to the origins of body positivity and the Fat Acceptance movement, encouraging individuals to acknowledge their bodies from an impartial place." It immediately continues with a quotation from Cara Bohon: "Body acceptance is a slight variation of body neutrality that has a somewhat more positive angle—accepting the body as it is in a nonjudgmental way."

6. Dr. Jordan B. Peterson (@jordanbpeterson), Twitter, June 20, 2022, 6:57 p.m., twitter.com/jordanbpeterson/status/1539019681125675009?s=20&t=kqOL9 Yy4HUFn9zBVwZvOvw. The tweet had received 1,409 retweets, 151 quote tweets, and 12,300 likes at the time of writing, June 23, 2022.

7. Tayler Hansen (@TaylerUSA), Twitter, June 20, 2022, 12:00 a.m., twitter .com/TaylerUSA/status/1538733481492094977. This tweet by Hansen, an independent self-described "gonzo" journalist who also recorded the footage, had received 1,884 retweets, 572 quote tweets, and 5,926 likes at the time of writing, June 23, 2022.

8. See, for example, Eleanor Klibanoff, "More Families of Trans Teens Sue to Stop Texas Child Abuse Investigations," *Texas Tribune,* June 8, 2022, www.texas tribune.org/2022/06/08/transgender-texas-child-abuse-lawsuit/.

9. Anna Louie Sussman, "Egg Freezing's BMI Problem," *The Cut,* June 6, 2022, www.thecut.com/2022/06/egg-freezing-bmi-limits.html.

10. Sole-Smith, "When You're Told You're Too Fat to Get Pregnant."

11. Richard S. Legro et al., "Effects of Preconception Lifestyle Intervention in Infertile Women with Obesity: The FIT-PLESE Randomized Controlled Trial," *PLOS Medicine* 19, no. 1 (2022): e1003883.

12. See Ryan Jaslow, "Obese Third-Grader Taken from Family: Did State Go Too Far?," CBS, Nov. 28, 2011, www.cbsnews.com/news/obese-third-grader-taken -from-family-did-state-go-too-far/, for one representative case of this in the United States; see Nadeem Badshah, "Two Teenagers Placed in Foster Care After Weight Loss Plan Fails," *Guardian,* March 11, 2021, www.theguardian.com/ society/2021/mar/10/two-teenagers-placed-in-foster-care-after-weight-loss -plan-fails, for a recent case in the U.K., where this had already happened in at least seventy-four other cases in 2014. And see Virginia Sole-Smith, "The Last Thing Fat Kids Need," *Slate,* April 19, 2021, slate.com/technology/2021/04/

child-separation-weight-stigma-diets.html, for an excellent critical discussion of this troubling practice.

13. Jason Rafferty et al., "Ensuring Comprehensive Care and Support for Transgender and Gender-Diverse Children and Adolescents," *American Academy of Pediatrics: Policy Statement* 142, no. 4 (2018).

14. Sarah C. Armstrong et al., "Pediatric Metabolic and Bariatric Surgery: Evidence, Barriers, and Best Practices," *American Academy of Pediatrics: Policy Statement* 144, no. 6 (2019). As this book was in press, the AAP released its first comprehensive set of guidelines for health professionals treating fat children, which also—horrifyingly—recommends that those as young as two undergo "intensive health behavior and lifestyle treatment" and that those as young as twelve receive weight-loss medications. See Virginia Sole-Smith, "Why the New Obesity Guidelines for Kids Terrify Me," *New York Times*, Jan. 26, 2023, www.nytimes .com/2023/01/26/opinion/aap-obesity-guidelines-bmi-wegovy-ozempic.html, for a compelling takedown.

15. Diana M. Tordoff et al., "Mental Health Outcomes in Transgender and Nonbinary Youths Receiving Gender-Affirming Care," *JAMA Network Open* 5, no. 2 (2022): e220978.

16. For the definitive treatment of this issue, see Sole-Smith's recent book, *Fat Talk*.

17. Virginia Sole-Smith, "What Instagram Gets Wrong About Feeding Your Kids," *Burnt Toast*, Substack, Oct. 19, 2021, virginiasolesmith.substack.com/p/ dor-diet-culture-instagram.

18. Jaclyn Diaz, "Florida's Governor Signs Controversial Law Opponents Dubbed 'Don't Say Gay,'" NPR, March 28, 2022, www.npr.org/2022/03/28/ 1089221657/dont-say-gay-florida-desantis.

19. For an important perspective on the role of kink at Pride, and an argument that it is actually valuable for children to witness in some forms, see Lauren Rowello, "Yes, Kink Belongs at Pride. And I Want My Kids to See It," *Washington Post*, June 29, 2021, www.washingtonpost.com/outlook/2021/06/29/pride-month -kink-consent/.

20. Barnes, *The Minority Body*, 181–82.

21. See Evette Dionne, "The Fragility of Body Positivity: How a Radical Movement Lost Its Way," *Bitch*, Nov. 21, 2017, www.bitchmedia.org/article/fragility -body-positivity, for characteristically brilliant commentary on this problem, among others.

22. Lisa Legault and Anise Sago, "When Body Positivity Falls Flat: Divergent Effects of Body Acceptance Messages That Support vs. Undermine Basic Psychological Needs," *Body Image* 41 (2022): 226.

23. Ibid., 227–36.

24. Ibid., 226.

25. See Karen Gasper et al., "Does Neutral Affect Exist? How Challenging Three Beliefs About Neutral Affect Can Advance Affective Research," *Frontiers in Psychology* 10, art. no. 2476 (2019): 1–11, for discussion.

26. Thanks to Alexandra Lilly for valuable discussion on this point.

27. Crucially, any adequate notion of bodily autonomy will uphold the right to have an abortion too. I explore these ideas in work in progress and mount an argument—drawing on a growing philosophical tradition—that a radical politics of autonomy does not have to take a backward and misguided stance against our communal *interdependence.*

28. Harrison, *Belly of the Beast,* 14–15.

29. Ibid., 13.

30. Eaton, "Taste in Bodies and Fat Oppression," 37–59. And see also Lindy West, who writes in her memoir, *Shrill,* that the question of where she got her confidence is one that she can answer in a single sentence: "There was really only one step to my body acceptance. Look at pictures of fat women on the Internet until they don't make you uncomfortable anymore. That was the entire process" (68). She writes, in particular, of discovering Leonard Nimoy's *Full Body Project* of photographs of fat, naked women dancing, talking, laughing, and just *being* in the world. ("I asked them," he explained, "to be proud.") West writes of feeling something start to unclench deep within her body in drinking in these images. "What if my body didn't have to be a secret?" she wondered (76).

31. Cheryl Frazier, "Beauty Labor as a Tool to Resist Anti-fatness," *Hypatia* (forthcoming). Note that Frazier takes the notion of "beauty labor" from important work by the Black feminist Shirley Anne Tate.

32. Tressie McMillan Cottom, *Thick: And Other Essays* (New York: New Press, 2019), 43.

33. Ibid., 58. And see also brilliant work by Jessica DeFino in this connection, via her *The Unpublishable* Substack newsletter, https://jessicadefino.substack.com/.

FURTHER RESOURCES

ON FATPHOBIA/FAT LIVED EXPERIENCE AND ITS INTERSECTIONS

J Aprileo, *Comfy Fat* (blog)

Jes Baker, *Things No One Will Tell Fat Girls: A Handbook for Unapologetic Living*

Hanne Blank, *Fat*

Susan Bordo, *Unbearable Weight: Feminism, Western Culture, and the Body*

Harriet Brown, *Body of Truth: How Science, History, and Culture Drive Our Obsession with Weight—and What We Can Do About It.*

Paul Campos, *The Obesity Myth: Why America's Obsession with Weight Is Hazardous to Your Health*

Ragen Chastain, *Weight and Healthcare* (Substack newsletter)

Evette Dionne, *Weightless: Making Space for My Resilient Body and Soul*

Amy Erdman Farrell, *Fat Shame: Stigma and the Fat Body in American Culture*

Roxane Gay, *Hunger: A Memoir of (My) Body*, and her "Unruly Bodies" series in Gay Mag

Linda Gerhardt, *Fluffy Kitten Party* (blog)

Aubrey Gordon, *What We Don't Talk About When We Talk About Fat* and *"You Just Need to Lose Weight": And 19 Other Myths About Fat People*

Sofie Hagen, *Happy Fat: Taking Up Space in a World That Wants to Shrink You*

Kate Harding and Marianne Kirby, *Lessons from the Fat-o-Sphere: Quit Dieting and Declare a Truce with Your Body*

Da'Shaun L. Harrison, *Belly of the Beast: The Politics of Anti-Fatness as Anti-Blackness*

Kiese Laymon, *Heavy: An American Memoir*

Marquisele Mercedes, Da'Shaun L. Harrison, Caleb Luna, Bryan Guffey, and Jordan Underwood, *Unsolicited: Fatties Talk Back* (podcast)

Tressie McMillan Cottom, *Thick: And Other Essays*

Ash Nischuk, *The Fat Lip* (blog and podcast)

Susie Orbach, *Fat Is a Feminist Issue*

April Quioh and Sophie Carter-Kahn, *She's All Fat* (podcast)

Esther Rothblum and Sondra Solovay (editors), *The Fat Studies Reader*

Abigail C. Saguy, *What's Wrong with Fat?*

Sabrina Strings, *Fearing the Black Body: The Racist Origins of Fat Phobia*

Sonya Renee Taylor, *The Body Is Not an Apology: The Power of Radical Self-Love*

Virgie Tovar, *You Have the Right to Remain Fat*

Marilyn Wann, *FAT! SO? Because You Don't Have to Apologize for Your Size*

Lindy West, *Shrill: Notes from a Loud Woman*

Rachel Wiley, *Fat Girl Finishing School*

ON DIET CULTURE IN RELATION TO FATPHOBIA

Aubrey Gordon and Michael Hobbes, *Maintenance Phase* (podcast)

Christy Harrison, *Food Psych* (newsletter and podcast)

Chrissy King, *The Body Liberation Project: How Understanding Racism and Diet Culture Helps Cultivate Joy and Build Collective Freedom*

Virginia Sole-Smith, *Fat Talk: Parenting in the Age of Diet Culture*, and *Burnt Toast* (Substack newsletter and podcast)

ON INTUITIVE EATING (AND ITS CRITICS)

Alexis Conason, *Diet-Free Revolution: 10 Steps to Free Yourself from the Diet Cycle with Mindful Eating and Radical Self-Acceptance*

Christy Harrison, *Anti-Diet: Reclaim Your Time, Money, Well-Being, and Happiness Through Intuitive Eating*

Evelyn Tribole and Elyse Resch, *Intuitive Eating: A Revolutionary Anti-Diet Approach*

Jessica Wilson, *It's Always Been Ours: Rewriting the Story of Black Women's Bodies*

INDEX

UNSHRINKING

A BOOK CLUB GUIDE

DISCUSSION QUESTIONS

1. Fat activists would have us use the word "fat" not as a bad word or as an insult, but as a merely neutral description of some bodies, much like the words "short" and "tall." How do you feel about the word "fat" after reading the book? Is it possible and realistic to reclaim "fat" in this way?

2. How did Kate Manne's relationship with her body—and specifically the way her fatness made her vulnerable—resonate with you? Have you experienced feeling vulnerable as a result of your appearance, either now or during childhood?

3. Do you agree that attitudes need to change, sometimes in radical ways, to accommodate fat bodies and make the world just for everybody—helping us all shrug off what Manne calls "the straitjacket of fatphobia"? Did the straitjacket metaphor speak to you? What are some of the injustices faced by fat people, according to *Unshrinking*? What are their implications? Can you think of other injustices faced by fat people not mentioned in the text?

4. What are some examples of the ways that fatphobia intersects with racism, misogyny, sexism, classism, ableism, transphobia, and more? Do you agree with these connections? Are there other forms of fatphobia's intersectionality not highlighted in the book?

5. Fatphobia is likely on the rise, especially when it comes to the implicit bias against fat people. Why do you think that might be? Are there other forms of bigotry that seem to be on the rise in your circles, and how, if at all, do they intersect with fatphobia?

6. Of the three strands of fatphobia—moral, sexual, and intellectual—described in the book, which was the most resonant for you? What was the most surprising? Do you think disentangling these strands is helpful, or are they all inextricably connected?

7. What did you think of Manne's argument that diet culture gaslights us into dieting, even when we know that dieting doesn't work to reduce people's weight in the long term in the vast majority of cases? Have you ever felt gaslit by a person or a whole social system? What are some of the other ways gaslighting might work systemically to make whole groups of people feel that they are crazy, lazy, guilty, bad, or otherwise defective?

8. Are you persuaded by Manne's argument that hunger is *authoritative,* and that we should grant our bodies' hunger cues the authority they deserve, rather than diet constantly? Why or why not? And if you're familiar with the idea of intuitive eating, how do Manne's ideas compare and jibe with that idea?

9. How does the idea of body reflexivity compare to body positivity and neutrality? Does body reflexivity resonate with

you? Why or why not? What about the idea of dismantling beauty culture completely?

10. What misconceptions did you have about fatness that were corrected by this book? What did you think the book's limitations were when it came to wrestling with our ideas of fatness and health and bodies? Who in your life, if anyone, would you like to read this book and/or absorb its main messages?

ABOUT THE AUTHOR

Author photograph: Simon Wheeler for Cornell University

KATE MANNE is an associate professor of philosophy at Cornell University, where she's been teaching since 2013. Before that, she was a junior fellow at the Harvard Society of Fellows. Manne did her graduate work in philosophy at MIT, and is the author of *Down Girl: The Logic of Misogyny* and *Entitled: How Male Privilege Hurts Women.*

katemanne.net
X: @kate_manne

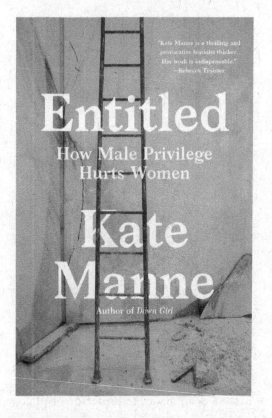